MW00633928

Other Brookledge Books

Milt Larsen's Magical Mystery Tour of Hollywood's Most Amazing Landmark: The Magic Castle
Written and photographed by Carol Marie

Hollywood Illusion: Magic Castle
Written by Milt Larsen
Edited by Carol Marie

Hockmann, the Great Exposes Himself! And Other Phony Magicians and Vaudevillians
Written by Milt Larsen, Illustrated by Paul Butler
Edited by Carol Marie

Peterkin, The Magic Rabbit
Written and Illustrated by Geri Larsen
Edited By Carol Marie

Fun With Hare E. Houdini
Compiled by Arlene Larsen

My Magical Journey

(The First 30,000 Days)

by

Milt Larsen

Copyright 2012 Brookledge Corporation
All rights reserved. No part of this publication may
be reproduced, stored in a retrieval system, or
transmitted, in any form or by any means, electronic,
mechanical, photocopying, recording or otherwise,
without the permission of the Brookledge Corp.

Archival research,
Designed & Edited by Carol Marie
Front Cover: Kendall Bennett photo of a 1924 gold Tiffany
desk inkwell from Milt Larsen's desk set, CM design
Back Cover: a Kendall Bennett design

ISBN: HB: 978-1-939178-00-8
SB: 978-1-939178-01-5

Published by:
Brookledge Corporation
7001 Franklin Avenue
Hollywood, CA 90028

Proudly Printed in the USA by:
Sinclair Printing Company
4005 Whiteside Street
Los Angeles, CA 90063
Jamie McCoy

Dedicated in loving memory to

William Larsen, Sr.
Geri Larsen Baker Jaffe
William Larsen, Jr.
and to the many dedicated members of the Academy of
Magical Arts who helped make the dream of a private
magic club become a reality

Acknowledgements: many, many thanks to Kendall Bennett, Paul Butler, Don Culp,
Allan Hayden, Dale Hindman, Dante and Erika Larsen, Al Rosson and the late Joe
Hoffman and Bruce Gordon. The hundreds of photos in this book are from personal
family scrapbooks and friends. We thank them all for their contributions.

Contents

How to Enjoy Life Without Ever Working

PREFACE

I am writing this while riding on the Amtrak Pacific Surfliner train that carries me from the Burbank airport to Santa Barbara, California. I usually drive from our home in Santa Barbara to the Magic Castle in Hollywood. It's a very pleasant ninety-mile drive if you happen to like freeways. I don't! So I often take weird alternate routes to see the cows and horses and smell the orange blossoms. I'm lucky that I don't have to punch a clock at the Castle, so my drive to and from paradise isn't too bad. But I really love the train. At this point in my life I can travel business class as a senior citizen. If it weren't for the fact that my car is always loaded with lumber and stuff that really doesn't work on Amtrak I'd probably sell my car (unheard of in Southern California) and ride the rails all the time.

The reason I'm saying this is that I have always considered my life as a journey on a railroad track. That track is magic! My brother and I were born in a magic family. We grew up surrounded with magic and magicians. The first credo of all magicians is that nothing is impossible. If you shoot for the moon you will get to the moon. What a life lesson!

Over the eight decades that I have been privileged to occupy space on this planet I have been on a fantasy train ride. The track always leads to magic and everything I have accomplished in life has been based on my upbringing in magic.

Wait a while! Every train track has switches, cross-overs and sidings. I'm an Aries person and that sign is well-known for people who love starting projects but then move on to more exciting things. My brother once said that I was the kind of guy that would quietly make a snowball, start rolling it up the hill all by himself and then, at the top of the hill, push it over the top and watch it roll down the other side as it gained in size and momentum. The giant snowball threatened to wipe out the village below. Then Bill said, "All of us who love Milt stood at the bottom of the hill trying to save the village and when we looked up we noticed Milt was rolling another snowball up the hill!"

I have always said that I have never worked a day in my life. That is because I have never had to do a job I didn't like. I never had to punch a clock for a boss I hated. Some jobs required endless hours and physical labor but I never considered it work. *I always respected the people I worked with and I always had the feeling they respected me. Every morning I awake to face the exciting challenges of the day.*

*As you read these pages you will see that my train gets sidetracked along the way. But somehow those sidetracks always lead back to the main track—*magic. *Please join me on this excursion of my life in magic. Throughout my life I have and will always be looking for a new light at the end of the tunnel. It won't bother me if I don't find it for a couple of hundred years.*

Okay: Conductor,
ALL BOARD! DEPARTURE APRIL 9, 1931

MAGIC!
THIS IS MY LIFE

I was born bald and overweight!
On top of that my parents were magicians!

My excursion through life began at the Huntington Hospital in Pasadena, California. As I understand it both my mother, Geraldine Francis Conrad Larsen and my father, William Walter Larsen, Sr. were there for the occasion. My dad was a very successful criminal attorney. (That's what they were called in those days. Now they are known as Defense Attorneys but, let's face it, a lot of Dad's clients were criminals.) By all rights Dad should have been a very successful pea packer. He was the son of William Larsen who founded the Wm. Larsen Packing Company in Green Bay, Wisconsin, which in later years was responsible for the brands "Veg-All," "Freshlike" and "Layer-Pak." Around 1905 the Larsen Packing Company employees organized a back-lot football team, eventually calling themselves the Green Bay Packers.

Dad grew up knowing that someday he might be head pea packer but he wanted to be a lawyer instead. He moved to California to attend Occidental College in Glendale where he found a beautiful lady by the name of Geraldine Frances Conrad. They met on stage at Occidental College when she was asked to assist him with his *Linking Ring* routine. Apparently he did a wonderful presentation because the lady he called

Proud grandparents in Wisconsin featured Brother Bill on the label of their newly introduced line of baby food of the Larsen Company, produced for HD Lee Mercantile, Co, Kansas, MO; and "Freshlike Corn" label.

up on stage stayed linked to him and became my mother. He married Gerrie in 1925. Originally from Traverse City, Michigan, Gerrie had never seen a magician before; it was love at first sight. I believe she made an excellent decision. If Dad hadn't gone to California he wouldn't have married mother, there wouldn't have been the Larsen Brothers, Genii magazine, "It's Magic!" and the Magic Castle might have been the Pea Castle in Green Bay, a social order devoted to the advancement of the art of pea packing in America.

From the very beginning of my life I was surrounded by beautiful theatres, magic and vaudeville. A California entrepreneur and Broadway impresario Martin Beck built the Palace Theatre in New York, designed by architects Kirchoff and Rose especially for vaudeville. The theatre opened in 1924 with headliner Ed Wynn. Throughout the course of The Palace's career in vaudeville *to play the Palace* meant that a performer had made it, had reached the pinnacle of his career. Sarah Bernhardt, Ethel Barrymore, Eddie Cantor, Fanny Brice, Ethel Merman, Sophie Tucker, George Jessel and Jack Benny were many of the legendary icons that performed at The Palace during the vaudeville years.

The official death of vaudeville as a main form of entertainment occurred when The Palace Theatre closed as a two-a-day house on May 7, 1932 then ran as a four-a-day theatre until November of 1932. The theatre had offered four vaudeville shows daily, seven days a week and even then wasn't profitable. With the Depression came an interest in film and radio. As fewer people wanted to see live performances, The Palace was converted into a movie house. I was born in 1931 so I figured the only reason I was put on earth was to bring back vaudeville. I've been trying to do that all my life; sometimes it worked, sometimes it did not.

Grandfather had made the mistake of buying young Bill a magic set to occupy the long and cold winter nights in Wisconsin. Dad became fascinated with magic which lead to his becoming an important figure in the world of magic, later being listed in the conjuring history books as an inventor, author and performer. He was a prolific writer and teamed with T. Page Wright, a brilliant writer with many film credits, to bring refreshing new ideas in magic to the pages of The Sphinx magic magazine in the '20's for Dr. A.M. Wilson. My dad had started writing for The Sphinx as a teenager in Wisconsin.

T. Page Wright came over to the Pasadena house every day. Dad and T. Page would work, far into the night, inventing tricks. They would circle the block working out their routines, pushing my brother, Bill Jr., in the baby carriage while Mother fixed dinner. When the magic inventors needed to stay in the house they rigged the baby carriage with a string so it would jiggle and lull Bill Jr. to sleep. Mother also became involved in magic and illustrated some of their tricks that were submitted to The Sphinx. Dad was so prolific he'd use the name of Dr. Straussberg or put his non-magic friends names as authors on his published tricks.

William W. Larsen Sr.

In 1931 Dad's writing partner tragically died in a car crash, at the age of twenty-five, a few months before I was born. T. Page was alone in the car when it hit a tree. Playing cards were scattered in the wreckage and Dad always thought he was probably practicing his famous *Page Pass* instead of watching the road. In honor of his best friend my middle name is Page: Milton Page Larsen. Upon my arrival on earth my brother, Bill Larsen Jr., was three years old and was already showing an interest in magic. He had had three years of being a captive audience for Dad and T. Page, watching them magish into the night.

There has never been any time in my life where magic wasn't a big part of it. Mother and Father were very, very clever. As magicians themselves, they always encouraged Bill and I **not** to go into magic, which, of course, became exactly what we wanted to do. When we were little kids in Pasadena, it was a regular, nightly occurrence to host magicians by inviting them to the house. It was very much like a mini-Magic Castle. I usually got sent to bed earlier than Bill but it was interesting to meet some of the truly legendary names in magic. Of course, we didn't know they were truly legendary names in magic, they were just Dad's magician friends: Caryl Fleming, Bert Kalmar, Mrs. Houdini, Edward Saint, Nate Leipzig, Bert Allerton, Dai Vernon, Max Malini, Johnny Platt, Leon "Popsy" Leon, Chester Morris, Harold Lloyd; all part of the magic gang that hung around our house. The magicians were the only ones in Pasadena who knew more about rice bowls than the Rose Bowl. Brother Bill and I went to magic stores, magic conventions, spent Saturdays at Thayer's Magic Shop and got to meet many great magicians. Avoid the magic bug? We didn't have a chance!

In the Beginning . . .
THERE WAS MAGIC

GERALDINE CONRAD LARSEN
presenting
MAGICAL MYSTERIES
"FASHIONS IN FANTASY"

A cultural entertainment of mystery thru the ages revealed intellectually, and with illusions, by America's Foremost Lady Magician

14

Surrounded by all the magical talent she observed on a daily basis in Pasadena, Mother thought she might have her own magical talent. In 1935 after watching a trophy winning Pacific Coast Association of Magicians (P.C.A.M.) convention performance, Mother was inspired. She had been bitten by the magic bug and knew she could develop a winning act. She was encouraged by Bill to work up a solo act for the following year. Dad helped her choose material and Gerrie worked on her routine. Next year, in San Jose, Mother won the big trophy. She honed her performances into three complete acts: a fifteen-minute act, a half-hour act, and an hour act. In her longer act, called "Magical Mysteries," she changed her gowns directly in front of the audience in a magical-like transformation. These acts became her solo lectures when we went on the road and material she later used in the syndicated "Magic Lady" series.

Dr. A.M. Wilson

When Dr. A.M. Wilson passed away in 1930, it was a great disappointment for Dad that John Mulholland took over the publication of The Sphinx. A regular contributor to The Sphinx magazine, Dad had entertained hopes of publishing The Sphinx himself. Over the next few years, he watched as the format and content of the oldest magic magazine deteriorated. So in 1936 Dad and Gerrie edited and published Genii, The Conjurors' Magazine, a new magazine for magicians that is still flourishing today. Dad's thought-provoking editorials in Genii inspired and challenged the magicians to update their magic instead of becoming complacent. The published tricks were innovative yet practical and the contributors increased in stature.

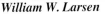
William W. Larsen

Mother penned "Paging the Ladies" under her maiden name. Dad often times would attribute the success of Genii to mother, who had taken over the mundane duties of subscriptions, accounting, proofing and solicitations to keep Genii afloat. She began receiving credit in the masthead as Editor in 1938. There was always news of the Larsen family in every issue, reassuring those in the trenches during the war and bringing a touch of stateside to them every month. Our family's life was in print on a monthly basis through Dad's editorials. In 1942 Dad began a new column, "Magicians in the Service" for all those magicians that now found themselves in service to United States.

In 1937 at the age of nine, Brother Bill wrote a newsletter for boys and girls ironically expounding on being nice to animals, especially magicians. Was that a prophetic omen that he would marry an animal activist later in life? Then in 1939, at the age of eleven, Bill Jr. debuted a new column in Genii entitled "Genii Juniors."

NEWSETTE

Edited and published by Billy Larsen, Jr.

**A Weekly Newspaper
For Boys and Girls**

Volume 1   Number 2   Week of May 17, 1937

OUR BEST FRIENDS

How many of you boys and girls have pets? I'll bet you all have some kind of animals at your home. You should treat all animals kind for if you don't they will run away and not like you. So, all of you readers that have pets treat them nice. You should always give them water and food, for if you don't, they will die and when an animal dies, he will not come back alive and then you would not have them. So, keep care of your pets and

BE KIND TO THEM

Brother Bill

Little Milt

If there were magicians within a few hundred miles of Southern California, Dad would haul off the family to see their act. In addition to the steady parade of famous magicians who seemed to live at our Pasadena home, I got to see acts like Cardini, Think-a-Drink Hoffmann, Gali-Gali, Paco Miller, Fu Manchu, A. Robins — the Banana Man and a host of others.

Larsen residence, 705 So. Hudson Avenue, Pasadena

Evenings at our house weren't filled with lectures, shows or parties—just magicians from all over the world who knew there was always an open door at 705 South Hudson Avenue. Jobs were tough to get in the depression so Dad's friend Harry Waterman became our personal butler, chef, chauffeur and houseman. Max Malini was one of Dad's favorite visitors, a wonderful guy with fabulous sleight of hand. In Dai Vernon's book "Malini and his Magic" Dai says Malini performed for more U.S. Presidents and foreign royalty than any other magician past or present.

Malini was a short, stocky man with a thick Austrian accent but his magic was flawless and Gerrie loved to tell Malini anecdotes. Every night Harry could be found in the kitchen making canapés for the visiting magicians. Max Malini loved to hang around the kitchen, eating the ingredients Harry needed for the hor d'oeurves. Harry told my father that the canapés were suffering and Dad pondered on how to solve the problem tactfully. One night Dad pulled Max aside after a canapé-ingredient-eating-binge and whispered a warning to Max that the guy in the kitchen was a man Dad had defended as a meat-cleaver-wielding-murderer. Harry had a short fuse and preferred to be left alone.

Max never went into the kitchen again. Instead, he'd bring his own snacks that he would hide somewhere in the house. Later in the evening he would mysteriously produce his stash of food. Now unfortunately, later in the evening he would be getting into his cups a bit. Max often brought his son Oziar and would call for him to help find the stashed tidbits. Sometimes it would take about two or three days before even Bill Jr. could follow the odd odor and find the moldy food hidden in a bookcase. Mother said Oziar would hang on to the back of Max's coat to help him keep his balance. In the middle of a routine Max would say, "Don't go 'vay, Ozzie... Don't go 'vay."

Max Malini

The second floor of the Pasadena house was the *living room* where Bill and I had a rather large electric train layout. Dad wasn't into model trains. I believe he was given the train set by a grateful client. Maybe that client was in jail and couldn't use it. Who knows? My grandfather, Sam Conrad, was a master carpenter and built a huge table for the trains that took up most of the upstairs living room space. The Hollywood Ring of the International Brotherhood of Magicians (I.B.M.) was founded in 1938. One of the Charter Members was Frederick Rickard, known as a master magic mechanic and inventor. Fred used to come over to the Pasadena house and drift away from the card crunchers and finger-flippers to play with our electric train upstairs.

My Brother Bill was not what you would call *mechanically inclined*. If something needed fixing he would simply give his younger brother the task. Bill loved pinball machines. He saved up his money and bought a used one. In those pre-WWII days, pinball machines were a festival of lights, contact switches and stepping switches. It was constantly breaking so Bill appointed me Chief Technician in Charge of fixing it. Between the trains and the pinball machines I got to know all about relays, solenoids and transformers. Fred was always there to help me before I blew up the old homestead. Another good friend of Dad's was Robert Stull, the famed inventor of the *Stull Watch*. He was an electronic and mechanical genius. During WWII he was in the Navy working on the then secret radar. I remember as a kid going to Stull's Magic Shop in San Francisco. I was fascinated with one of his new inventions, an automatic dice throwing craps shooting machine. Like all great inventors, Stull and Rickard were kids at heart and loved playing with our model trains upstairs.

William W. Larsen Sr.

Dad, as a criminal attorney, defended many shady characters left over from the days of prohibition. One night he ushered us quickly out the back door of Nikabob's Restaurant on Western Avenue in Los Angeles seconds before some bad guys came in and shot a few of their enemies. In 1938 Dad defended his mother's chauffeur. It was during the depression and the chauffeur had become a family friend. He was brought up on false charges of cold-blooded murder of his wife and two children (or so my father preferred to think the charges were false). Unfortunately last minute evidence was introduced, one overlooked little slip of paper found in the chauffeur's pocket that totaled the chauffeur's net worth; how

18

much he had saved, how much his salary was, how much the insurance would be, how much his wife's salary was—crossed out because he realized she wouldn't be bringing home a salary after he had killed her. My mother said that Dad kind of slid under the defendant's table when the net-worth list was introduced by the prosecutor. It affected Dad very much; he had liked this man and really believed in him. Even though he was genuinely disenchanted that our chauffeur could have eliminated his entire family so brutally, Dad did his best to defend him. His excellent defense saved the chauffeur from the death penalty; he was sentenced to life with no parole, a difficult sentence to obtain in those days. It was then Dad decided to go on the road as a professional magician and give up his criminal law practice.

Dad took the entire family touring the lecture circuit as "The Larsens—A Family of Magicians" presenting *a cultural background of magic*. My dad had wisely figured out that the only audiences who could afford shows during The Depression were wealthy resort hotel patrons who would buy entertainment if it were presented as *culture*. So for three years, we crossed the country three times and put on a two-hour show. Most bookings were in Southern California and Arizona that kept us closer to home and made it possible for Dad to continue publishing Genii.

...The LARSENS...

Photo by Rex

A Family of Magicians
presenting
The Cultural Background of Magic

19

THE LARSENS
A FAMILY OF MAGICIANS
Presenting
The Cultural Background
of Magic
★
Management
MAE NORTON
143½ SOUTH BEVERLY DRIVE
BEVERLY HILLS, CALIF.

The lecture was really a full evening stage show. A recording of Offenbach's "Gaite Parisienne" reached a stirring climax as the curtains parted, revealing Mother, center stage. She wore a white sequin-studded hoop skirted dress, ala "Gone With the Wind."

Magic's Foremost Family of Magicians
The photo, above, portrays the Larsens as they appeared on the stage. To the left is Milton Page Larsen, the younger son, Geraldine (Mrs. William Larsen). Third is William Larsen and to the right of him, Bill Jr. The photo was taken in 1942 as part of Mae Norton's publicity campaign.

On her hands were thin net-laced gloves popular long, long ago. She carried a large feather fan. As the music faded, Mom quoted from John Northern Hilliard's classic book, Greater Magic: "In the beginning there was magic in the air. The magic of day and night, of winter and summer…" Father would then take the stage and begin the evening's entertainment. There were four acts in all; each began with a short lecture sketch.

William W. Larsen Sr. and Geraldine with cups and balls

The first act addressed the evolution of magic from ancient times.

Dressed in stylish cutaway tails, Dad presented antique magic effects: *Cups and Balls, Skittle and Vase, Die and Box*; Mother produced *Flowers from the Shawl* and performed a beautiful *Butterfly Silk* routine.

The second act was Magic of the Orient; Dad spoke about the *Hindu Rope Trick* and performed an entertaining *Cut-and-Restored Rope* routine, then the *Chinese Linking Rings*. Mother performed the *Rice Bowls* and wore a gorgeous Chinese robe with one of Dante's original Japanese headpieces.

In the third act, Modern Magic, Dad started with the *Paper Tear,* and then went into the classical *Solid-through-Solid* while he discussed the difference between illusion and delusion. Mom

Geraldine Larsen

Bill Jr., Bill Sr., and Milt

produced a *Mutilated Parasol* and introduced her famous *Peterkin, the Magic Rabbit* puppet that took on almost human qualities while finding a selected card. Bill Jr. had a star spot with a red band of cloth and a slate routine.

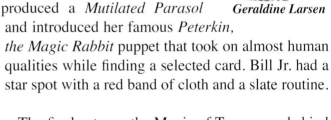

The final act was the Magic of Tomorrow, behind the curtain of the mind. Dad's mentalist act was different from any other mental performer that I had ever seen. He amazed his audience while keeping them laughing, "A laugh is worth one thousand mysteries." He closed with the *Magazine Memory* trick, always a show-stopper. For every story Dad had a quip or joked as though the audience were visiting friends and Mr. and Mrs. William Larsen were the charming, gracious hosts; it was a fast-paced program with an appearance of utmost leisure. We had a ball.

My father had a unique attitude towards performing. While other magicians made an art out of their magic—perfectionists who worked up a silent act performed to musical accompaniment, Dad loved to get the audience totally involved. He would engage the spectators in almost every effect he did, like his *Chinese Linking Rings*, where he started the routine saying "When the sailors accompanied Marco Polo on his travels they came back saying they had seen a Mongolian magician that could pass a solid human being through a solid wall. The passing of solid through solid is one of the oldest tricks in the world." He would then bring up a lady from the audience to handle the rings with him. It was this same routine that had endeared him to my mother when they first met.

At one point in the lecture Mother displayed a coach cup that had been given to her by the legendary magician Silent Mora. The cup was once the property of Adelaide Herrmann who took over the Herrmann Illusion show after Alexander Herrmann's death in 1896. The cup had been fashioned from a large Brazilian nut, rimmed with silver and had the name *Addie* engraved on it. We had it on display in The Magic Castle with some other magical treasures but the cup had vanished. One day Mother, thinking the cup was still on display at the Castle, wanted to present it to James Hamilton who was doing a remarkable recreation of Herrmann, the Great. She mentioned it to Jim and he was elated. Then we had to break the news that the rare piece of magical history had been permanently borrowed. When James Hamilton was doing his act at the Magic Castle years later the missing Herrmann coach cup mysteriously appeared in his dressing room. No explanation, it just magically appeared!

Geraldine Larsen

With United States' involvement in World War II looming in the near future the Larsen Family Magical Tour in 1941 performed the patriotic *Stars and Stripes Forever*. Bill Jr. and I produced three large handkerchiefs: red, white and blue. I attempted to turn them into a

Bill Jr. and Milt with flag

flag, via a tube. Unfortunately I dropped the blue handkerchief on the floor and the flag emerged with the blue field missing. Then I discovered the missing handkerchief and placed it in with the rest, producing a large *Old Glory* flag. The *Mis-Made Flag* was my first star spot and the resort audiences loved it. Bill Jr. had his own star spot. Attired in a many buttoned bellhop-type jacket he performed the *Skittle and Vase* routine with Dad in the first act.

Bill Jr., Bill Sr. and Milt

We carried our own sound equipment. The introductory and incidental music was all specially recorded on one 16" transcription record. Radio stations at the time used this type of record. This meant that all the music was on one side of the large disk, which Bill Jr. handled throughout the show. Lacking stagehands, on many occasions, Brother Bill and I became electricians, curtain pullers, prop men and assisted on stage as well. All during the program those who were offstage, while others were performing, were packing: that was mostly Bill Jr., and myself. When the last trick was done, we were ready to depart.

Occasionally Dad booked a solo lecture, entitled "Evidence of Deception," that was based on his experiences as a criminal attorney. "'Evidence of Deception' was a study of courts and witnesses presented from both a legal and psychological viewpoint. It was predicated upon the hypothesis that the majority of witnesses, in lawsuits, wished to tell the truth but were incapable of so doing because of defects in their own senses of perception. Mr. Larsen demonstrates that no one with five senses may be entirely trusted; that error in observation is the rule rather than the exception."

"Mr. Larsen has studied the functioning of courts as a writer, a student of psychology and a lawyer. His studies in the field resulted in his attaining a degree in law and being admitted to the State Bar of California. However, his vocation had been that of a magician and mystery writer. He reasoned that the senses of a witness at the scene of an accident or crime are deceived in precisely the same way as they are at a conjurer's performance. It's simply a case of *not believing anything you hear and only half of what you see*."

"The lecture illustrates a number of experiments in sleight of hand, proving that every human sense may be deceived. Likewise, there was a full discussion of the results of observation tests conducted by advanced psychology classes in the largest universities of the world. Other lectures available are: Fantasies, Frauds and Fakers (reviewing magic of the past); Only Fooling; Miracles in Books; The Question of Spiritualistic Phenomena." The above was quoted from Mae Norton's publicity flyer enticing patrons to book William W. Larsen's deception lecture.

Although we traveled with a small house trailer pulled by a Woody station wagon, we stayed at some of the grandest resort hotels on the West Coast: The Hotel Del Coronado, in San Diego; the El Mirador and Desert Inn, in Palm Springs; the Casa D'Manana, in La Jolla; the Del Monte Hotel, in Carmel; the San Marcos in Chandler, Arizona; all fabulous oases of wealth in the depression era. We were always treated as honored guests. I grew accustomed to castle-like dining rooms and posh surroundings. I never knew you had to pay attention to the right-hand side of a menu. So you could say, I was born with a silver spoon in my mouth. Of course it wasn't *our spoon*, but what was the difference?

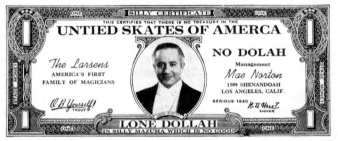

I don't think Dad ever told us there was a depression. I never quite understood the realities of the day. For a big outing we would to go to the Pasadena train station and watch the trains come in. In those days many of the Hollywood stars would get off the train in Pasadena to avoid the paparazzi at L.A.'s Union Station.

There was a theater on Pasadena's main drag, Colorado Boulevard, which showed serials and westerns on Saturday mornings. The train passed within a few feet of the theater. When the train rumbled by the theater would shake and the kids would react accordingly. That was real surround sound! Of course the real thrill was going to the Glendale Central Airport on Sundays to see people actually departing from those shiny passenger airliners. Thanks to our parents the *Great* Depression was pretty great.

When we were home in Pasadena Mother would convince us that Creamed Tuna and Peas was a great delicacy. When we were on the road playing the resort hotels we could order caviar milk shakes. It was quite a wonderful life.

While on tour, The Larsen Family of Magicians would stay five or six days in one resort, in their finest rooms and sign for their meals. The house trailer served as storage for the large hoop-skirted costumes and theatrical props. Arrangements could be made to have Dad give private readings by palm, horoscope, cards or crystal after the lecture or as a novelty entertainment feature in itself.

The Larsens, A Family of Magicians. L-R: Bill Larsen Sr., Gerrie Larsen, Jack Trepel, John Mulholland, Swan, and Richard Cardini; Milt Larsen, front.

William W. Larsen palm reading

Although Dad disclaimed any psychic ability, he read with surprising accuracy. His work showed years of study. The resorts paid enough to keep us on the road but Dad picked up all his extra money reading palms and performing cold readings on the verandas of the hotels at $10 a shot. In the '30's that was not too shabby!

Often Dad would do a special mentalism act. One of the bits was summoning a little spirit that happened to live in an antique wooden teakettle. Once a week I got to be the little kid. I hid in the bathroom and become the voice in the *Talking Teakettle*. In the '30's radios were still cumbersome things.

Gerrie Larsen and the Thayer Talking Buddha

The Thayer *Talking Teakettle* had a radio receiver, akin to a crystal set, built into its spout. The base of the kettle contained an induction cable. In order for the talking teakettle to work we had to lay another induction cable about fifteen feet in diameter inconspicuously around the edge of the room.

My broadcast studio was usually an adjacent bathroom or closet. When Floyd Thayer built the Thayer Studio of Magic theatre he installed a radio induction coil under the floor. Radio was a novelty in the early '30's so talking teakettles and Buddhas were quite amazing!

I was also the hidden modus operandi in Dad's version of a small haunted house. Magicians reading this will know the *Magic Doll House Illusion*. If you don't know, well, let's say the doll house was a little house shown empty from which a full-sized beautiful girl would appear. Dad had the Owen Brothers build one that looked like a small haunted house. Objects placed in the interior would float up, bells would ring and all sorts of spooky effects took place. Spoiler alert! Non-magicians, please skip to the next paragraph. The secret was I was hidden in a secret compartment in the house. It was fun until I couldn't fit into the doll house any more.

Starting to get the picture? I was a kid with a love of magic living in a castle-like atmosphere, living a fantasy life. Maybe this would lead to something big!

Bess Houdini was a family friend and a captive audience. So that cute little six-year-old kid (me) took advantage of one of my first audiences and performed a fabulous coin trick for Mrs. Harry Houdini! I'm sure the lady was impressed with the trick even though she had probably seen her share of magic in her day but I knew it was fabulous by her reaction and delight. Mrs. Harry Houdini was a gracious audience. She was a charming, diminutive silver-haired woman and an active force in magic. Dad was Mrs. Houdini's lawyer in her later years when she lived in an apartment on Vermont next to the on-ramp of the Hollywood Freeway. Every time I use that ramp and pass the Frostonya Apartments I think of Dad and Mrs. Houdini.

Little Milt and Bessie Houdini

Bessie Houdini

Bessie Houdini devoted her life to keeping the name of Houdini alive. Harry died in 1926 and Bessie lived until 1943. For ten years, every year on the anniversary of Houdini's death, Mrs. Houdini held a séance to prove whether or not Houdini could come back. The tenth and final Houdini Séance was held on the rooftop of the Hollywood Knickerbocker Hotel just a few blocks from the Castle on Ivar Avenue. The fact that Houdini died on Halloween helped make the séances a publicity natural. Mother and Dad attended the final Houdini Séance in 1936. Houdini did not come back… or did he? That night it rained in Hollywood—but only over the Knickerbocker Hotel!

Crystal Ball

One of Dad's very successful lectures was "The Final Houdini Séance." His lecture was the basis for our very popular Houdini Séance at the Magic Castle. We recreated the last original séance from the Knickerbocker Hotel in our Houdini Séance Room. It has proved equally as successful and for the past four-plus decades we have been trying to contact Houdini… sometimes twice nightly. The Houdini Séance Room has been noted for providing guests with some very fine *spirits*.

Center, seated: Bessie Houdini, Gerrie Larsen behind on left.

Mother was a co-founder, with Jennie Thayer, Carolyn Trask and Mrs. Houdini, of the only woman's magic club called "Magigals." She served as the club's President in 1939 and again in the '60's. The club was composed of many wives of magicians who got together while their magician husbands had their magic meetings. The group provided material for her Genii column, "Paging the Ladies." The organization quickly grew and had chapters in many states.

Gerrie Larsen in front of Houdini's portrait

About one hundred years ago Harry Houdini published his twenty-fourth and final issue of Conjurer's Monthly Magazine. There are interesting stories about Houdini and the Tsar of Russia in the days prior to World War I. The Tsar wanted Houdini to become his spiritual advisor and expose the evil Mad Monk Rasputin. At a dinner party to celebrate the event the Tsar proposed a toast however Houdini did not drink and refused. It was a social affront to the Tsar who withdrew his offer. Rasputin gained enormous power in the Russian revolution and had a controversial death, purportedly murdered by the royal family in

Tsar of Russia's brooch

1916. I was reminded of all this because there is a little walnut gavel on my desk that was turned by Floyd Thayer. It has a small emblem on it signifying that it was made to present to the President of the Magigals, the club started by my mother. One of my mother's most treasured possessions was a ruby and emerald brooch that was given to Beatrice Houdini by the Tsar of Russia. Mrs. Houdini gave it to Mother who, in turn, gave it to my wife, Arlene. The little Magigals gavel was added to the Magic Lady display in the Academy of Magical Arts library but the brooch is still worn by Arlene.

My mother was the first lady to perform magic on television in 1939 for the Golden Gate International Exposition. She presented her *Peterkin, the Magic Rabbit* card magic in front of a television camera to demonstrate television before it even existed! Gerrie Larsen had found a charming, saucy, twinkling-eyed hand puppet—a veritable

Gerrie Larsen and Peterkin

young Peter Rabbit—that she called Peterkin, who has achieved international fame. It became Peterkin's duty to find three selected cards from a shuffled pack. The first card Peterkin always found with alacrity. The second necessitated the use of telepathy. The third he couldn't find at all, with the result he cried and, needing a handkerchief with which to dry his eyes, pulled forth a crumpled hanky from Mother's sleeve. Eye dabbing attended to, the handkerchief was opened to reveal the name of the missing third card depicted brightly on the handkerchief itself.

The Larsen home on Hudson Avenue was only a short walk to the Red Car platform. The Red Cars were Henry Huntington's answer to rapid transit in the early part of the

20th century. His Pacific Electric streetcars were the primary mode of public transportation up until World War II. After the war the track right-of-ways were where our freeways are today. Maybe that's where I got my love for trains.

We could jump on a Red Car in Pasadena and go to Balboa, Venice Beach, Downtown LA and Hollywood in minutes. Although they traveled at a high speed mo-

Pacific Electric Railway Red Car

torists always respected that the Red Cars had the right of way. That was because the bed of the cars were filled with granite rocks to provide ballast. Red Cars never tipped over. In 1903, the Union Rock Company founded a quarry at the end of Bronson Avenue in Griffith Park. Caves were the result of excavation of crushed rock used in the construction of city streets and the Red Car ballast. Pacific Electric tracks led up to three entrances where they were filled with rocks. The quarry ceased operation in the late 1920s, leaving the caves behind. The "Three Way Caves" were a favorite location for early science fiction films.

As a kid the Red Car ride was a real excursion. From Pasadena to Los Angeles

Selig Zoo Entrance

we passed the Alligator Farm, the Ostrich Farm and the old Selig Zoo in Lincoln Park, East Los Angeles. Col. William Selig was a pioneer filmmaker back in the silent movie days. He specialized in animal pictures, lions, tigers and elephants. His zoo was a fading landmark in the forties but it was still a great place to visit. At the entrance to the zoo was a statue depicting trumpeting elephants. I always loved those elephants and they were still there in the sixties. I wanted to buy them and use them as the entrance to the Magic Castle. Of course it was one of my better totally impractical ideas.

THIS IS UNION STATION LOS ANGELES, CALIFORNIA THE FORTIES – GO WEST, YOUNG MAN

A New Life in the Wild West

When I'm called upon to talk about my life I have gotten a great deal of mileage from this line, "Many people don't realize that I was born in the Far East… (Wait for it…) PASADENA!" (For those who don't know, the Far East, Pasadena, California is just a few miles from Los Angeles.) I made the tedious trek across the Arroyo Seco in a covered wagon at the age of eleven. (Actually I think it was our Woody station wagon.)

Faced with the end of the magic tours and lectures, Dad made an unusual deal. He traded our home in Pasadena with Floyd Thayer's property in the posh Wilshire District of Los Angeles and bought the world's most prestigious magic manufacturing company in the bargain. Floyd Thayer had opened Thayer Quality Magic at 334 South San Pedro Street back in 1907, (ironically the same year they started construction plans of the Lane Mansion which is now the Magic Castle and Dad's father started the Green Bay Packers). We used to visit the shop when we were little kids. The store and shop were upstairs. It had a small demonstration stage in the showroom area next to a very large woodworking shop. In those days all the machines were driven by a series of pulleys and big overhead leather belts. It was a sight more interesting to me than the illusions next door.

Floyd Thayer

Dad was very friendly with Thayer and wrote a great deal of patter for the Thayer tricks. Floyd Thayer and his master mechanics, Carl and Emmet Owen, used only the finest hardwoods and made truly quality magic. They took enormous pride in their work. Carl Owen's wife, Lillian, hemmed all the silks and the Humphrey Brothers made quality metalwork. Thayer's was indeed a name to conjure with—a trademark that has long been the symbol of that exceptional quality and service.

When Thayer moved to the new studio address in 1931, most of the manufacturing was still done at the 334 San Pedro shop manned by the Owen Brothers. During World War II the Owens were contracted by the government to make thousands of little airplane spotter slide film viewers. Each one was made of walnut and looked like something out of the Thayer catalog. The little viewer was typical of the Thayer Quality Magic.

Floyd and Jennie Thayer lived in the large Mediterranean-style house built in 1923 when the Wilshire/Hancock Park area was a new subdivision in the primitive bean fields. The property was blocks from the famous LaBrea Tar Pits where dinosaurs once roamed.

Floyd and Jennie Thayer's Longwood Avenue house

It was this elaborate new residence and Studio Theatre on Longwood Avenue in Los Angeles that became our new home in 1942. Thayer's Magic Studio was a far cry from the little enterprise founded by Mr. Thayer in 1907 to this present, up-to-date three level structure he built behind his home called The Brookledge. The theater building spanned a natural fresh water brook, which in itself is considered magical in Los Angeles, and therefore the appellation: The Brookledge. The building originally housed a complete theater, showroom, stockrooms, shipping department, woodworking shop and a large office. Not bad for an R-1 residential zone! We used to visit the studio as youngsters, never dreaming that someday we would call it home. Thayer's Magic Studio was, without a doubt, the finest of its kind to be found anywhere; it was a veritable magician's paradise.

About 1938 a major flood hit Southern California. I still remember the horror of vacating our home near Santa Anita and watching Dad nearly swept away trying to get our Woody station wagon over a swollen stream. We were living just below the Santa Anita Dam, constructed in 1927 to prevent seasonal storm floods, and the Dam was overflowing—causing us to evacuate. It's right up there with my childhood memories of the time Dad went down in the basement because he smelled gas and lit a match to see where it was coming from! He proved, even during a depression, there could be a boom! Fortunately, he escaped relatively unscathed on both occasions.

During the flood of l938 the little stream beneath The Brookledge became a *Mini-sippi* river. Floyd Thayer saved The Brookledge by sending in his crew with axes to chop out both side walls, letting the water run through the building rather than sweeping it away. When we moved into the building a few years later we wondered why an old upright piano didn't play. We opened it up and found it was filled to the brim with dried, caked mud. For years neighborhood kids were finding old billiard balls and magic gimmicks downstream from the house. Collector's alert: There are probably some still buried there!

After five years in publication, Genii's subscriptions had more than quadrupled. The daily operations for the magazine were still being performed in the house in Pasadena, while Dad wrote many articles on the road. All family members had to participate. One of the Magigals, Evelyn Kaps and her husband, Fred, used to join Bill and Gerrie once a month to sit around the dining room table to address the mailing envelopes for Genii magazine—by hand. (By the way, Fred Kaps should not be confused with the very famous Danish magician Fred Kaps. At that time, the inventor of the *Salt Pour* trick would have only been about twelve years old.)

Before the Larsen family moved into the Thayer home Bill Jr. and I used to spend many a Saturday afternoon at the Thayer Studio of Magic. In the late '30's the Thayer Studio was considered *way out west* in Los Angeles. When Thayer bought the property in the '20's it was considered a new development in a bean field. Often on Saturday we would stop by the lake in Westland (now MacArthur Park) to ride in the little electric boats. Then we would spend the afternoon at Thayer's. Saturday afternoons at the studio became the meeting place for the great names in magic. At four o'clock in the afternoon Jennie Thayer served fresh lemonade and homemade cookies to her guests. The Thayer home was like home to Bill and I before we knew that someday we would call it *home*.

Floyd and Jennie Thayer

The Brookledge

In those days there were no electric clothes dryers so there was a clothesline rigged with pulleys that stretched from the back door of the house to the stage door of The Brookledge theater. If someone got a message Jennie would yell out the back door: "Ah Falloyd... ahh... FALLLLLOYD!!! And then she would send a message to him via the clothesline.

Floyd and Jennie Thayer were wonderful people but I'm not sure Mr. Thayer was terribly bright. For instance, the paint-spraying booth was next to a small bathroom in The Brookledge. In those days all magic props were beautifully decorated and sprayed with layers of lacquer, a highly flammable paint. In a cabinet under the sink in the bathroom Mr. Thayer stored his supply of *Flash Paper*. Nothing wrong with that—if the sink should leak it would keep the flash paper wet. The problem was another magic effect that was also stored under the sink, an old trick called the *Red Hot Ball*. This was a brass ball, which was cold until the magician handed it to his unsuspecting assistant chosen from the audience. Then the ball would heat up to a point of the helper juggling it like the proverbial hot potato. The effect worked because of a method of separating a load of potassium from the water in the ball. When water and potassium mix it creates extreme heat.

THE RED HOT BALL!

A beautifully made brass ball is given to any person to hold. Immediately the ball begins to warm up, and in a few moments becomes so hot that the spectator is forced to drop the ball to the floor, much to the merriment of the audience. The ball is simplicity in working, and can be used over and over again. Great for comedy interlude, or burlesque hypnotic stunt. Price complete, Ball and Instructions **$3.50**

Guess what was also stored under that sink, right next to the *Flash Paper*... next door to the spray booth? That's right... enough potassium for years of *Red Hot Ball* orders. Luckily, that sink never leaked!

Talk about a kid in a candy store? I was eleven years old in 1942 when we moved into the Thayer Studio of Magic. All the tricks were stored in shoe box-sized wooden drawers and there were over a thousand, four hundred effects listed in the Thayer catalog at the time. I would open a drawer, unwrap the trick, play with it and carefully wrap it up again. I was fascinated by the mechanics of magic, unwrapping every listed trick in the catalog! By the time I was twelve I was an expert in magic gimmickry. It was an accidental education that proved to be the foundation for a future life in comedy writing and a large factor in creating a place called The Magic Castle.

Dad started publishing the Thayer Quality Magic catalogues in 1943, dividing the large Thayer catalogue into five parts. Catalog 1, No. 9 dealt with pocket tricks, rope effects, thimbles, coins, cigarettes, card experiments and tricks with billiard balls. Part 2 dealt with silks, general club, stage and night club magic. Part 3 offered large stage illusions, escapes and magician tables. Part 4 was devoted to items of a psychic nature. Part 5 was a supplementary catalog, bringing the first four up to date.

Thayer Quality Magic
Catalogs No. 9

I learned wood turning from Floyd Thayer, a master from the old school. I used to watch in awe as he turned a square block of maple into a perfectly round billiard ball. Then the *miracle*—turning the billiard ball into a paper-thin shell! My Grandfather, Samuel A. Conrad, was a master carpenter and cabinetmaker. I guess that's where I inherited my love for woodworking. I became a student teacher in the wood shop at John Burroughs Junior High School and showed other kids how to make birdhouses and bookends. Then I returned to The Brookledge to turn blocks of maple and manufacture Lucite magic thimbles. The picture sharpens: The kid that likes magic, mechanical gimmickry and old buildings gets interested in carpentry.

I built my first bar when I was about twelve years old. It wasn't really a bar. It was a working soda fountain, which I built in a corner of my bedroom at The Brookledge family home. While Dad would socialize with Benny Chavez and the young kids at the Chavez School of Magic like Channing Pollack, I would go across the street to a restaurant supply house and get stuff for my home soda fountain. Later I built a bigger and grander bar at the house. Believe it or not I didn't drink as a teenager. I just enjoyed the look of old-time bars.

The Larsens: Geri, Bill Jr., Bill Sr. and Milt

The Brookledge was built with seven garden terraces. Floyd said he wanted a different sitting place for every day of the week. I remember Dad getting angry with Harry Blackstone's kid for playing in the fishpond. Harry Jr. was a rascal and got into a lot of mischievous trouble and he was only eight years old! He loved the pond and would wade shoeless through the mucky water. Floyd probably chased me out of the wishing well more than once. My mother always thought she had a few extra sons when George Falcon, Red Baker and Dick Sherman showed up at The Brookledge. Much later George Falcon became the publisher of Key Magazine, a very popular Southland entertainment and dining guide, and never missed a chance to plug whatever we happened to be doing in the world of show biz.

The Brookledge garden terraces

Adjacent to the theatre at the Thayer Studio was Floyd Thayer's personal shop. That is where he would work at the lathe turning those perfect billiard balls. When he moved to our house in Pasadena he took his shop with him. At that time magician Jim Conley went off to fight WWII and, rather than put his tools in storage, he lent them to Dad to allow us to outfit the shop. During the war Dad farmed out most of the manufacturing to other skilled craftsmen like Ben Wallace and Homer Hudson as well as the Owen Brothers. My grandfather, Sam Conrad used the studio shop from time to time but I really thought it was my turf. As a kid I was always inventing gags and building things.

No. 714. Thayer's Billiard Ball
Rack

This useful article will appeal to all billiard ball manipulators. It consists of a neat
stand to which a cross arm is attached and
has ball cups for holding three balls and a
shell. It offers an attractive means of displaying balls obtained during any "multiply-
ing" ball routine.
Size for 1½" or 1¾" balls as desired. It
comes in black and gold finish and takes
apart for packing.
Price, stand without balls $5.00

One day when I was ten years old I remember my dad being very disturbed about something he had heard on our car radio. We happened to be driving near grandmother's house, Gertrude Larsen, my father's mother, and we rushed in. Grandmother also was glued to the radio. There had been an attack on a place called Pearl Harbor. Although at the age of ten years old and even though we had traveled to every state of the union, I had no idea of where or who Pearl Harbor was. The awesome possibility of war didn't mean too much to a ten-year-old kid but that announcement changed our lives.

World War II travel restrictions put an end to the Larsen Family resort tours. Most of the grand old resort hotels had become military hospitals during the war. Although we still performed for the troops, the resort tours and lectures had ended. During the war years the Larsen Family of Magicians performed in the Hollywood U.S.O. and Camp Shows. Sgt. Ben Oakland organized the camp shows. In civilian life he was a well-known Hollywood composer, writer of "Java Jive" and "I'll Take Romance." He was also a magician and member of Los Magicos, a celebrity magic club with members like Harold Lloyd, Edgar Bergen and Chester Morris. Gasoline was rationed and there was no way to get extra gas to take the Woody station wagon to Camp Pendleton, Fort Ord or Camp Roberts. So Ben Oakland would send a bus to pick us up, take us to the camp and bring us back… then the bus would have to return to the motor pool. Four people and one bus driver in a fifty person bus drove twice the distance our faithful Woody would have had to, burning four times the amount of gas. I guess nothing has changed too much with government spending.

Hollywood U.S.O.

Hollywood, USO California

C. Merle Waterman,
Director

THIS CITATION IS PRESENTED TO:

The Magical Larsen Family

In Appreciative Recognition of Assistance in Maintaining Our Program of Entertainment, Hospitality and Fellowship for Service Men and Women of World War, II.

Rexford Bellamy, Program Director

Performing for the troops was always interesting. I still remember when our entire family broke into tears while doing a show at the desolate Desert Center in the middle of the Mojave. It seems the Quonset hut where we were to perform had recently been used for tear gas testing. We had to evacuate and perform on a flat bed truck outside.

The camps throughout California were often beset with power failures. For emergencies Dad put a *Comedy Light Bulb* in the footlights for that contingency. When the lights failed he would simply reach down and light a bulb by magic. He always received a standing ovation. Of course, most of the guys were standing anyhow!

One day, at Williams Air Force Base in Arizona, I vanished. We had just finished a show and were returning to the bus. I was carrying our wind-up *Snake in the Basket* trick and walked between Dad, Mother and Brother Bill. Suddenly all the lights on the base went out. It was pitch black on a moonless night in the middle of the desert. When the family got to the bus the driver had a flashlight and someone noticed that the Larsen family of four had become a family of three! A small search party retraced our steps and found that little twelve-year-old Milty had dropped into a deep pit as the rest of the party walked past on either side. According to eyewitnesses at the time, I was sitting in the bottom of the pit with a wind-up *Snake in the Basket* trick on my lap rising up the Queen of Diamonds... I guess you had to be there!

President Franklin Roosevelt's WWII USO plea for support

Then there was the time Orson Welles broke the glass on the studio door because he needed a small prop. He left a note about where to send the bill for the prop AND the door repair! At that time Orson was doing a magic show for the troops under canvas called "The Mercury Wonder Show" in Hollywood. It was a carnival-like affair that combined magic, carnival and humor. Orson used The Brookledge's red curtained stage to rehearse with Marlene Dietrich, Joseph Cotten, Agnes Moorehead and Rita Hayworth and kept his props in our garage.

Orson Welles' Mercury Wonder Show

"The Mercury Wonder Show" was a U.S.O. event where 1,500 servicemen got in free and 500 big celebrities got to pay big money for the Sucker Seat behind the front pole and the Super Sucker Seat behind the back pole of the tent. Orson took a stripped-down version of the show to military facilities around the nation. "Orson the Magnificent defies the laws of science in feats of legerdemain never before presented in America. The occult secrets of antiquity and the present day reproduced for your delight and fascination are: Born in Flames... The Devil's Orchard... The Fourth Dimension... The Strange Aquarium... The Hindu Mango Mystery and the Haunted Aviary with invisible pigeons and transparent doves."

*The Magic Crystal: Due to the unbelievable strain on the prac-
tioner of this incredible feat the management must reserve the
right to change this portion of the program without notice.*

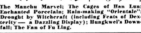

*The Girl with the X-Ray Eyes: An extraordinary demonstration
by Miss Rita Hayworth of strange powers recognized, but unex-
plained by science, featuring thought transmission and projection, extra-sensory perception, lightning calculations and second
sight.*
*The Great Joseph: The Wizard of the South presents split sec-
ond escapology. The redoutable J. Cotten risks his life at every
performance.*
*Million $ Mystery: Miss Hayworth and Mr. Cotten make you
doubt your senses in a bewildering display.*

*Joseph Cotten performed the Grand Finale: Voodoo! billed as a
re-enactment of Mr. Cotten's interesting experiences among the
witch-doctors of Dark Africa.*

The Larsen Family of Magicians performed for the Masquers Servicemen's Moral Corp.

THE MASQUERS
SERVICEMEN'S MORALE CORPS
One Hundred fiftieth Weekly Function
in honor of
OFFICERS AND MEN
of the

U. S. S. Wilkes-Barre
Com. Philip W. Mothersill, C.O.

Host

Frank Morgan

At the Dinner
Presiding- Edward Earle

Toastmaster
Fred Niblo

On the Stage
Director- Wm. B. Davidson
Stage Manager- Clint Urtubees

Mark Breneman- M.C.
William Ellfeldt- Musical Director

Hollywood, California
In The Masquers Club - February 23, 1946

Chef Bill Nylund Presents
DINNER
Masquer Service
✿ ✿ ✿

Entertainment
In the Lounge
JEANNETTE REAUME   MARIO SILVA
RONNY MANSFIELD
—
THE NATIONAL ANTHEM

On the Stage
THE LARSEN FAMILY
MARK BRENEMAN & JEANNETTE REAUME
CARMINA CANSINO & ROY
DALE MELBOURNE
LARRY STORCH
THE TODDS
CHARLES KEMPER & HENRY O'NEILL
with GEORGE BOYCE
in "THE INDUCTION"

CONSTANCE KRONKOWSKA
JEANNETTE REAUME at the piano
LOUIS DaPRON
JOHN LORENZ & FULTON McGRATH
DANNY BECK
✦ ✿ ✿ ✿

Thanks to the Baldwin Piano Co. for the duo pianos.

Marvyn Roy used to work at Thayer's Studio demonstrating magic with Brother Bill. Marvyn was a teenage sensation with a beautiful act called "Marvyn, the Silk Merchant." He was a protégé of the late Ray Muse, grandfather of Academy of Magical Arts Past President Dale Hindman. Later Marvyn teamed with another brilliant young magician, Alan Wakeling. They became Wakeling & Roy and they knew the value of staging and choreography in an act. Marvyn and Alan Wakeling used to work out new routines and rehearse them on The Brookledge stage. I helped them by running the sound and lights. One act they were rehearsing was really clever and beautiful but a little on the artsy side. The next day when they showed up for rehearsal they found one of those old vaudeville enunciator signs at the side of the stage: *Dancing, Prancing and Necromancing by Wakeling and Roy.* I think they got the point!

Alan Wakeling

Marvyn had been trying to figure out how to light a household light bulb without having to stick his foot in a light socket. I presented him with two 67.5-volt batteries I had taped together and wired in series, producing 135 volts. The future "Mr. Electric" didn't know much about electricity at the time so he was astounded by the discovery. It was easy for an avid Popular Science reader like me—a miracle to an artistic magical genius like Marvyn. I have often wondered if I hadn't helped him when I was kid, would Marvyn have gone down in magical history as "Mr. Gaslight"? Marvyn met a beautiful dancer and ice skating champion trick rope spinner while performing in an ice show at the Palmer House in Chicago. Alan was out, Carol was in and Mr. Electric was born.

Marvyn & Carol Roy publicity

Le Lido de Paris
Talk of the Town
The Latin Quarter
The Empire Room
London Palladium
The Liberace Show
Stardust Las Vegas
Radio City Music Hall

"In All The World There Is Only One!"

Mr. Electric & Carol

The Thayer Studio was located on a quiet residential street behind the main house in an area of big estate-type homes north of Wilshire Boulevard but a trickle of large homes followed the picturesque stream, the Rio de la Jardin de las Flores. Floyd Thayer had run the business from the large building in his backyard as a mail order firm with the showrooms open only on Saturdays. Dad expanded the business to the point that the neighbors started noticing the presence of hordes of people, fifty-seat buses and trucks invading their turf. After the war, Dad decided to move the retail activities to a building on LaBrea Avenue, half a dozen blocks from The Brookledge. The Thayer Studio of Magic then simply became our home, a little place with a theater in the rear. That theater would become an important part of my life in later years.

William Larsen Sr. demonstrating magic in the Thayer Studio

School days, school days… We moved from Pasadena just in time for me to start John Burroughs Junior High School and for Bill Jr. to attend Los Angeles High. Both were within walking distance from our new home. Brother Bill, was an excellent student. In fact, he excelled in everything he did. He was my senior by only three years. In Bill's three years at Los Angeles High School he was an "A" student. He was popular with the teachers and popular with his fellow students—especially the girls. After Bill graduated it was my turn to spend three years at Los Angeles High School. I was a lousy student. I spent three years listening to: "Why can't you be more like your brother?" Brother Bill went on to college (Occidental College in Glendale and USC in Los Angeles). I was lucky to graduate high school. But, after all—I knew EVERYTHING!

I just wasn't all that interested in furthering my academic education. After all, when you are in your mid-teens—you know everything! Because of our growing up in theaters Bill became the stage manager for the school's very professional theater. That was one thing I loved and the one thing I did well so I immediately inherited the job at Los Angeles High. I received A's in Drama 1 & 2, Play Production and Stagecraft and barely passed everything else. I flunked English but at that time Harrison "Red" Baker and I had published three joke books and Snag Werris was teaching me the fundamentals of comedy writing. I knew about bookends, blackouts and "Here we are in sunny Spain." To me, syntax was an extra charge at the Follies Burlesque Theater.

While Gerrie was nurturing and editing Genii, providing material for her column and occasionally providing comic relief with her cartoon comic strip "The Hocus Family" with Tom Lawless, she continued perfecting her magic.

THE HOCUS FAMILY

by TOM and GERRIE
(LAWLESS) (LARSEN)

Gerrie was the first lady magician to perform on her own weekly show, "The Magic Lady" on KTLA in the late '40's when that station was still called W6XYZ. Television was very primitive in those days. I remember the excitement of going to the studio, then at Marathon just above Melrose, to watch the show. It was kind of a shock to see Mother in her green makeup and dark green lipstick… which, of course, made her look beautiful on film as green photographed a deep red.

In 1948 Dad went back to his successful practice of criminal law with his offices in the back of the Thayer stores. His office consisted of one big roll top desk. Roll top desks are fun. I inherited the roll top desk where I replaced my old typewriter with a Mac computer and keyboard. This electronic device of the 21st century resides on Dad's beautiful roll top desk. The desk, which dates back to the 1890's, belonged to the legendary lawyer Henry Huntington. His offices were in a little two-story building at Broadway and Temple that is now part of the sprawling Los Angeles Civic Center. When they tore down the building Dad bought Henry Huntington's desk and moved it to the Thayer store.

Gerrie Larsen, The Magic
Lady of Storyland

The polished oak desk has thirty-four drawers and the simple act of pulling down the roll top locks each and every one of them! The desk is an organizational marvel. There are twelve drawer/bins across the top, one for each month. A cluster of four bins represents the quarterly files. There is an area for reports, incoming items requiring action and dispensers for stationary and invoices. Then there are the little drawers for stamps, cards, pencils, pens, and other trash. With a desk like this you would never need a staff of employees. And if the I.R.S. ever questioned your business you could just crate up the entire desk and send it to them.

Milt sitting in front of the Huntington roll top desk

The desk has a very nice home in my office at our home in Santa Barbara. There's a certain incongruity about the state-of-the-art Mac computer that has found a home on the 1890 desk, but what's a hundred year or so gap in the life of office furniture?

My dad loved the practice of law. Although he gave it up for about ten years to practice his even greater love of magic, he was still a very fine attorney. He often used magic in his legal cases. Dad once defended a guy who was accused of stealing a lion from a circus. His client didn't deny that he had the lion but claimed he had rescued it from a horrible life at the circus where the lion was mistreated and starved. The Jury wasn't exactly buying it until Dad had the lion brought into the courtroom as evidence. After the courtroom settled down it was obvious the lion had a great affection for the accused lion-napper and a huge dislike for the circus owner. Dad won the case.

Dad defended another hapless magician friend who was wrongly accused of driving under the influence of alcohol. He had flunked the breath test, which at that time consisted of blowing into a balloon. If the balloon changed color the poor soul was busted. Dad's defense was that his client was a magician returning from a gig and had been performing the *Smoke-from-Clay-Pipes* trick. The pipes were coated with two chemicals. When the bowls were placed together it produced smoke. Dad had a bonded witness stay with his client for hours before his trial to prove that he had not consumed a drop of booze. The magicians did the trick then blew into an official test balloon. It changed color and Dad won the case. The prosecutors were forced to re-think the entire drunk test system.

Sitting at the desk brings back memories of the Thayer shop on LaBrea. Magician Harry Mendoza and Brother Bill Jr. managed the store. I was at Los Angeles High School at the time, flunking English in my ambition to become a truly fine writer. I got to hang around Thayer's after school and on Saturdays. One of the Academy's first Board Members, the late Harry "dog meat" Mendoza, was the official manager of the Thayer shop for quite a while. Harry got his nickname because Dad would often invite Harry to join him in the quest of dog meat from a butcher stop across the street. There was also a friendly tavern next to the butchers where Dad and Harry held frequent mini-magic conventions in its environs. Brother Bill managed the store and would tell visitors Dad and Harry were out buying dog meat.

Harry Mendoza

Harry was very involved with the Masquers Club that used to have a grand clubhouse around the corner from the Magic Castle on Sycamore. Its members included some of Hollywood's best known actors like Alan Mowbray, Joe Frisco and George Burns who hung around its carved mahogany bar with two slightly erotic murals by the famed artist Henry Clive (who was also a magician). I was only twenty-five years old when I started writing for "Truth or Consequences." I was thrilled when Harry told me the Masquers had started a junior membership drive. (At the Masquers Club a junior was anyone under the age of thirty.) A junior could join the club for a nominal fee and then convert to a full membership with much higher dues at any time.

I had always loved anything having to do with vintage showbiz and this was my chance to rub and bend elbows with some of the legends of Hollywood. I got the impression that the older members of the club resented the fact that some young whippersnappers were invading their space. The old-timers kept to themselves and the kids felt awkwardly out of place. After about a year I dropped out of the club. Later I was interested in joining the Players Club in New York. The dues were very high and one needed seven letters of recommendation by other members to join. I produced letters from Leonard Sillman,

Cary Grant and Gordon Davidson among others. I remained a member for a few years but I found myself spending very little time in New York. I figured every drink I had at their bar cost me about five hundred dollars. Unlike the Masquers and the Players Clubs, The Magic Castle will remain forever young because our older professionals embrace our young members.

Bert Kalmar and Harry Ruby were prolific songwriters with such hits as "Three Little Words" and "Who's Sorry Now?" and all those crazy tunes for the Marx Brothers. Bert Kalmar was a very active amateur magician. He was one of Dad's best friends and I saw him often at Brookledge. Kalmar ran away from home to join a tent show as a magician. He helped, with Bill Larsen Sr., form a small exclusive magic organization, Los Magicos, where meetings were held at Harold Lloyd's mansion in Benedict Canyon. Nicknamed Greenacres, the estate consisted of 44 rooms, a golf course, and a canoe run on 15 acres — not bad for a clubhouse!

Harold Lloyd and his Benedict Canyon mansion

Bert loved practical jokes and magic gags. He would go to any extreme for a laugh. He would capture a large Miller moth and keep it in a compartment in his wallet. When it came time to pay the check he opened the wallet and let the moth fly out. He would go to the bank and get brand new bills that he glued together end to end. Again, at a restaurant, when the check came he'd reach in his pocket and remove a roll of bills, reel off the proper amount and cut the last bill off the roll with a pair of scissors. He would hand the startled waiter a long strip of bills. Kalmar would sneak his own doughnut into a restaurant and then do a whole routine of switching chocolate and plain doughnuts, driving the waitresses crazy. He was a generous tipper and did it all without being obnoxious.

Edgar Bergen was a founding member of Los Magicos, a club made up of many celebrities: Orson Welles, Chester Morris, Peter Godfrey, Bill Larsen Sr., Harry Usher, and Bernie Giannini. Bergen's mentor was a vaudeville headliner vent by the name of The Great Lester. Harry Lester was a frequent visitor of Thayer's Magic Shop in the '40's. There was one of those old-fashioned pay telephones hanging on the wall just inside the front door. Dad had it rigged so he could push a button behind the counter to cause the phone to ring. In those days the earphone and the mouthpiece were separate. When The Great Lester was in the store full of customers the phone would ring and The Great Lester would conduct a hilarious conversation with a non-existent party, throwing his voice into the earphone. At one point he would ask a bystander to hold

The Great Lester

the phone for him while he searched for a piece of paper. The voice in the phone would continue to talk even though Lester walked away to the other end of the store. He was a true illusionist! Edgar Bergen was a member of the Magic Castle and used to drop in often. He was a walking encyclopedia of magic and vaudeville.

Gerrie Larsen, Edgar Bergen, Jeannie, Charlie

Harlan Tarbell wrote the book for aspiring magicians, "Tarbell Course of Magic," originally a mail order correspondence course very popular in the late'20's. In 1941 Louis Tannen, the founder of Tannen's Magic in New York, took on the monumental task of publishing the work in book form and the first of five volumes became available. "Doc" Tarbell was a great friend of my dad's and was a frequent visitor to our home. I had never seen Tarbell perform on stage. Like the Larsen family he did his magic on the lecture circuit rather than in theaters and clubs. In the early '50's he presented a one-night only show at the old Philharmonic Auditorium in Los Angeles. The Philharmonic was a grand theater with an arched proscenium, very much like the Radio City Music Hall. Built around the turn-of-the-century it was home to the Los Angeles Civic Light Opera. It was the kind of theater where Klaw and Erlanger's "Ben Hur" was staged, complete with live horses. Like most big theaters of the day it had several balconies. From the upper peanut gallery, where I used to usher as a kid, performers on stage looked like ants.

"Doc" Harlan Tarbell

It was with great expectation that I sat in the best seats in the house with my dad, mother, brother and many of the greatest names in magic to watch this icon of magic perform his art on the great stage. It promised to be a night to be remembered. There was no overture—the orchestra pit was empty. The curtain rose to disclose a couple of card tables loaded with simple props. Tarbell entered in a tuxedo probably discarded after Al Capone's funeral. No dancing girls—no assistants in sight—somehow I knew this wasn't going to

be an extravaganza. Then Doc Tarbell started to perform and it was truly a night to remember! He did things with ropes and rings and silks.

He filled that big stage with personal magnetism and real magic. It was one of the more memorable nights of my life. Since I was born in a magic trunk, I have probably seen more magicians than most living humans. Harlan Tarbell is at the top of the list as one of the greatest magicians I have ever seen.

Richard Cardini played a monocled British gentleman, a trifle over served, who seemed rather surprised when objects appeared at his fingertips. He was widely imitated but never copied. His wife, Swan played the part of a bellboy and the act was sheer perfection. Cardini and Swan traveled a lot and The Cardinis also worked the lecture circuit with Larsen family of Magic.

My life was magic and magicians. I think my love for magic gave me the curiosity to explore the world of show business beyond the trap doors, smoke and mirrors. Long before the high rises and the Grand Avenue downtown we know today, when I was a mere lad in the '40's, I used to have a Saturday afternoon ritual. I would park at the top of Bunker Hill and admire the old Victorian mansions and hotels. Then I would spend my nickel to ride the world's shortest railroad, Angel's Flight, to the bottom of the hill to see what treasures could be found at the Goodwill Store, primarily to check out the piano rolls, 78 records and their amazing system of shooting baskets filled with money up to a cashier's cage in the center of the ceiling. I got my first player piano there for $50. Then I would walk through the wrought iron fantasy of the Bradbury Building. It was a sight that made me want to build a Magic Castle. My Saturday

Richard and Swan Cardini

Angel's Flight

odyssey continued with a visit to the Million Dollar Theater in time to catch the Mexican vaudeville stage show. Although I couldn't understand a word of Spanish, the visual gags and variety acts were hysterical. I loved the singers, dancers,

Bradbury Building

acrobats, jugglers and magicians. The orchestra pit contained eight musicians and occasionally scurrying rats. After the show I would walk through the Grand Central Market for the freshest crab in town, exit at Hill Street and return to my car via another ride on Angel's Flight.

Our magician/criminal attorney father used to have some mighty interesting clients. One was a rather remarkable entrepreneur by the name of Jim "Shamus" Fay. In the late '40's Shamus was producing a play at the Beaux Arts Theater, a gem of a small legitimate theater in the Halliburton Building at 9th and Beacon. The play was called "Lazarus, the Headless Rooster." The play wasn't doing too well. Shamus figured he needed some cheap publicity so he borrowed a big stake bed truck and filled it with live chickens. On the side of the truck was a banner plugging the show.

6th and Broadway was probably the busiest intersection in Los Angeles—especially during the rush hour. By some freak accident that truck full of chickens, driven by Shamus Fay, broke down at exactly 5 p.m. in the middle of that crowded intersection. Not only that, but the tail gate of the truck fell off unleashing the chickens, creating a traffic jam that made every newspaper in town! Shamus was hauled off to the biggest chicken coop, aka Lincoln Heights Jail. Dad got him out of the slammer and off with a modest fine. It was still cheaper than paying for advertising!

It was Shamus Fay who inadvertently started me on a life of producing major theatrical disasters for the American stage. Fresh out of Los Angeles High School I had an idea for creating a *Gay Nineties Music Hall* and took the idea to Dad's friend and client, Shamus Fay. I knew his Lazarus show had just folded and the Beaux Arts Theatre was dark. He said he loved the idea but had other big deals cooking and didn't have the time. He did, however, have the key to the Beaux Arts Theater. He explained that I could take possession of the theater, fix it up and turn it into a Victorian Music Hall and, at some time in the future, he was sure I could make an equitable deal with the building owners. By the way, Shamus needed fifty bucks, cash! I gave him my fifty bucks and he gave me the key to the front door.

I spent the next six months of my life carefully painting, gilding, and re-rigging this fine old theater. I had cards printed that proclaimed "Milt Larsen's Gay Nineties Music Hall." I put a poster in the showcase. One day the manager of the building popped in. He admired the work I was doing but said he was a little confused. Who was I and why was I restoring a theater they had just rented out as a warehouse? I still have one of the business cards to show for my efforts. In fact, that's *all* I have to show for my efforts! I thank Shamus Fay for that first step into the real world of show business.

About this time my friend and writing partner, Harrison "Red" Baker and I started working together. Dr. Zomb needed two assistants for his midnight spook show, "Séance of Wonders." Dr. Zomb was an absolutely wonderful magician and hypnotist named Ormond McGill. Ormond, in real life, looked more like a dentist than a menacing spook show host. When he was on stage though, he became… "Dr. Zomb!" Now for those of you underprivileged few who may not remember the great days of midnight spook shows, this was a great form of live stage shows that utilized the fact that most of the old cinema palaces still had big stages… and that kids loved to stay out late and have an excuse to grab their date when the spook show got too scary.

Ormond McGill

The Dr. Zomb Show played the old Fox West Coast Theaters in the late '40's. Because they were generally booked to begin at midnight after the day's theatrical film run, theater owners stood to lose little by allowing live spook shows to be presented. In fact, they were able to make a lot of money from these programs for long periods at a time. We would play two and three shows a weekend. Red Baker and I got the job because Ormond McGill knew my father, Bill Larsen Sr.—I didn't have a car. Red had a Pontiac Convertible and I had the father—so we got the job. Red was a really talented writer but his love was performing. It was easy for me to convince him that he should play the part of a gorilla. All he had to do was put on a lifelike gorilla suit and run up the aisle. I knew a little about spook shows. Something my old pal Red didn't know was the guy in the gorilla costume was fair game for the young stud in the audience who wanted to show how well he could protect his girlfriend. Running up the aisle in a gorilla suit was something like being a living armored car in a war zone.

Dr. Zomb did a great hypnotic act. He would get about thirty volunteers on stage. Most of them were those same young studs on a beer break. McGill would line them up across

the stage in chairs and interview them. Invariably they would fake cooperation and the moment Dr. Zomb's back was turned, they would make faces and obscene gestures. As assistants, dressed as ushers, Red and I carried large five cell battery flashlights. When we spotted a troublemaker we simply stood behind him, holding our five-cell as a club. Dr. Zomb would turn to the offender and say, "I don't think you will do," and we would escort the guy back to the audience. It was a very effective means of crowd control.

I think I got my interest in physical theatres as a teenager when we worked on these midnight spook shows. I really enjoyed going through the back stages of these wondrous old theatres. There were very few live stage shows then but the dressing rooms were usually full of old, discarded playbills, posters and theatre ads. I would ask the manager of the theatre if they were going to throw the memorabilia away and they would always let me have whatever I wanted; thus began my collection of old vaudeville ephemera. We were paid twenty bucks a show. In the late '40's, twenty bucks was a whole lot of money for a couple of teenage aspiring writers. It's interesting how this chance employment opportunity for a couple of kids affected our future.

Why would a kid, growing up in the '30's and '40's, have any interest whatsoever in a dead entertainment form? And why would that kid find himself devoting most of his life trying to convince the world that more people should take time to enjoy, appreciate and utilize the untapped mine of valuable knowledge that is rapidly being lost forever?

Milt's first gramophone

Why me? I was stage manager for a Los Angeles High School production of "Pygmalion." The prop list called for a gramophone. I found a beauty at a junk shop in Hollywood. It was an old Edison with the traditional morning glory horn, and I paid a whopping $25 for it—complete with a bunch of old cylinder records. The records had an acoustical sound I had never heard before. I had discovered something that was so old it was brand new, a philosophy that is still uppermost in my crusade to preserve the variety arts. When I added ephemera of theatre history to my ever-growing record collection, I found that some of the vaudevillians listed on the playbills made phonograph records and many of the great stars of the day started in vaudeville, Jack Benny, Burns & Allen, Eddie Cantor, Sophie Tucker, Red Skelton, Lucille Ball and Bob Hope—all started at the bottom. They learned from their elders and honed their craft through thousands of live performances and the careful application of the basic principles of showmanship.

While my high school friends were listening to the contemporary hits of the day on their fifty pound *portable* radios, tuned in to disk jockeys playing "Open the Door, Richard," "Nature Boy," "On a Slow Boat to China," and Frankie Lane's "Mule Train," I would go home and listen to "Yes, We Have No Bananas," "Mister Gallagher and Mr. Shean," and "Does the Spearmint Lose It's Flavor on the Bedpost Overnight?" Yes, I was considered something of a nerd in love with comedy. That was the start of my never-ending obsession to collect things.

Remember the old mimeograph machines, the pre-Xerox copiers that printed material by cutting a stencil? My early life seemed to be very connected to this miraculous invention. Red Baker and I had put out a comedy booklet titled: "In The Aisles." Red had a great gift of thinking up jokes and, of course, I had the father with a mimeograph machine. Dad gave us space for an ad in Genii magazine and we scraped together a few bucks to advertise in Billboard Magazine. The little book sold for a buck and we took in a bunch of bucks. Our first pamphlet was a little mimeographed book; we had literally cranked out our first joke book. With our next pamphlet we got classier and put out a printed book. Finally we got even classier and had them commercially printed.

Red Baker and Milt Larsen's comedy booklets

We clearly decided being comedy writers was a fun way to make a living. A little of my father's writing talent had rubbed off on me. I loved all forms of comedy. Baker and Larsen started writing jokes and publishing more comedy books.

We didn't know much about radio or TV script writing and we wanted to learn. Because of our weird schedule playing midnight Dr. Zomb's "Séance of Wonder," we would return home about three or four in the morning. This meant we could visit the radio studio trash cans before the trash collectors arrived. In those days the CBS and NBC studios were side by side on Sunset Boulevard. We would finish our gig with Ormond McGill and stop by the trash cans to pick up any discarded scripts of the radio comedy shows from that day.

One day the head janitor at CBS caught us upside down in the trash bins. He explained that rummaging through trash bins was immoral, illegal and, not to mention, unsanitary. We explained we only wanted to study script-writing form and become comedy writers. Leo, the janitor, said in the future he would save all the comedy scripts for us. Later, Leo introduced us to a bright new radio personality by the name of Steve Allen. Steve was very helpful and introduced the two garbage-can-raiders to some of the CBS people inside the studio.

Brother Bill thought he wanted to be an attorney and went to U.S.C. Law School for a year. He just didn't like it. About this time Bill decided he wanted to get in show business. He made the rounds to ABC, CBS, NBC, and William Morris Agency and filled out applications. CBS gave him a call from the script-typing department and made an appointment with Bill to see Walt Dunnin. Bill took a typing test, passed with flying colors, and then they started talking about magic. Bill got the job! He worked back in the bungalows at CBS, from eight a.m. to two a.m. in the morning, typing stencils for the scripts of the next day.

The Thayer Studio of Magic became the Larsen family funhouse in 1948. Dad rented three stores on nearby LaBrea Avenue for the commercial operations. That left a teenage kid with the world's greatest toy: a theater in the backyard! I quickly turned the balcony, once the Thayer library, into a projection room. I loved collecting old 16mm sound films and, at one time, the projection room housed two 35mm projectors, two 16mm projectors and other pro equipment. We were the neighborhood movie palace. I should have been a theater projectionist. While our friends were watching films I enjoyed changing reels and watching for those little dots every twenty minutes. I ordered trailers from a coming attraction maker in Chicago. I would make weekly trips to *film row* on Vermont Avenue to buy lobby insert posters for the Brookledge lobby cases. I installed electric curtains and later a CinemaScope screen. The Brookledge became the gathering place for our pals. Of course many magic clubs used to meet at the Brookledge and many magic social events continued to be held there.

HOUSE POLICY

Admission to all parts of the theatre is free of charge. This programme will admit you and one guest. (It is our theory that any friend of yours is not necessarily a friend of ours . . . please do not give this to anyone without checking with the management.)

Doors open at 8:30 — entertainment begins precisely at 9:00 — come early and be assured of a choice seat.

Refreshments will include copious quantities of grand old Eastside Beer— on the house, of course.

(The proprietors of the Brookledge Music Hall find no objection to the drinking of other alcoholic beverages. However, after pricing other booze, we have decided to limit the "on the house" goodies to beer. If you want something else you are admonished to provide your own.)

After the performance the main theatre will be referred to as the Grand Ballroom. . . . Those who dance will take especial notice. Also you may visit the "museum" to sing to the music of the Mighty Automatic Nickelodeon. Our informal "After-the-night-clubs-close-at-two-show" will begin at 2:30 Surprise acts will sneak over from the Band Box, the Purple Onion, and other saloons.

ONE NIGHT ONLY!

LARSEN'S

BROOKLEDGE

MUSIC HALL

929 South Longwood Ave. • WYoming 5912

ANNOUNCING the ANNUAL GALA FAREWELL DEBUT of the BROOKLEDGE BREVITIES... An evening of VAUDEVILLE ENTERTAINMENT in the finest TRADITION of the BROOKLEDGE THEATER, HALL of MERRIMENT and PALACE of VARIETIES !!!

SATURDAY, SEPTEMBER 22nd

- - - IN PERSON - - - ON STAGE

Our Master of Ceremonies will be the very popular personality MR. ART BAKER who will introduce the following impressive list of clever and exuberant performers!

the UNIVERSALS - Rockin' at the Brookledge
MISS SALLY KAY - Popular Recording Star
MR. FRANK BRESEE - Witty Remarks
MR. JOHN CORDA - Direct from Europe
the DORAN TWINS with MR. MIKE at the BANJO
MR. MILT LARSEN - Let's humor the host!
MISS GERRIE LARSEN - (Relatives!)
MISS LORAY WHITE - star of "Joy Ride".
VERNON, RYAN AND BAKER - Songs & Dances
the DUNCAN SISTERS - Only the Greatest!

EXECUTIVE STAFF

MILT LARSEN	Impresario
BILL LARSEN	Manager
GERRIE LARSEN	} Hostesses
DOTTIE LARSEN	}
EUGENE POINC	Scenic Master
DICK SHERMAN	Musical Director
RED BAKER	Indian Guide

HEALTHFUL SPRING WATER
from the Rio De Los Flores
on the theatre premises
10c the barrel
(cheaper during floods)

IN THE PIT
Mr. Johnny Graves conducts his ad-lib orchestra —
(one piece and up)
AFTER THE SHOW
JAM SESSION
(bring your own jam!)

From time to time we would stage the Brookledge Music Hall variety shows. The Brookledge gang included many aspiring show biz types as well as Mother and Dad's stellar friends like Buster Keaton, Harry Richman and Rudy Vallee. My Castle non-magician regulars included Red Baker, my writing partner; Oliver Berliner, whose grandfather invented the disk phonograph and microphone. Ollie would become my future partner on the first "It's Magic!" shows; Dick and Bob Sherman and their songwriting Dad, Al Sherman; George Falcon, who would become the publisher of Key Magazine, Frank Bresee, host of "The Golden Days of Radio;" Harry Coles, Jerry Singer, Steve Markham and many others. They were all part of the Larsen family.

Eugene Poinc was a classmate at Los Angeles High School He was a very talented actor and a brilliant artist. For many years he was the staff artist for Genii magazine. Gene painted the vaudeville *olio* drop that we used for our shows. Magicians loved the small Brookledge stage and we also had some pretty amazing guests stars like the famous Grock. Grock was a Swiss clown, composer and musician. He was billed as "The King of Clowns." He was once the most highly paid entertainer in the world.

On one of our Brookledge Music Hall shows Mother performed her classic *Mutilated Parasol*. (The umbrella fabric vanishes and colorful silks take its place.) During the act Geri would sing the popular song "Umbrella Man." At that time I was terribly impressed with Gene Kelly's "Singin' in the Rain" dance routine. I built a rain gutter drilled with holes and suspended it like a border across the stage. For the finale of her song real water poured from the ceiling. To accomplish the effect cheaply I had to carry two buckets of water to an awaiting funnel on the stage roof.

Grock, "The King of Clowns"

After the Thayer store moved out of the Longwood address the entire building became my personal bachelor pad. Bill and Irene and the family lived in the front home and I was given a free hand to build bars, secret doors and even a swimming pool. I converted the business office over the garage into a lavish office and apartment. Naturally I built a small bar in the corner. It is wonderful that Dante and Erika Larsen are now recreating those great days of variety with their series of Brookledge Follies shows.

Milt's Brookledge museum bar

THE FIFTIES

I grew up surrounded by magicians in a home built by a magician that was home to magicians from all over the world. Dad had the Thayer Magic Shop on LaBrea Avenue in Los Angeles and the Genii magazine was very successful. And I wanted to be a gag writer.

Red and I had just graduated from high school. My dad would have, very happily, sent me to college to follow his course of being a lawyer. But I didn't want to do that. I was only interested in being a comedy writer. I had lucked out because of the little books Red and I were writing. We got to know some people who had no idea that we were just kids until they met us. Upon first sight, of course, they found out the awful truth even when I smoked cigars and grew a moustache in an attempt to look older.

We took our hard earned gains from Dr. Zomb and rented an office at Sunset and Vine. Well, not really Sunset and Vine… everybody knows that was the address of NBC's Radio City. We rented a former film vault in the old Otto K. Oleson building at the corner of Selma and Vine next to the NBC parking lot. At that time it was kind of a Brill

Corner of Sunset & Vine, NBC's Radio City

Building West, filled with struggling and out-of-work writers, directors, producers and songwriters. The building was left over from the days when Jesse Lasky, Sam Goldwyn and Cecile B. DeMille made Hollywood's first film "The Squaw Man" on the site in 1913. In the late '40's and '50's Hollywood's Vine Street was the center of show biz.

The theater now known as the Avalon Hollywood had opened in 1927 as the Hollywood Playhouse and housed "Ken Murray's Blackouts" as well as television staples such as "This Is Your Life" and "The Merv Griffin Show." When Ken Murray opened his record-breaking long run show in 1942 Henry Duffy's Hollywood Playhouse was renamed El Capitan Theater. The original El Capitan Theater across from Grauman's Chinese changed its name to The Paramount Theater. After Murray's run and World War II, NBC took over the theater and in addition to Ralph Edwards' "This Is Your Life" it was also the home of NBC's "All Star Revue" and "The Colgate Comedy Hour," both starring the greatest names in comedy and variety.

Henry Duffy built another theater originally called The Vine Street Playhouse. That theater was better known in the '30's and '40's as The Lux Radio Theater featuring dramatic radio versions of movies, hosted by Cecile B. DeMille. Later it became The Huntington Hartford Theater, then The James Doolittle Theater and it is now called The Ricardo Montalban Theater. Next to that playhouse was a marvelous landmark restaurant Mike Lyman's Grill. Mike Lyman also had a fine restaurant downtown and at the Los Angeles airport. Incidentally, the Henry Fonda Theater was originally the Music Box Theater built by actor Carter DeHaven. It was the home of the "New Faces of 1938" revue. Carter DeHaven, father of actress Gloria DeHaven, was a former vaudevillian magician and was a friend of my father's. Then there was the Hitching Post movie theater across the street from the Pantages where kids had to check their toy guns before going in to see Tom Mix and Hopalong Cassidy. Next to the Hitching Post was Bert Wheeler's Hollywood Magic store, a hangout for magicians.

Across the street from our office was a drug store where you could get a great blue-plate special lunch for under a buck. In those days struggling writers ate at the drug store. When you got work you lunched at Nickodell's at Selma and Argyle. You lunched at the Brown Derby only to impress people that you were really working. One of the big gimmicks at the Brown Derby was a telephone jack at every booth. Public Relations folk would page their clients at the Derby whether you were there or not. It was very impressive to be paged and then have the waiter bring a telephone to your table (in the days before cell phones). The Brown Derby was a really classy place. They even had crushed ice in the men's room urinals.

Our office was a teeny, tiny 10' by 10' room with no windows and a door that opened in. We wanted an executive-type desk to impress our future clients. We couldn't afford one so, using my woodworking skills, I made one. It was a great desk but it took up most of the space in our tiny office. There was barely room for two chairs, the desk, and that door that opened in. We started the Comics Information Service and put out a monthly bulletin of topical one-liners. The only real writing job we could get was writing some gags for a local radio show. We got paid in product instead of money.

One of our satisfied CIF (Comics Information Service) gag buyers was an upcoming radio personality Reed Browning. He was a staff announcer at ABC. One day we got a call from Reed that he had landed a network ABC radio audience participation show. It would be a daily show starring Reed, feature guest stars, and emanate live from the old Tom Breneman "Breakfast in Hollywood" ABC-Radio studios on Vine Street in Hollywood. They would even have vocalists Art and Dottie Todd and the twenty-five piece Rex Koury house orchestra! Big time! Would we like the job of writing the show? Wow!

In the '50's, the large building on the west side of Vine Street between Sunset and Selma was the home of the American Broadcasting Company. It had been a former bowling center and then Tom Breneman turned it into a restaurant when he moved his "Breakfast at Sardi's" radio show there and called it "Breakfast in Hollywood."

Red and I met with the executives at ABC. The ABC Program Director for the West Coast at the time was Dresser Dahlstead, a very impressive silver-haired former announcer with a golden voice. The producer of the show was Harfield Weedin, a well-known producer/director of top radio shows. We signed a contract to provide material for the show. Our salary? They explained they didn't have writers in the budget but Reed really liked our work and felt he needed our material. There would be no money but we were allowed to inject three commercial plugs a week.

What is a commercial plug, you ask? Back in the days before the payola scandals it was an acceptable art form to sneak commercial plugs into scripts. There was nothing illegal about it. It was simply a perk that was available to the clever writer. If a writer mentioned the name of a product like *Chicken of the Sea* tuna that was worth a dozen

cases of the product. In some instances you received gift certificates or even money! If you wrote a joke about Mobil Oil, you could get vouchers for 100 gallons of gasoline. That would be worth a lot of money today! In those days, if a writer didn't have a case of Coca-Cola on his doorstep every week, he wasn't a working writer.

Our deal allowed us three plugs a week and we made the best of them. Our office got to be known as *The Plug Kids Store*. The other struggling artists in the building walked by our office and couldn't help but notice it was filled to the ceiling with left over prizes and payment of product. They knew they could buy everything in our office from toothpaste and shoe polish kits to chicken soup at big discounts. We had so much merchandise we finally had to get rid of one of the chairs. That exposure led to various small writing jobs.

The Plug Kids Store was doing well. Red and I were working for plugs but we were working. Later we would share real writing credits and get paid in real money. But for now we appreciated our first wonderful credit of a national radio show.

The Sherman Brothers would become legendary Academy Award wining songwriters later but in the early '50's, Robert B. and Richard M. were just Bob and Dick. They were living in a small apartment above a cleaning shop on Pico Boulevard. Dick was writing songs with other collaborators. Bob was more interested in being a novelist or radio writer. I interested ABC Radio to spring for a pilot for a new radio series: "Hear the Year." It was written by Bob Sherman and Milt Larsen and hosted by Reed Browning. Each show would focus on the music and sounds of a particular year. The pilot year was 1927—year of Lindbergh's solo flight and Paul Whiteman and the Rhythm Boys featured a new singer by the name of Bing Crosby. The network liked the show but didn't see fit to purchase it.

At that time Dick and I collaborated on a song "Concert in the Park" which was performed by the Bobby Hammack Trio, regulars on the Reed Browning Show. Dick and I wrote a couple of songs that we thought would be naturals for the great Jimmy Durante. Jimmy was famous for remembering his two pals Lou Clayton and Eddie Jackson. They starred in vaudeville as "Clayton, Jackson and Durante." After Jimmy became a star he kept his two pals on his payroll and often referred to them in his radio and TV shows. One of the songs we wrote for Durante was "Two Soft Shoes:"

Just two soft shoes, a hat and cane…
A little white piano and a funny refrain
Simple props you see,
But they meant the world to me
They meant Clayton, Jackson and Durante

The other was a song based on the popularity of the first big CinemaScope hit "The Robe." Our song was "There's Only Eighty-Eight Keys on the Piano." The idea was for Jimmy Durante to create a new piano "Pianna-scope" which had 176 keys. Through Dick's father, we set up a meeting with Jimmy Durante at his Beverly Hills home. He was wonderful, gracious and said he really liked the songs but he had his longtime writer Jackie Barnett penning his special material. "Thanks kids, but no thanks."

Red Baker and I shared a passion for collecting and running films. Back in the pre-historic days before home video rentals every movie mogul's mansion had a screening room. Some had sliding panels that would reveal big screens. Many homes had a sophisticated projection room with both 35mm and 16mm equipment. If you were a big enough celebrity the studio would send over a print of their latest work complete with a union projectionist. Seeing a movie in the privacy of a home screening room was the epitome of class.

One of the greatest film buffs was Lou Costello of Abbott and Costello fame. As one of Universal's top money-makers Lou had a clause in his contract that allowed him to take home a 16mm print of every film Universal released. That was unheard of in the '40's and '50's! Many of the home screening rooms ran films authorized by and borrowed from the studios. Most of the films on the shelves of collectors, called the Bel Air Circuit, were illegal. Not that many of the prints were stolen property but by merely showing them it constituted a copyright violation. Thus the FBI was on the constant prowl for this peculiar brand of renegade. Raids by the FBI were not uncommon. It was a bit like prohibition. Most collectors were honest and upright citizens of Hollywood who would never think of doing anything against the law. On the other hand, who could resist a brand new Technicolor print of a movie classic? Today you can buy or rent almost any picture and run it on your huge home video screen. Like the movies themselves, some of the excitement has dimmed.

Red had a 16mm sound projector and we made extra money by working for a man who would rent out movies to churches and retirement homes. We would set up a screen and run the film. Usually it was something like "Ben Hur: A Tale of The Christ"—the 1925 silent version with Ramon Novarro and Frances X. Bushman. God! We got tired of watching that film.

There was a big music store on Hollywood Boulevard. Bill Denels owned Denels Music. Bill was a film buff and turned the second floor of his building into a film library for his pals. His film-collecting-friends included people like Donald O'Connor, Director William Dieterle, Mel Torme and others. Anyone that stored their collections at Denels had access to all the films. Bill even hired a librarian to take care of the collections. We got to know Bill and became his official *runners*. If someone in the group wanted a film we would deliver it. We didn't make any money but we got to be members of this very elite club. One time Donald O'Connor borrowed a print of Bing Crosby's "Bells of St. Mary" to run for some friends. It turned out the friends were a group of nuns. Everything was fine until they discovered someone had spliced some explicit porno into the print. Donald was not happy.

After the Thayer Studio of Magic moved to the commercial location, the family lived at The Brookledge that just happened to have a theater in the backyard. That theater was another reason there is a Magic Castle today. My very patient parents allowed me to practice my primitive building skills on a very fascinating building. They were somewhat miffed when I sawed one of the legs off our grand piano so it would fit under the stage to make it look like an orchestra pit. When I heard they were tearing down the historic Westminster Hotel on Main Street, I bought the ornately carved ballroom balcony façade where President William McKinley had spoken from and made it into the front of the Brookledge stage. Ernie Evans saved two angels holding gilded torchieres from a church demolition, which now adorn each side of the proscenium.

The Brookledge theatre

The Brookledge bar

Pretty soon the balcony of the theater became a projection room and our friends were treated to frequent showings of Hollywood's latest films. In order to compete in the game of one-upmanship you had to be more like a real movie theater than the next guy; this included electric curtains, atmospheric lights, popcorn, lobby cards for the evening's event… the whole enchilada. I had dual 35mm and dual 16mm projectors andtheater-type speakers and CinemaScope lenses. We got to know film collectors and people with great studio contacts. I had invented a method by which our twelve-foot screen would rise from the basement with the push of a button. It was this very invention that later convinced Tom Glover I could make something wonderful out of his Victorian house on Franklin Avenue.

The Brookledge projection balcony

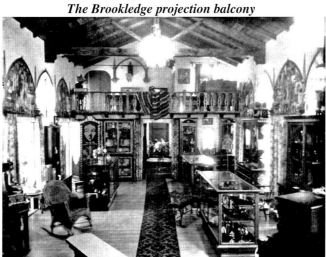

The late George Boston worked with many of the great magicians. He wrote a fascinating book with Bob Parrish called: "Inside Magic." Just after I graduated from Los Angeles High School, I got my first real job working for George who was the manager of the Abbott Magic Shop at 6505 Sunset Boulevard. This was a branch of the world-famed Abbott's in Colon, Michigan. It was a pretty good job: hard work, long hours and $35. a week. It was a nice shop though, with real magic and no joke store stuff. George had a well-known local artist paint portraits of famous magicians on the walls. I assume those portraits are still there under a coat of Kem-Tone.

George Boston

Working for George was a bit of an experience. He would have been a great General, expecting a lot out of his troops. And I was *his troops*. George wasn't afraid of hard work… but he preferred that somebody else do it… that somebody else was me! One day George took off for a few hours and asked me to mind the store. My first and only customer came in and cheerfully asked what was new. I demonstrated a new version of the *Dime and Penny* trick. He acted as though he had never seen it before and wanted two of them. This enthusiastic customer bought at least two of everything I showed him. He stayed about an hour and said he had a great time chatting with his teenage salesman.

By the time he left the bill was over two hundred dollars… a huge sum in the late '40's. (In fact, I was curious—that would have been the equivalent of $1,872.80 in 2012.) When George came back he asked if I had sold anything. I showed him the multi-paged sales slip. He was amazed when I told him all the sales were to a sole customer. Did I know who it was? Sure, George, everyone knew Cary Grant! George was not amused. He had always wanted to meet Cary Grant. George was one of our first Academy of Magical Arts Board Members.

While I was working at Abbott's I came up with pretty funny gag. At that time a standard gimmick was a little ratchet that would make a loud sound while the magicians wound his watch, a *Watch Winder*. I soldered a *Joy Buzzer,* a gimmick that used to get a laugh when you shook hands with an unsuspecting victim, and a *Bingo Shooting Device*, which shot off a loud cap when you released it onto the watch winder. When the magician pretended to wind his watch, it would sound as if a spring had broken, and the whole thing exploded. It was a great gag until they invented battery operated watches. George suggested that Percy Abbott put it in the catalog and there it was: *Milton's Buzz Bang*. Percy believed in giving name credit rather that money.

Milton's Buzz Bang

Great as a gag among your friends or in your Act. Calling attention to your watch, you proceed to wind it. The noise that ensues is a clackity-clack, and a whir — as the spring breaks (?). It's screamingly funny. Gimmick is flesh color and is concealed in hand. The finish is a bang.

ALL CHANGE – ALL CHANGE – ALL ABOARD FOR HOLLYWOOD!

In the '50's, Brother Bill had graduated from Occidental College and had decided that his year at USC's Law School was enough. He wasn't cut out to be a lawyer. Dad totally agreed. My brother was managing the Thayer store on LaBrea and was very involved with Genii magazine.

William W. Larsen Sr.

In 1952 Brother Bill married Dorothy Davis. Bill had met Dorothy in college and she assisted him in his magic act. Their marriage was announced in Genii, of course. And when they had their first child, Wendy, the following year—that too, was announced in print. The Genii readers were able to follow the activities of the Larsens through the pages of Genii.

Governor Earl Warren tapped Bill Sr. for judgeship. Before he decided whether to accept the post, Dad died suddenly in 1953 at the age of 48 from a cerebral hemorrhage. When Dad passed away the family decided to continue to publish the patriarch's magazine and rallied; the staff of Genii changed. Mother was still the editor and publisher, Bill Jr. and I were Associate Editors, Bill's wife, Dorothy, became Advertising Manager, and Eugene Poinc was staff artist. In Bill's first editorial, he promised Genii would go on as Dad would have wanted. Bill made good on that promise.

William W. Larsen Sr.

Mother said that God threw away the pattern when he made Bill. There could never be anyone quite like him. Faults he had aplenty, but he was the first to admit them. His heart was bigger than the world and from it he gave so much to the world of magic, to his family, to his friends, to living. He had had an incredible love for the art of magic and he had passed that love on to his family and to magicians throughout the world.

Mother had her own filmed syndicated show "The Magic Lady" for Telemount Pictures (a joint venture with Paramount Pictures) in the '50's, one of the first shows filmed in glorious color—which the television audiences enjoyed in black and white because CBS and NBC were arguing about whose color system was going to be used. We all remembered the excitement of watching the ticker tape news go past with the Paramount mountain logo in the background. What a miracle of modern technology! Mother's show paved the way for lady magicians in the future. Dell O'Dell and Gerrie Larsen were the only female magicians televised at the time. The ten-minute show was produced and directed by Henry Donovan with Jerry Maren, a little person actor who had played one of the Munchkins in MGM's classic "Wizard of Oz," as the impish Boko. It was endorsed by the Southern California PTA and ran for thirteen weeks.

"The Magic Lady" sets were very impressive. Her primary set was the Magical

The Magic Lady, Geraldine Larsen

Garden of the Moon with a rocky moonscape, crescent moon, stars and a bubble machine worthy of Lawrence Welk. Dressed in her "Gone With The Wind" flowing white gown and a sparkling star tiara, Geraldine performed magic and sang original songs to organ accompaniment. Dick Sherman had been a family member since the early days at The Brookledge and he was delighted to work with Mother putting several of her poems to music.

Gerrie was first to utilize audience participation from the television audience at home! When the entire set appeared to be underwater, boys and girls at home were asked for magic words to help rescue The Magic Lady and Boko. She performed her favorite routines: *The Mutilated Parasol*, *The Indian Rope Trick* that Boko climbed up and disappeared from and *The Butterfly Routine* where Boko chased an elusive butterfly and The Magic Lady made it appear as a beautiful silk. Her famous *Wishing Tree* was a P&L Blooming Rose Bush that granted wishes of children who wrote to The Magic Lady.

Using black art principles, The Magic Lady placed Boko into a large sack, drew the strings closed and made him vanish only to reappear riding a Shetland pony through a huge golden frame behind her. Bill McIlhaney located some of these shows and reproduced them through the Miracle Factory "as a lasting tribute to Geri's radiant spirit, beauty and remarkable talents." The images below were captured from the actual videos of "The Magic Lady."

Geraldine Larsen as "The Magic Lady" with Jerry Maren as Boko.

69

The Magic Lady, Geraldine Larsen, loved to sing. She incorporated her own original melodies on her television show and took every opportunity to break out in song. My mother hammed it up on occasion in my little showbiz museum at The Brookledge circa 1950.

Geri Larsen hamming it up at Brookledge

As an English major from Occidental College, Gerrie wrote and published three books on puppetry, in addition to two novels: "Diary of a Magician's Wife" and "Nothing Up His Sleeve."

Unfortunately Mother had a few show business setbacks. She had signed a seven-year exclusive contract with a producer who sat on her contract without producing anything and as a result Mother missed out on commercial work. Warner Brothers wanted to purchase the rights to "The Diary of a Magician's Wife" for their Blondie television series. The book exposed some magic secrets and Dad felt that exposing magic on television was not a good idea. They agreed not to release the rights. It was published, instead, in the pages of Genii under her maiden name, Geraldine Conrad.

The Diary of a Magician's Wife

Illustrated By Tom S. Lawless

By Geraldine Conrad Larsen

Within the pages of this book I refer to our mother as Geraldine, Gerrie and Geri. Her names swing depending upon whether she was a performer—Geraldine Larsen "The Magic Lady;" Gerrie Larsen, the author, writer, housewife and mother; or Geri, the artist. She was also Gerrie Larsen, Baker & Jaffe and Geraldine Conrad. Bill and I had three sensational fathers and one magnificent mother.

NOTHING UP HIS SLEEVE

A MERRY MELANGE of Mystery and Magic

GERALDINE CONRAD LARSEN

ILLUSTRATED BY TOM S. LAWLESS

Dell O'Dell

Dell O'Dell also had a show on KTLA about the same time. Dell and Mother were total opposites. Mother was the "Magic Lady From Make-Believe Land" while Dell was a great nightclub performer. Dell O'Dell's husband was a fine juggler, Charlie Carrer. When I was a kid, Charlie taught me one of my odd, strange, unique and little-known talents: yanking a tablecloth from under a fully loaded table. One day I received a call at the Castle asking if I knew anyone that could perform the table yank trick. I recommended myself. I was asked to demonstrate the bit for the producer of the very popular series, "Bewitched."

The following morning I met the producer Bill Asher in his office at the old Columbia Studios lot. He asked if I really did the gag and wondered if there was some place we could go to demonstrate it. I said "no problem." He let me do it right then and there. I asked permission to clear off part of his big executive desk. I spread out a large napkin and a few glasses and dishes. I yanked the napkin and he was impressed. "That's great kid, now can you do that with a bigger table and whole lot of dishes?" I assured him it was no problem. I got the job.

The next day I got a call from the prop man on the show. Did I need a special table? Rigged glasses? Magic dishes? What??? I told him all I needed was a smooth table, glasses and dishes with smooth bottoms and a smooth tablecloth. I didn't bother telling him I had never done a big table yank before. I also mentioned that it might be cool to have some extra dishes and glassware on hand, just in case we had more than one take. The big day came and I reported to the studio where I was issued my duplicate Paul Lynde suit. My bit would be doubling for Paul. The prop master showed me the set where I would be doing my act. The table was fully set up and looked great. I checked the tablecloth, glasses and dishes and told him I didn't see any problems. He also assured me that he had cases of extra breakables for *when* I failed. (That gave me a lot of confidence.) I met Paul Lynde and watched them shoot all day. At the end of the day they apologized and said to return again the next day. Again, no problem… I was getting paid by the day.

My crowning achievement was when I doubled for Paul Lynde on "Bewitched" and yanked the tablecloth from under a complete five-place setting dining table with crystal goblets, fine china and even two large candlesticks. I did it on the first take. I still have my AFTRA (American Federation of Radio and Television Artists) and SAG (Screen Actors Guild) membership cards. Throughout the years my main acting credits have been yanking tablecloths as a stunt double.

Dad had been the President of the Society of American Magicians, Assembly 22, at the time of his passing in 1953. Snag Werris took over as President and I became Secretary and started writing the newsletters for the organization. I wasn't a very good secretary so they made somebody else the Secretary and asked me to keep writing my interesting and fun newsletters.

I remembered the great annual stage shows that the P.C.A.M. and S.A.M. produced in the '40's. I felt it was a shame that the big shows were now being held in school auditoriums and parks. At that time the wonderful world of magic wasn't so wonderful. The biggest club in town was the S.A.M. with its seventy or eighty members. Some of the energetic spark plugs of the organization had already passed on. Those old shows were put together by people like Ray Muse, Claude Leaf, Peter Godfrey and, of course, Bill Larsen Sr. When Dad died the annual shows also passed on. In 1956, Mark Wilson had just broken the television barrier with his "Magic Land of Allakazam" shows on CBS but, other than that, the magic show biz was really no biz!

The S.A.M. had been producing their annual public show in a five hundred-seat flat-floored community auditorium in Plummer Park. They produced a good show with local talent and usually turned a net profit of about five hundred dollars. I offered to produce the S.A.M. Annual Show of 1956. I wanted to bring back the big shows, lights, scenery, and a band in the pit—glamour... all that jazz! After all, in 1956 I was twenty-five years old. I knew everything! If the S.A.M. would provide the acts, my good friend Oliver Berliner, who happened to have some money, would provide everything else and guarantee the S.A.M. their five hundred dollars. Oliver and I produced the show and called it "Hocus Pocus '56." We rented the then famous landmark: the sixteen hundred seat Carthay Circle Theater in Westwood.

Carthay Circle Theatre postcard

74

It was an absolutely beautiful theatre with a very long forecourt to Wilshire, perfect for premieres. A flagship for Fox, it had been a presentation house for movies, fully equipped with an orchestra pit. Sadly, they tore it down to build two dreadful office buildings in 1969.

John Filbert of the Filbert Company, one of Hollywood's biggest dealers in theater equipment, told me a funny story about the immense fire curtain of the Carthay Circle Theatre. B.F. Shearer, another major theater supplier and Filbert's main competitor, a theatrical wrecking company, purchased the theatrical equipment from the theatre. Cleveland Wrecking took everything else. The two guys from the wrecking companies argued about who was going to take down the huge and very heavy asbestos fire curtain from the Carthay Circle Theatre. B.F. Shearer said they didn't want it and it wasn't their job to remove it. Cleveland Wrecking said that it was considered theatre equipment and it was their job. It would be costly to take it down.

An Emigrant Train at Donner Lake

A man appeared on stage announcing he'd like the curtain. Both Shearer and Cleveland Wrecking immediately claimed the curtain as theirs and said they would sell it. The man replied that he had just heard them both arguing about whose responsibility the fire curtain removal was. He would get the crew and remove it for free if he could have it.

Later on, both companies found out that the beautiful hand-painted fire curtain had been painted by famous Western artist Frank Tenney Johnson and was dedicated to the Donner Party "An Emigrant Train at Donner Lake." It would have been worth thousands. It now resides as a backdrop at Dr. Eugene Scotts' United Artists Theatre at 9th and Olympic.

CARTHAY CIRCLE
THEATRE

THIS EVENING
SATURDAY, JANUARY 28, 1956

THE SOCIETY OF AMERICAN
MAGICIANS
SOUTHERN CALIFORNIA/ASSEMBLY Nº 22 *INC.*
IN THEIR ALL NEW MAGICAL EXTRAVAGANZA

HOCUS
POCUS '56

Program
SUBJECT TO CHANGE WITHOUT NOTICE
in the order of their appearance:

1 □ ORCHESTRA UNDER THE PERSONAL DIRECTION OF MR. RAY STEWART
A FEW WORDS FROM MR. SNAG WERRIS (PRESIDENT S.A.M. ASSEMBLY #22.

2 ART BAKER

3 TENKAI & OKINU

4 PHIL BAUER

5 EVELYN RUSSELL
WITH
SNAG WERRIS AND SID FIELDS

6 GERALDINE LARSEN

7 THE CHAUDETS

INTERMISSION

8 CHOP CHOP & CHARLENE

9 SKIPPER FRANK

10 AUBREY & COMPANY

PRODUCED FOR OBERLINE INCORPORATED BY MILTON LARSEN

FIRE NOTICE—Look around now, choose the nearest exit to your seat, and in case of disturbance
of any kind, to avoid the danger of panic, WALK (do not run) to that exit.
☞ SEE OTHER SIDE ☜

CNTR — CARTHAY CIRCLE THEATRE — 6316 W. San Vicente — LOS ANGELES 8:30 P.M. CALIFORNIA — ORCHESTRA — JAN'RY 28 1956 — SATURDAY EVE. — THE SOCIETY OF AMERICAN MAGICIANS IN — HOCUS POCUS '56 — EST. PRICE $2.00 FED. TAX .20 $2.20 — GOOD ONLY SATURDAY EVE. JAN'RY 28 — CARTHAY CIRCLE THEATRE — ORCHESTRA — GLOBE TICKET COMPANY, LOS ANGELES — CNTR — ORCHESTRA — ROW SEAT — 1 6 — 1956

"Skipper" Frank Herman

Frakson

Tenkai & Okinu

Chop Chop & Charlene

The Chaudets

Geraldine Larsen

Art Baker

Even if I do say so myself, our first show was pretty amazing. Art Baker emceed and Mom performed as "The Magic Lady." Ollie Berliner and I were proud of the line-up: Frakson, Chop Chop & Charlene, Phil Bauer, Aubrey & Company, The Chaudets, Harry Mendoza and Tenkai & Okinu—all classics. It was an artistic but not financial success. We ended up paying the S.A.M. their fee of five hundred dollars and we lost a few bucks in the transaction.

The following year "It's Magic!" moved to the 1,033-seat Wilshire Ebell Theatre in Los Angeles' swank Hancock Park area that was to be our annual home for the next nineteen years! Art Baker emceed again. Art was the star of "You Asked For It!" At that time Art and mother, Geri Larsen, were seeing each other but not yet married. John Calvert was a major star in magic traveling throughout the world with a big illusion show in his sixty-five foot, one-hundred-ton yacht called The Magic Castle II. John was very well-known to the general public as the dashing star Falcon, a detective series of

the movies. Ollie Berliner, Brother Bill and I talked about the idea of asking Calvert if he would perform in the show. No way! We thought. Why would a big star like John Calvert do a show for a twenty-six year old producer with no budget for the talent? But what the heck, it never hurts to ask!

John Calvert's Magic Castle II

I remember the day as if it was the day before yesterday. I had just started working on Bob Barker's "Truth or Consequences." I dialed a number from a phone booth in the hallway of the old NBC Radio City Studios at Sunset and Vine. Much to my surprise John answered the phone personally. I started with the line, "You don't know me, Mr. Calvert, but…" I didn't get to finish the sentence. John interrupted, "What do you mean I don't know you? You're Bill Larsen's kid!!!"

Then he went on to say how much he admired my dad and how much he missed him. Bill Larsen Sr. had passed away just two years earlier. Then he said he would love to do the "It's Magic!" show but I would have to agree to his price. I choked and asked what that price would be. He said it would be $10,000. But he would knock off $10,000 for old times sake so the price would be zero! We immediately added John Calvert to the show.

We had several celebrities, Frank "Skipper" Herman and NBC's new star, Ernie Kovacs as hosts. Aubrey & Company, The Chaudets, Harry Mendoza returned and we added Leo Irby & Company and Jim Conley to the show. We were producing the show for S.A.M. again but we had renegotiated. This time we offered no guarantees. Ollie and I loved the show, so did the audience. However, there was more enthusiasm than audience. We lost money again and S.A.M. made no money at all. The next year their annual show went back to Plummer Park and Ollie and I went on to produce the 3rd Annual "It's Magic!" at the Wilshire Ebell as an independent production.

"Skipper" Frank Herman, who had appeared on the 1957 show, said there was nothing wrong with the show that good publicity wouldn't cure. He knew the answer—he had a friend who had seen the last two shows, loved the concept and happened to be a fantastic publicist. That was the year "Skipper" Frank Herman introduced me to Norman and Shirley Carroll. Norman was the ringmaster of the Ringling Brothers Barnum and Bailey Circus. The Carrolls were also the West Coast publicists for the circus. Ollie and I were about ready to throw the concept of bringing big time magic to L.A. in the dumpster. Frank insisted that we meet the Carrolls first. I met Norman Carroll and he said, "You've got a great show, let me show you how to sell it!" The next year we produced the show and Norman and Shirley did the publicity—at absolutely no charge. They wanted to make a point and they certainly did. That year everyone in Los Angeles knew about the "It's Magic!" show. We turned people away.

Shirley Carroll receiving Academy of Magical Arts Award of Merit from Milt (L) and Bill (R)

THE SOCIETY OF AMERICAN MAGICIANS

SOUTHERN CALIFORNIA ASSEMBLY 22
PRESENTS
ITS SILVER ANNIVERSARY PUBLIC SHOW

IT'S MAGIC!

PRODUCED BY MILT LARSEN
in Association with Oliver Berliner

PROGRAM

OVERTURE: "IT'S MAGIC!" (Cahn-Styne)
Manny Harmon and the Orchestra

Master of Ceremonies
MR. ART BAKER
"YOU ASKED FOR IT"

The Incomparable
1. CONLEY and His Company

2. HARRY MENDOZA
In His Famous Characterization
"ATA SUN GAI"

Today's Most Famous Escapologist
3. LEO IRBY and Co.

PROGRAM CONTINUED NEXT PAGE

PROGRAM CONTINUED

4. **SKIPPER FRANK HERMAN**
   Courtesy KTLA-Paramount Television

THE FABULOUS
5. **AUBREY & COMPANY**
   Television's Most Popular Illusionist

INTERMISSION
15 MINUTES

7. **ART BAKER**
   "THAT SING THING!"

8. **THE CHAUDETS - Bill & Mary**
   Magic's Favorite Couple

OUR SPECIAL GUEST STAR
9. **ERNIE KOVACS**
   Courtesy NBC Television

The Internationally Known Star
10. **JOHN CALVERT**
    And His Hollywood Cover Girls

STAFF FOR "IT'S MAGIC"

DIRECTED BY - - - - - GEORGE L. BOSTON
ASSISTED BY - - - - - FRED RICKARD
(A Presentation of Oberline, Inc.)

WILSHIRE-EBELL THEATER

MANAGER - - - - - HAROLD PETTIJOHN
STAGE MANAGER - - - - - BILL MANHOFF
ELECTRICIAN - - - - - BILL MANHOFF, JR.

The producers wish to express special thanks to Mr. Snag Werris, Mr. Don Slater, Mr. Joe Lepselder, Mr. Julian Neilsen, Miss Mary Markham, Mr. Phil Bauer, Mr. Ben Hunter, Mr. Dave Starling, and Mr. Don Allen for their kind efforts in behalf of "It's Magic."

It was Shirley Carroll who suggested we produce "It's Magic!" closer to Halloween. The press was always looking for unique stories to tie into the wonderfully fun holiday. One of her best promotions was with Hughes Market, a local grocery store. She sold Hughes Market on the idea of putting four or five different cartoon face masks on their paper bags. The eyes could be punched out and children could wear the bag as a Halloween mask. On the back of the grocery bag was a tear-off coupon, courtesy of Hughes Market, for two dollars off the "It's Magic!" ticket price. 200,000 bags were printed which cost next to nothing for the local market. Kids were parading around Hollywood with these bags over their heads and their parents used the coupons. We sold out that year.

Shirley also warned me not to even try to get articles in the Calendar section of the Los Angeles Times because the movie studios had all the clout and took up most of that section. Instead, she suggested the local "City-Side" section. By taking our magicians to a hospital to perform for the patients or underprivileged, we'd end up on the first page of that section with a six-column spread. She was a brilliant, brilliant lady.

The Carrolls were singularly responsible for the success of "It's Magic!" And the "It's Magic!" shows paved the way for the creation of the Magic Castle. Norman Carroll was on the original Board of Directors of the Academy of Magical Arts. Unfortunately, he passed away before the Castle opened.

Irene Stolz met her first husband, John Daniel, when he performed a magic show in Germany, 1956. She was asked to assist him on stage. (It seems to be a curse of Larsen women as the same thing happened to Mother.) When John returned to Los Angeles Irene came with him. Shortly thereafter Irene married John and performed *Thin Model Sawing* for the first time in America. She performed in a spook show "Dr. Satan's Shrieks in the Night," demonstrated magic at Abbott's Magic Shop on Hollywood Blvd. and performed with Orson Welles as the *Disembodied Princess* on the "Dean Martin Show."

It was no accident that famed radio and TV personality, Art Baker, hosted the first "It's Magic!" ("Hocus Pocus '56") and subsequent shows like "They Called It Vaudeville." A few years after Dad's death, Gerrie met Art Baker, star of "You Asked For It," the successful audience participation TV show that he hosted for most of its nine year run in the 1950's. Mother met him through George Boston. Yes, the same George Boston who gave me my first job.

Art Baker

This wonderful man became my second father August 11, 1957. Geri and Art Baker were the perfect couple. They shared a love for singing and they both loved magic. Married in London, they continued their honeymoon by traveling throughout Europe. Together they traveled extensively and were great ambassadors of good will for the Magic Castle and the Academy of Magical Arts. In addition, Bill and Dorothy had now separated. Genii had become Bill's baby with most of the work being handled by Bill alone.

Art Baker, an aficionado of magic, took his "You Asked For It" audience through Abbott's plant in Colon, Michigan and then presented Aubrey performing one of Percy's effects, without exposing the effect. George Boston made sure that conjurors appeared with considerable regularity. Art was born with a wonderful set of pipes. For many years he was an outstanding evangelistic singer and song leader. Radio was his next field.

Art Baker and Geri

Shortly after his marriage to Gerrie he put out "That Sing Thing." He was very involved with SPEBSQA (The Society for the Preservation and Encouragement of Barbershop Singing Quartets in America) and hosted most of their National events. He hosted "Art Baker's Notebook" on syndicated radio for over two decades. He was identified with Chevrolet as the announcer for Dinah Shore's NBC TV shows and appeared in many movies.

My mother loved to write poetry. When she was asked to do a pilot as "The Magic Lady" in 1957 she asked Dick Sherman to write the lyrics and music for "The Magic Lady," opening and closing themes, as well as create music for several of her poems so she could use them in her show.

Milt, Geri and Dick Sherman

THE MAGIC LADY OF MAKE-BELIEVE LAND
Words and Music By DICK SHERMAN (BMI)

Opening

I'm the Magic Lady of Make-Believe Land
Hello little friends, Hello
Come along with me
And such wonders you will see
In my magic garden of the moon
With a tiny wave of my stardust wand
Your dreams become re-a-li-ty
So put on that smile
And for a little while
Come and wander through
Make-Believe Land with me.

Closing

I'm the Magic Lady of Make-Believe Land
Goodbye little friends Goodbye
It's been so much fun
But the clock was on the run
And alas it's time to say Goodbye
With a tiny wave of my stardust wand
Your dreams became re-a-li-ty
So be good and sweet
And then next time we meet
We can wander through
Make-Believe Land again.

85

Ralph Edwards created a show in 1940 based on an old parlor game called "Truth or Consequences." The show became a huge success on radio and television, and the only game show that an entire town in New Mexico was named after. When Ralph Edwards introduced to the "Truth or Consequences" radio audiences the *Mrs. Hush* and *Walking Man* fund-raising contests, the ratings soared. America's radio fans stopped everything to listen. Ralph was able to raise astounding donations for the March of Dimes in 1947 with the *Mrs. Hush* contests. The American Heart Association made its public debut in late 1948 during a network radio contest, *The Walking Man*, also hosted by Ralph Edwards. Millions of Americans sent contributions to the American Heart Association along with guesses of the walking man's identity. The contest/carryover kept the entire nation in suspense. The effort netted $1.75 million before Flo Hubbard of Chicago finally identified Jack Benny as the *Walking Man*, and Ralph Edwards got the ratings!

By 1956 "Truth or Consequences" was an institution. Ralph was the host until he left to star in "This Is Your Life" that became one of TV's number one hits. Jack Bailey was the host of the nighttime "Truth or Consequences." A new daytime version of the show made its TV debut on December 31, 1956. The star of the new show was an unknown radio personality Bob Barker.

Bob Barker, Ralph Edwards

My old boss at Abbott's Magic, George Boston, worked for Ralph Edwards Productions as the manager of their prize promotion department. George told me they were looking for idea men for the new show and I submitted some material to Ralph's brother, Paul Edwards. Paul very politely told me the submissions were not what they were looking for, but George Boston had recommended me for the new job as George's assistant in the prize department. It would be a chance to put my foot in the corporate door and be part of the Ralph Edwards organization. It wasn't exactly what I wanted but it was a job.

As I left his office, Paul introduced me to the writer that they had hired as an idea man. He was a short blonde kid from Texas who looked like he was about fifteen years old. His name was Robert Lauher. How could they hire this snotty-nosed little kid when they could have had a twenty-five year old seasoned professional like me?! Later Bobby Lauher became one of my closest friends and was my writing partner until his untimely passing in 1973. But, at that moment, I hated him.

The years of writing for merchandise instead of money paid off. I knew about promoting prizes and I did a good job—too good, in fact. The Ralph Edwards organization was very happy with my work in the prize department, too happy! After a few months of promoting prizes while watching the organization hire and fire a number of new writers I complained to Paul that I had only taken the job in the prize department to get my foot in the door. Now my foot was getting stepped on by a herd of incoming and outgoing writers. He talked to the show's head writer, Bill Burch, and they came up with a plan. While working in the prize department I could submit acts to Burch. If an act was used on the show I would be paid a fee. This would be a way to prove myself.

The Edwards Productions warehouse was a secret treasure chest. Beyond the stacks of toasters, ovens, grooming kits and prizes was a stack of Kinescope copies of the first "Truth or Consequences" nighttime shows, pre-video tape. Remember the theatre at The Brookledge? Well, it would come in handy once again. I asked if I could look at the old Kinescopes. George Boston knew about the theatre, knew I had really good equipment and knew I would take care of the old films. He allowed me to take them home overnight and review them.

Those early shows were pure gold. Actually, pure Old Gold since Old Gold cigarettes was the sponsor at the time. If Snag Werris had taught me *anything* about gag writing it was the theory of switching a joke; an act that played with a Sergeant and Private could be switched to an act that would play equally well with a Bank President and a new Teller. I studied the Kinescopes and wrote acts using the concepts the show had aired before. My acts were new and fresh but, somehow, they had a guaranteed feeling about them. The nightly showings of the old nighttime "Truth or Consequences" had paid off. It wasn't too long after that when I received a call from Paul Edwards. I was being fired from the Prize Department and hired as an idea man. You see, they were paying me a lot of additional money for my acts. I took to the gag writing easily. The reason I got this neat job was I thought upside-down and all the other writers thought right-side up—a magician starts with the climax and works backwards.

People thought of "Truth or Consequences" as a game show, but it really was a comedy-variety show, requiring players to perform elaborate stunts when they almost invariably failed to answer a trick question before Beulah the Buzzer sounded. What made Ralph Edward's "Truth or Consequences" different from any subsequent audience participation show was the fact that Ralph always insisted the show was produced in impeccable taste. Yes, we threw our fair share of whipped cream pies, crushed cars with wrecking balls and dropped guys wearing old-fashioned bathing suits into tanks of water but it was always done in a way that never, ever embarrassed the contestant. It was a valuable asset instilled in me from my early years of comedy writing with Ralph Edwards and one premise I held to when I produced vaudeville and magic shows. My role models were Ralph Edwards and Walt Disney.

We were often asked what the writers did on a show like "Truth or Consequences." We certainly didn't write lines for the contestants to say. And if we didn't know what the contestants were going to say, how could we write lines for Bob Barker's response? We wrote gags and situations. Every gag or idea had to have a beginning, middle and a great payoff. Then Ralph Edwards said, once you have that, look for one more topper. Ralph's standing credo for us was simply to come up with gags that would have viewers talking about the show the next day around the water cooler.

For the on-camera rehearsal the writers stood in for the soon-to-be-selected contestants in what we thought they might do. It was great fun because nobody could really predict what a person facing the TV cameras and lights for the first time would do. Bobby Lauher, Jerry Payne, and I wrote situations for reunions, hidden camera remote jokes, silly stunts, carry-overs, contests, sketches, songs, games, heart acts, star acts, kid acts, in other words, just about everything under the sun. There was no limit to the wild things we were allowed to think up. The only set rule was that it had to be funny. Remember also that the show was live.

When I started on the show in 1957 the coaxial cable only carried the TV signal one way! We did our show to air in New York at 11 a.m. That meant we had to go *on-the-air* at 7 a.m. The show would be filmed by a 35mm camera of the TV screen by a process was called *Kinescope recording*. Then the negative was put on a special NBC plane that was outfitted with a lab and the film was developed in-flight. Once landing at the Burbank airport the film was sped to the NBC Studio at Sunset & Vine and put on the projector so it could play the West Coast at 11 a.m. The film was dubbed a *wet kinnie* because the chemicals dripped into a bucket under the projector. Later we saw the advent of amazing breakthroughs in TV technology. Black and white gave way to color. Videotape became common and electronic editing was made possible. But "Truth or Consequences" was always aired as a totally live show.

In 1957 most NBC's TV shows were produced at the old NBC Radio City Studios at Sunset & Vine in Hollywood. "Truth or Consequences" held forth for six years in Studio D, an intimate 250-seat theater at the Sunset and Argyle end of the NBC block-long studio complex. Ralph Edwards hated to move from those studios to the new NBC Burbank lot in 1962. We had the advantage of doing an audience participation show in an area where there were thousands of tourists. At that time in Burbank, it was easier to find horses than people. The wrecking ball was already working on Studio A at Sunset and Vine while we were still producing "Truth or Consequences" from Studio D.

We never knew what was going to happen next and no matter what happened Bob Barker would always be there to save the day. Some of our funniest shows were ones that didn't go as written. A typical script would often be: Bring on contestants, interview and question, play act. As writers, we had *house numbers*:

LAMBERTI ACT: This was based on a great old vaudeville/burlesque act. Professor Lamberti would come out as a classical musician and play the xylophone rather badly. The audience would applaud and shout for more and Lamberti would accept the applause and do many encores. What he didn't know was strippers were doing their stuff behind him to the cheers of the audience. We used that device doing things like having a lady's husband swing back and forth on a rope behind her in a Tarzan loincloth picking up gifts until, of course, the lady spotted him. The variations were endless.

OBSERVATION ACT: How long would it take three ladies being interviewed by Bob Barker to notice that a fellow contestant's knit dress was being unraveled by a prop man with an offstage winch? It took a long time for one lady contestant to notice that writer Jerry Payne, who was bald, deftly switched toupees until one of the other lady contestants spotted him. I did a bit once playing the part of a fellow contestant and my necktie kept getting longer and longer. Yes, many years later I marketed the *Growing Necktie* as a magic comedy prop.

HALLWAY ACT: Usually a practical joke or a reunion took place in the hallway outside the studio with the *pigeon* unaware that a "Truth or Consequences" act was in process. We had some delightful hallway kid acts like a little kid being left to watch over a *talking puppy*. The puppy's voice was provided by Bobby Lauher.

Milt Larsen's Growing Tie

CARRY-OVER: Ralph Edwards started this classic art form in the '40's on radio. A *carry-over* simply was an act that started on one show and went on for many shows.

PRACTICAL JOKES: When we did practical jokes on the show "Truth or Consequences Strikes Again," they were done live. In the build-up to a hidden camera gag, Bob would describe exactly what was going to happen or what we hoped would happen! Here are a couple of my favorites:

Cement truck:

Bob Barker explained in our build-up that a husband was going to play a joke on his wife. Our hidden camera took us to the scene of the crime. Across the street from our studio on Argyle Avenue, a large cement truck was parked on the street in front of a really nice-looking convertible. Behind the convertible was a small car with a driver in it. Bob went on to say that at this moment, the husband was circling the block looking for a place to park. Just as the husband turned the corner our henchman in the small car pulled out, leaving a splendid parking space. Except, of course, the husband's large car was a little too big for the parking space. He proceeded to do what any normal male would do—he pushed the convertible forward with his car which caused the convertible to bump into the cement truck which, in turn, released a chute of mixed cement into the empty convertible. The husband and his wife got out of their car to inspect the damage when they were met by the convertible's owner working on a sign—it was Jerry Payne of our writing staff. I'll never forget Jerry's great ad lib as the cement poured into his car, "What have you done?—I had my lunch in there!" The wife joined in the fray, swatting Jerry with her purse, until Bob interrupted over the loud speaker. Once again the elaborate payoff was hilarious.

Airliner Arrival Gag:

When Los Angeles celebrated the opening of the new LAX airport we were on hand to play an elaborate gag on a poor unsuspecting passenger. At an unused gate we built a large platform with festooned flags, a microphone, some chairs and a high school brass band. In the build-up Bob explained that, at our signal, a plane that had just landed would taxi over to this area. The crew of the airliner had picked one person out of all the passengers whom they thought would be a good *pigeon* for our gag. They had radioed ahead with his name and we had banners on the bandstand and a few of our people carried signs, *Welcome Joe Jones* (or whatever his name was). When the plane came to a stop in front of the bandstand the band started playing and Dresser Dahlstead of our staff, dressed in military regalia, greeted this bewildered passenger and led him to the platform where other official-looking dignitaries greeted him. He was then led to the microphone. The minute he started to say something, the band packed up their instruments, the dignitaries left the stage, and the crowd dispersed. It was a priceless moment. Bob entered and explained this was our way of welcoming him to Los Angeles' new airport. Funny!!!

Piano Drop:

We hung an expensive-looking but straight-from-the-junkyard grand piano suspended from a block and tackle three floors above the entry to a building adjacent to the NBC Studios at Sunset & Vine. I played the part of a mover holding the end of a rope attached to the pulleys holding the piano. My job was to stop a passerby and ask him to hold the rope while I went in the building to look for my missing partner. All he had to do was keep the tension on the rope. I found a likely Good Samaritan, gave him the rope and left. While the world watched on our hidden camera, the man became a little impatient as Bob described the scene to the audience. Finally, at our cue, we released the piano, which came crashing to the cement below in a cloud of dust! I dashed out and accused the Good Samaritan of letting go of the rope. And as Bob was on the speaker explaining it was a "Truth or Consequences Strikes Again" stunt, the Good Samaritan took off and I had to chase him half a block down Vine Street.

"Truth or Consequences" became more than a job, it became a career. Writing the show was a daily challenge and a daily joy. It was an incredible experience that lasted, onc way or the other, for about twenty years.

"Truth or Consequences" inspired other Edwards hits: "It Could Be You," "Name That Tune," and, of course, the greatest spin-off of them all, "This Is Your Life." Most of the contestants were chosen from the studio audience just prior to the show. In the early days, "Truth or Consequences" was a live show. The

Milt and Bobby Lauher as bit players

audience participation shows of the past were based on talented hosts getting the most out of talented people, whether they were variety acts on Ed Sullivan or the Hollywood Palace or whether they were common folk on Tom Breneman's "Breakfast Club" or Bob Barker's "Truth or Consequences." Bob Barker had an amazing aptitude for instantly recognizing hidden talent in people. Our "Truth or Consequences Strikes Again" hidden camera remotes were unique in that they were always done as an elaborately set-up situation building to a payoff that was totally unpredictable.

Robbie Robertson provided the audiences. Bob Barker, the world's greatest emcee, picked the contestants from the studio audience. He had an uncanny talent of picking just the right people for our crazy acts. One day he went up into the audience to find

Bob Barker and Chang, the Magician

Bob Barker loved magic and magicians. We featured magicians whenever we had the opportunity.

Bob Barker, John Daniel and Irene

92

that Robbie had booked an entire audience of sailors. There is nothing wrong with that, except all the sailors were from the Japanese navy, none of which could handle the English language very well. All of the scheduled bits could not play with this group so we instantly rewrote the entire show with stunts that would work for the Japanese sailors.

Charlie Kohrs was an accomplished magician and had mastered the art of voice throwing, a totally different form of ventriloquism than the art of making a figure come to life and have a voice without the ventriloquist's lips moving. Charlie could actually create the illusion of a voice coming from across the room or any place he might desire, called *throwing your voice*. One of his favorite tricks at the lunch table was to spin a half dollar and then place his fingernail over it like a phonograph needle as if it was a very small phonograph record. You would swear a voice came directly from the half dollar. His voice could be heard caught in an empty bottle. He could make you think someone was calling from the next room. I wrote a bit for Charlie in the late '50's for "Truth or Consequences" that remains one of the funniest gags ever done on that classic show. We put Charlie in a waiting area with an unsuspecting stranger. We had conveniently left some workman's tools on a nearby couch. On a secret cue from Bob Barker, we watched through the lens of a hidden camera as Charlie went to work. A frantic voice was heard coming from an air conditioning vent up near the ceiling. Charlie's voice throwing was so convincing that he had the guy unscrewing the vent cover to save the imaginary victim. It was hilarious!

"This Is Your Life" was a totally honest surprise show, hosted by Ralph Edwards. Ralph unexpectedly called a guest on stage and then proceeded to take him through his life in front of an audience that included his friends and family. No one knew what subject was being worked on. Their ability to keep the bits a secret was much tighter than any United States security system, even now. Although I was not on staff on "This Is Your Life" once in a while I would get a call from Ralph Edwards who asked me, "Milt, would you mind terribly taking Ed Wynn to lunch, keep him busy this afternoon?" The show needed to get Ed out of circulation to do what they needed to do for the show. I had the opportunity to meet wonderful people like Buster Keaton, Mack Sennett, Stan Laurel and a lot of old timers who were around in the 70's and 80's.

Ralph Edwards

At The Brookledge, I got into where Thayer's shop used to be with my hammer and saw and converted it into a museum. I moved into the former office which made a nice studio apartment. I installed a television set into a niche I built into the wall of the

Milt in his Brookledge museum

bedroom. I had forgotten how much heat was generated by an old tube-type television and the bedroom, where I also stored years of old TV Guides, caught on fire… good thing the Thayer *Flash Paper* and *Red Hot Balls* had been removed! I took where the stage was and made a bar in the little theatre at Brookledge. Everyone said it was a really nice bar. Then I built a museum bar. On the 7th level of the garden I built a pool bar… oh yes, then the barbecue bar. At one point people said I had the combined length of fifty-eight feet of bars on the property. We used to invite everyone over to the house, quite often.

Being a fanatic record collector, I collect old recordings of show business personalities and vaudeville stars. Ray Avery of *Ray Avery's Record Roundup* hired me to work in his store. I liked working there because instead of paying me with money, Ray paid me in phonograph records. Some ten years later, Ray Avery took a photo of an old house on Franklin Avenue for a Halloween sounds album he was producing. He felt the old house was the epitome of a haunted house. As coincidence would have it, he took the photo the very week I started to work on turning that spooky house into the Magic Castle in 1961.

I met Dick Sherman in 1951 through our mutual interest in old phonograph records when Dick wandered into Ray's old, rare record store where I worked. I had an old 78 Harry Richman record playing in the store. Dick asked me, "What's a young man like you playing this ancient record for?" As I replaced the record into its cover, Dick tried to pull it away from me. We had this tug-of-war over the old disk. It was lucky the record didn't break. I asked Dick why he had wanted this particular song and Dick replied, "Because my father wrote it."

That was good enough reason for me. I handed him the record. Dick was collecting all the hit songs his father, Al Sherman, had written. Al wrote so many big hits in the '20's and '30's: "You Got To Be A Football Hero," "Wanita," "No, No, A Thousand Times No," "Potatoes Are Cheaper," and "Now's the Time to Fall in Love;" great songs that were very, very popular in his time. I told Dick if he liked Al Sherman he should see my vast collection at home. I had a whole room full of records; it turned out I had dozens of Al Sherman recordings.

Ragtimers Milt and Dick Sherman

In that one little short meeting at the record store, Dick and I formed a friendship that has lasted over sixty years. Who knew my best friend would become the Academy Award winning creator of songs with his brother, Robert: "Mary Poppins," "Chitty, Chitty, Bang, Bang," "A Spoonful of Sugar," and "It's a Small World."

When I first met Richard M. Sherman, he was Dick Sherman. The use of his full name came when his brother, Bob, wanted to avoid being confused with others with similar names. Thus Bob and Dick became Robert B. and Richard M. Sherman—the Sherman Brothers. When Dick and I write songs, it's Sherman and Larsen. Richard M. Sherman and Milt Larsen. Maybe it should be Milton P. Larsen but we're both too old to change.

Always the aspiring entrepreneur, I had an idea for opening a Roaring '20's Speakeasy in Hollywood in 1957. The concept of the show was that the producers had found a score for a revue "Spangles of 1927" under the seat of a thirty-year-old paddy wagon used in a raid. Dick and I wrote a dozen songs in the style of the '20's. We were able to get

THE WHOOPEE KID

THE HILARIOUS NEW SATIRE OF THE FILM MUSICALS OF THE THIRTIES

Book by
Milt Larsen
Richard M. Sherman
Roger Dittner

Music & Lyrics by
Richard M. Sherman
Milt Larsen

a great jazz musician to record a demo for us, Rosy McHargue and his Ragtimers. That was also my first meeting with a banjoist that would become one of my closest friends, Spencer Quinn. The speakeasy never happened but we used the songs later—adding a book and re-naming it "The Whoopie Kid." Even later we brought it back as a live staged radio show at the Variety Arts Roof Garden. At that time we called it "Charlie Sent Me." As you will see in my writing about shows and albums we produced over the years, if we couldn't sell something the first time around, we'd simply change the name and try again.

I used to take some of my old records up to the CBS Radio studios at Sunset and Gower and guest on Jim Hawthorne's popular late night show. His other guest was Andrew White, the founder of CBS Radio, who had fascinating stories about the old personalities. Hawthorne replaced Steve Allen on CBS Radio in 1952 and then went on to his own network series on ABC radio. He was also the first late-night comedian on television when he did a show on KLAC-TV.

Just after I escaped from Los Angeles High School (Class of Summer 1949), Red Baker and I had our own radio shows on KVAC. It was a closed circuit radio station that operated to send aired programs to the veterans at the Sawtelle Veteran's Hospital in Westwood. Red's shows had very little music and were very funny. He was well on his way to becoming a successful comedy writer and nightclub comedian. My show featured me talking about my collection of old records. Although the shows never went on the air we got a taste of what it was like to be behind professional microphones and professional turntables. That started my lifelong passion for radio. One of my high school chums was Frank Bresee who later became well-known for his "Golden Days of Radio" shows on *Voice of America*.

A very good friend by the name of Steve Markham was the staff announcer at the prestigious classical radio station KFAC. He allowed Frank and me to visit him on the late-night shift and use the studio to record comedy bits for our own amusement. Steve is an incredible collector. He collects stage draperies dating back to the days of the old Fanchon and Marco stage revues. We often take advantage of his generosity and borrow some of his spectacular drops for our various stage shows.

Another high school pal was David Berger. He was interested in magic and also had jobs as a radio announcer. Later in life we got together to do a show for Bill Bragg's satellite radio superstation. As of this writing, the show is still on the air every week and we've been doing it for almost three decades. The show is called "The Music Museum" and we have fun playing those old records. Since David moved to Las Vegas we record the shows at our convenience at his studio in Las Vegas and mine in Hollywood. For information, check it out: www.yesterdayusa.com. The Texas station plays nothing but old radio shows and nostalgia twenty-four hours a day.

One particularly fun item was a "You Asked for It" show bit featuring prolific Genii magazine contributor Gene Poinc in a version of the old rag picture act which was aptly named *Artistry in Garbage*. George Boston contributed a great deal to the "You Asked For It" series. George was one the original Board of Directors of the Academy of Magical Arts. I used to come up with an occasional idea for the show back when I was an aspiring writer. When host Art Baker introduced Gene Poinc, my teenage graduation yearbook face was in the irised-photo on the Skippy Peanut Butter jar. Gene was there because Milt Larsen Asked For It! Gene Poinc was a dear friend from Los Angeles High School days. He was a fine artist. I thought of the act, Gene created it, and the

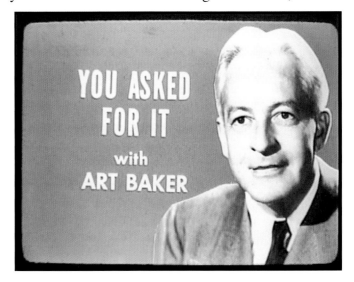

show's producers bought it! The other ironic part of all this is that I didn't realize at the time that the host of the show, the very popular TV star Art Baker, would be my stepfather!

As a teenager I became fascinated with a time before my time. Through my upbringing in magic, I had gotten to see, know and admire many of the vaudevillians. My dad would take us to see any magicians anywhere near our home, nightclubs, theatres and conventions. I loved the magic but I also loved seeing the great old variety acts that were still around. I think my favorite was "A. Robins—the Banana Man." He would come on stage in a really large coat and simply keep emptying his pockets with such things as vegetables, musical instruments and bunches of bananas. He threw them into a trunk, which he happened to have inside his larger trunk. Then, while singing a little La-Te-Da-Te-Da song he would pull another cart from the trunk… and then another, constantly filling them with bananas. The coat never got smaller. Finally he changed the original trunk into a small locomotive engine that he attached to the front of his carts and drove off, while smoke lofted from the engine's smokestack. In later life he was popular on some of the kid's shows and you can still see his act on YouTube. When I was a kid—A. Robins, the Banana Man was real magic and real vaudeville.

A. Robins—The Banana Man

Because Dad would always take us to see magicians I grew up seeing headliners like Sophie Tucker, Paul Whiteman, Harry Richman, Bill Robinson, Jimmy Savo, Ted Lewis, Eddie Peabody and many, many others. At that time the legendary Pickwick Bookshop on Hollywood Blvd. was the place to find books of anything on the theater or Hollywood. From time to time they would have special estate sales on the second floor. One of those estate sales was one of Hollywood's greatest character actors, Walter Catlett. He had a great collection of posters and books—all for sale. There were Strohbridge theatre posters for five and ten bucks each! (Those are the ones that go for hundreds and thousands today.) I bought a few but that was a lot of money when I was a kid. One thing I really wanted but could not afford was a set of bound volumes of The Theatre magazines from 1900 to 1931. They priced the full set at $600. Not too much and a very fair price but no way could I find that kind of money. The salesmen at Pickwick were great people and liked the fact that a young kid respected books. They offered to keep the books for me and let me pay them off over a period of time. No deadline—"When you pay for them, they are yours."

Every week I stopped by Pickwick and gave them twenty dollars. I never missed a week. When I got to the 30th week I brought in my twenty dollars and had the surprise of my life. The employees had gotten together and bought a big cake, balloons and serpentine. They had packed up my forty or so books as gifts and served champagne for all the customers in the store that night. I didn't realize I had become some sort of ideal for the employees and the customers who were hoping I'd make that last payment. At that party they had also invited some representatives of the Troupers Club, a club of old performers who were also excited that some kid was actually interested in what they had done over the years. That moment started me on my life's quest to respect the pioneers of show business. Through the Trouper's Club I got to meet some of the true legends of the theater, headliners like Elsie Janis, Trixie Friganza and Grace LaRue — names from the Gay'90's that were still around in the early '50's.

In my quest to become a comedy writer, I had the great opportunity to meet my father's friend, Snag Werris, one of Hollywood's most prolific gag writers. Snag was a wonderful gentleman, a good magician and would hang around Dad's shop. He had a tremendous comedy-writing career as the head writer for Jackie Gleason for many years. Before that he had written for Bob Hope, Red Skelton, the Old Colgate Comedy Hours, The All-Star Revues, the Ritz Brothers and just about any major comedian and any one of note in the business, including Eddie Cantor, Jerry Lewis and Jimmy Durante. His writing credits ran from burlesque to radio to films to television.

Snag became my comedy writer mentor. He had me write scripts and then would grade them like a professor, ruthlessly tearing apart my work. He taught me about comedy construction: "You're putting the punch line in the middle… you idiot! One-Two-Three-Joke… One-Two-Three-Joke. The straight does the set-up, the comic gets the laugh." Simple rules but how do you learn them without having a teacher who has been there? He

Snag Werris and Jerry Lewis

was a night owl and sometimes his wife, Charlotte, would be making the morning coffee as I'd be leaving for home, always a little wiser in the ways of writing comedy.

I got to know a number of the best burlesque comics and straight men in the last days of real burlesque. The first rule in proper burlesque sketch writing is that you have to establish the entire scene in the first line; thus the set-up line: "Well, here we are in sunny Spain waiting for that bullfighter who stole my wife." In those days I was more interested in "Well, here we are in sunny Spain," than in the strippers who, incidentally, were always lovely, caring ladies who didn't seem to mind a kid gag-writing protégé being backstage. Rule number two is, if you want to be a writer, write something! Sit down every day and write something… anything: a sketch, a book, a screenplay… anything!

Snag's background came from burlesque in the Catskills of upper New York where vaudeville burlesque survived. Weber and Fields had a theatre in New York in the 1880's and 1890's devoted to burlesque. The term burlesque was not what you think it is today, not the bump and grind burlesque shows of the depression era but real live genuine burlesque, as in travesty or parody. When "Quo Vadis" was a huge hit on Broadway, down the street the Weber and Fields theatre would be doing "Quo Vass Iss." While New York audiences flocked to see Clyde Fitch's new play "The Stubbornness of Geraldine" the Music Hall audiences were laughing at "The Stickiness of Gelatine." Producers of Broadway shows would lavish Weber and Fields with gifts to get them to parody their shows. It was the greatest compliment a show could receive if they were successful enough to have Weber and Fields parody their show. They had some of the biggest stars of the day in their little variety music hall theatre on Broadway; Lillian Russell, Faye Templeton and David Warfield. Dick Sherman and I would write a musical about them later, but that's later, right now…

One of the early burlesque theatres in Los Angeles was the Burbank Theatre on Main Street and 6th. The Follies Theatre was at 3rd and Main. The Burbank outlasted the Follies. And then there was another burlesque theatre down the street, The Gaiety. They all operated as legitimate theatres then went into burlesque in the '30's. When vaudeville was on its way out, these theatre houses started introducing strip teasers and comics doing burlesque acts. Burlesque, as we know it today, was non-existent up until that time. In a B.F. Keith or Keith Albee show performers were not allowed to even use a swear word like damn or hell on stage. Early burlesque shows were very clean and, of course, burlesque strippers never totally stripped.

Burbank Theatre

Snag knew all the comedians and he taught me how the burlesque theatres worked. There was a large blackboard backstage with lists of a performers' play list. Everyone backstage knew all the sketches: the top banana, the second banana, the straight and the juvenile. The comic would select one sketch they wanted to perform, circle that sketch on the blackboard and perform it. I was only eighteen years old when Snag took me backstage to the Burbank Theatre. I found lovely ladies in very filmy negligees doing their nails. These ladies were grandmothers and mothers and I had no idea they were going to go onstage and strip. Sally Rand and Gypsy Rose Lee were consummate burlesque performers who utilized balloons and feathers to tease the audience and let their imaginations have full reign. The burlesque theatres from the turn-of-the-century were legitimate theatres that specialized in comedy and burlesque. The naughty burlesque came much, much later.

Broadway is the main north/south street through downtown Los Angeles. Los Angeles' Broadway theatre district represented the largest concentration of pre-World War II movie palaces in America. Some of these theatres had deceptively simple exteriors but breathtakingly lavish interiors with sweeping marble staircases, ornate balconies, velvet plush seating, spacious gilded ceilings, rococo design; flamboyant palaces fit for a king.

Mason Opera House

It's amazing how many beautiful theatres met an early demise in the Los Angeles area. In 1955 yet another theatre was scheduled to meet the wrecking ball—the Mason Opera House located where the Los Angeles courthouse is today. Opened in 1903, it was designed by Chicago architects Marshall and Wilson and was the first large theatre on Broadway to provide a prime venue for some of the most prestigious entertainers visiting Los Angeles, hosting the likes of Lillie Langtry and Helen Modjeska.

Hippodrome Theatre

I went in to see if there was anything I could scavenge from The Mason Opera House before it was destroyed. I remember it was scheduled for demolition in 1955 because Walt Disney bought the majority of the theatre seats for his soon-to-be-opened Disneyland. I bought six of the theatre seats; Walt bought the remaining fourteen hundred but apparently never used them.

Whenever I traveled in a strange city I always headed downtown to look for a tall building with a fly loft among the old buildings. Even though the building was not a theatre anymore, perhaps turned into an indoor swap meet, warehouse or movie house, you can always tell if it was once a theatre. The ones that used to be theatres were obvious because of the fly lofts and balcony doors, usually visible from a number of vantage points. A fly loft is the space that houses rigging for raising and lowering stage sets, lighting and curtains toward the back of the theatre. They are integral to the operation of a theatre. I always had a keen interest in physical theatres and would do anything I could

Downtown L.A. flyloft

to get inside the building, short of breaking down the door, to see what the interior looked like. One of the most interesting theatres I was ever in was the Hippodrome Theatre on Main Street, across the street from the Follies. It was a 2,100-seat theatre, once known as Adolphus, (named after the builder Adolph Ramish), and the largest of the theatres on Main Street in the downtown area of Los Angeles. Ramish would later partner with the Gore Brothers, Sol Lesser and San Francisco impresarios Turner, Dahnken and Langley, to form the Fox West Coast Theatres.

At that time, Main Street in Los Angeles was like Broadway in New York. To make sure the Hippodrome entrance to the theatre was on Main, the patrons were forced to walk through a façade theatre-front on Main Street into a half-block-long courtyard before reaching the actual theatre entrance on Los Angeles Street. That façade remained for years and years as the Main Street Gym long after the theatre was razed. There were grand marble staircases going up to the balconies. The design of the complex provided a little 400-seat theatre beneath the main theatre to run silent movies for the children of the vaudeville show patrons upstairs, animal cages and an Olympic-sized swimming pool.

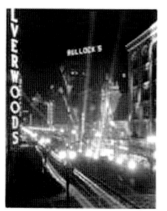

Downtown L.A. theater lights at night, Orpheum Theater interior

A typical vaudeville show had progressed from the kind of shows at the turn-of-the-century to a fully structured playbill of a series of unrelated acts in the '20s and '30's. Most New York vaudeville shows were lengthy with as many as fourteen acts per show. People would literally stay an entire day, packing a lunch. When producers changed the standard show into a two-a-day vaudeville schedule, they reduced the number of acts to eight or ten.

The whole theory of vaudeville was that every act was self-contained, was in itself an act: dance act, men's chorus, magician, singer, animal, acrobat and novelty. A vaudeville performer could go in the theatre, open a trunk and do his act, pack up the trunk and go to a different theatre to perform yet another show. The average vaudeville show was well structured. The first act was a silent act, called a flash act. It was a non-speaking act that allowed the audience to find their seats, accommodated the ones coming in late. It was usually a ten-minute act that was designed to get the audience's attention. Normally the next act was a talking act—a comedian or comedy sketch, then a dance or novelty act. When the hour-and-a-half shows changed to *two-a-day* there was no intermission. The second to closing act was the headliner: a Sophie Tucker, an

L-R: Houdini, Eva Tanguay, Sophie Tucker, Al Jolson

Al Jolson, or an Eva Tanguay who performed for thirty-five minutes. Harry Houdini was a huge headliner in vaudeville.

The last act was usually the animal act, called the chaser. The producers wanted to *chase* the audience out of the theatre. After the headliner, the chaser was anti-climatic. That was done on purpose; unlike today where you buy a ticket to the first show **or** the second show, in those days you could come to the first show and stay for the next one.

Later when *two-a-day* gave way to *four-a-day* that was very much the case. People took advantage of the daylong entertainment. The animal acts diminished in talent and substance as the four-a-day shows became popular to ensure the audience would leave.

The Ed Sullivan variety show, which ran from 1948 to 1971 on television, had a vaudeville-like structure. Ed introduced new talent every week. Every act was a separate act. There was something for everyone, from the novelty band to the opera star; if you didn't like one act and you waited long enough, you found one you did like. There were a few recurring characters who appeared many times a season. The Little Italian Mouse puppet, Topo Gigio, and Senor Wences, ventriloquist were two of the repeating favorites. The whole nature of vaudeville was variety. In theatres, vaudeville performers could hone the same act for twenty years. One day on television and every one had seen the act. Television destroyed the live theatre variety performances; the performers lost their stages and couldn't find work. No one wanted to learn the variety arts, become a performer and become unemployed. That's why there's no such thing as an old vaudevillian. The wonderful thing about vaudeville and the vaudevillians was that for several decades variety entertainers were numerous and gainfully employed.

I used the vaudeville formula when I started the "It's Magic!" show in 1956: open with a great silent act, then comedy, a sleight of hand artist and a flashy illusionist. After the intermission: a magical novelty act and a big illusion finale. The formula has never changed and I think it accounts for the longevity of the show.

During that time, we taped two shows a day for three days at "Truth or Consequences." That gave us six shows and occasionally we took a break when we got ahead. I was a kid in my '20's with essentially four days off every week. Ralph Edwards was an Executive Producer of the daytime "Truth or Consequences" and oversaw all production elements of the show. It didn't matter how the writers came up with the material as long as we showed up at the writers' meetings on Tuesday morning with great ideas. Happily

L-R:
Jerry Payne,
Bobby Lauher,
Milt Larsen

Ralph did not insist on our punching a clock or sitting at a desk all week. Bobby Lauher, Jerry Payne and I were the three basic writers on the show. We were fondly dubbed the "Redlighters." We wrote better under the pressure of a deadline while stopped at red lights on the way to work Tuesday mornings.

Jerry, Bobby and I went to Portland, Oregon to broadcast "Truth or Consequences" live on a new NBC affiliate in 1958. We were supposed to be there for a week but, as luck would have it, NABET called an engineers strike during that week. Since the show was already out of town when the strike was called, the union allowed the show to go on as long as we stayed in Portland. Our one week turned into six weeks. At that time we had about seven writers on the show but only Jerry, Bobby and I wrote the show while we were in Portland. We proved we worked well as a team. Shortly thereafter "Truth or Consequences" was canceled because of the popularity of a quiz show "Dotto," coincidentally a creation of our old friend Snag Werris. I didn't even have time to get to the unemployment line because "Dotto" got caught in one of those messy quiz scandals and NBC immediately put "Truth or Consequences" back on the air. This time the writing staff was trimmed to three: The Portland Gang—Milt, Jerry and Bobby, all thanks to a twist of fate.

When we moved to Burbank, the show was handled by MCA and they insisted the writers wear MCA type suits and show up every day. That's the last thing a writer wants to do. So to rebel against the new policy, we would have the writers' meetings on the merry-go-round in Griffith Park: three guys riding 'round and 'round on the carousel animals. We would take our secretary along with us sometimes and she would ride on a horse next to us, taking notes.

Griffith Park Merry-Go-Round

In 1958 Bill wrote for the Genii readers: Wilshire Ebell Theatre, "'It's Magic!' with Ollie Berliner—you only have to read the list of acts to know that this was one of the finest magic shows ever presented, including the best the conventions have ever offered. The reason for the success of the show is simple. Milt limited the show to six professional acts, provided them with a professional orchestra in a comfortable legitimate theater, gave each enough time to accomplish something, and spared them the problem of having to re-establish the magic spell after some second class variety act by having the show all magic. Art Baker did himself proud as Master of Ceremonies with audience-tested material… always in good taste. Art has the knack of building up his personality without getting carried away. His distinguished appearance added dignity to the show and things got off to a very fast start as he introduced the first act,

Bottom L-R: Senor Ermando, MacDonald Birch, Bill Larsen, Blackstone, Jr., Aubrey, Art Baker

Senor Ermando. Harry Blackstone Jr., Kirk Kirkham, Aubrey, Dottie and Bill Larsen followed. MacDonald Birch closed the show."

One day, a few years after I had met Dick Sherman, I played a 1927 record written by Dick's father, Al Sherman, entitled "Lindberg, Eagle of the U.S.A." It was a great tribute to that lone flyer that flew across the Atlantic. Dick explained to me, after the record had finished playing, that his father wrote the song while Lindberg was still in the air. If Lindberg landed successfully, they would publish it. "Lindberg, Eagle of the U.S.A." became a smash hit. I wondered, out loud, what would have happened if Lindberg hadn't made the flight, had had the misfortune of falling into the ocean and perishing. It was a possible outcome of a trans-Atlantic flight back in those days. No one would have been interested in "Lindberg, Eagle of the U.S.A." It would have been a smash flop!

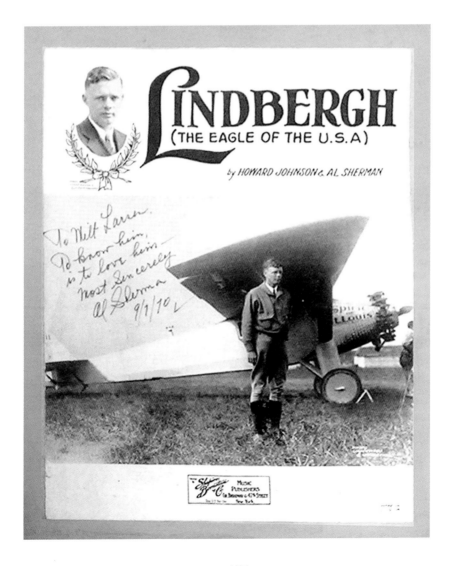

BON VOYAGE TITANIC
and other songs that sank!
SHERMAN & LARSEN'S
SMASH FLOPS!

CELEBRATE
THE SUCCESS OF

The Hindenburg
President Dewey
The Spruce Goose
Tucker Automobile
Custer's Last Stand
Confederate Victory
Neville Chamberlain
and other winners...

Magic Castle Records - Hollywood

And that was how "Smash Flops" came about in 1959. The secret to good songs is the concept. If you have a brilliant idea you're three-quarters the way home. Without great ideas it's just another song and people will soon forget. Dick and I would write happy, upbeat songs about events that went slightly askew, or more than slightly askew —events that became downright disasters or tragedies: "Bon Voyage Titanic," "When the Hindenburg Lands Today," and "General Custer." So our first collaborative effort ended up as a successful album of comedy satire entitled "Smash Flops." Our first hit was a flop!

One of my favorite "Smash Flops" songs, "Congratulations Tom Dewey," was used for the theme song in the stage production of "Give 'Em Hell, Harry!" a one-man stage play about the United States President Harry S. Truman, starring James Whitmore. The stage play was later made into an Academy Award nominated film in 1975.

I spent many happy years across the street at the old Radio City Sunset and Vine studios of NBC where I was writing "Truth or Consequences." On the corner was Wallach's Music City. This was probably the most popular record store on the West Coast. To make it on the Music City *Top Ten* list meant you had a hit. We had a direct line to the Vine Street window, which we used occasionally for our "Truth or Consequences Strikes Again" gags. One day I slipped a copy of our then new LP, "Smash Flops" into the display in the window. The management didn't catch it for weeks. Sure enough, we ended up on the top ten list—number eight!

Over the years, a lot of things have gone right with "It's Magic!" But there were a few things that went wrong… Once a well-known magician thought it would be funny to sabotage Bill Larsen Jr.'s sub trunk. Another magician friend of Bill's found out about it and told Bill that he didn't thinnk it was funny. Bill agreed with him, fixed the prop and never mentioned the prankster's name in Genii—a punishment worse than death! Once a visiting magic dignitary ventured backstage during intermission, tripped over a control wire and set off three flash apearance flashpots just before the second act curtain. A well-known escape artist failed to make a timely escape from a pair of borrowed challenge handcuffs. After twenty minutes the stage manager, George Boston, made the call to lower the first act curtain on him. He never quite forgave us.

Dante was a great, great magician. Both Bill and I thought Dante was the greatest magician we'd ever seen. The Fountania was a major stage production with beautiful Japanese costumes. The set and the gorgeous appliqué drop were originals from the Dante show provided by Al Jansen. Robert Towner had the rights to perform the act and

Dante's Fountania

Al Jansen assisted him. It was a poetic dance act with Japanese ladies and a magician in a Japanese kimono. He'd take a little water from a fountain, put it on a fan, then take the water from the fan and place it on stage where it would spurt water until the entire stage was filled with dancing waters. The climax of the act centered on a coconut shell that was supposed to control a stream of water, causing an umbrella effect. Without revealing any magic secrets, I can only say that the stream of water became uncontrollable and the large stream of water hit hot stage lights, showering glass upon the stage amidst electrical popping and sparks. Bob Barker was in the audience that night and said that it was the funniest act he'd ever seen. I don't think Robert Towner thought it was terribly funny but it was spectacular. We ended up having to pay several hundred dollars to replace the stage lighting.

One year on "It's Magic!" Chen Kai performed a manipulation act with a fire bowl and mouth coils. At one point of his act he pulled a serpentine out of a bowl, the bowl caught on fire and a dove flew out of the bowl. What he hadn't noticed was that one of the pieces of serpentine lit like a fuse. Chen Kai had come directly from Mexico where they don't think about fire retardant paper as much as we have to here. Chen Kai stood in front of the olio drop, downstage and produced this fiery bowl. The audience saw the serpentine aflame and Chen Kai standing in the middle of a mound of serpentine on the stage floor. There was a certain amount of anticipation as the audience wondered if they were going to watch a magician go up in flames. Dick Zimmerman, our stage manager, picked up the curtain directly behind Chen Kai and the CO_2 fire extinguisher swooshed loudly. There was a great amount of applause from the audience and to this day I don't think Chen Kai ever knew why he got such a reaction to his fire bowl routine.

John Daniel performed twice on "It's Magic!" The first time was in the sixth edition and he performed the *Chefalo Kitchen Scene*. It was the first time the Alan Wakeling *Thin-Sawing* had ever been seen by anybody. He received a standing ovation. We brought John back in 1963. He was previewing a show he wanted to bring to Las Vegas, his Shazam show, based on scenes of Hades. "It's Magic!" has always been a family show. To this day, you can bring your kids and grandkids. We never questioned John in rehearsals but by the time he got on stage, it was a Vegas show,

John Daniel in Chefalo Kitchen Scene

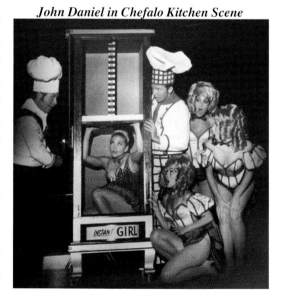

with the ladies dressed for the occasion. John opened the second act with this great production number in Hades, in fog. When the curtain went up, the entire audience only saw a sheet of white. They had turned on the fog effect a little early and the fog, heavier than air, had no place to go except into the audience and orchestra pit. The musicians couldn't see the music, the audience was coughing and the actors couldn't see their marks on stage.

John Daniel's "Hades"

Some mishaps weren't so funny. In the 1975, on the 22nd edition we had to make numerous last minute substitutions for such reasons as Harold Taylor getting stopped by immigration and Johnny Thompson landing an important Flamingo contract in Las Vegas. Harold, on his way to Los Angeles, had stopped to see a friend in Canada. He made the mistake of telling somebody at the border crossing in Canada he was going to go to Los Angeles to work on a show. Unfortunately, he never made it to Los Angeles… they sent him back to England.

We took "It's Magic!" to the Pasadena Civic Center one year. I believe it was Billy McComb's first trip to America. "Skipper" Frank Herman emceed. The interesting thing about that show was the union situation. We had always played with an eight-piece band. The Pasadena Civic Center had a twenty-one musician minimum and they were adamant about it. There were 2,400 seats and 21-man orchestra in the pit. Oliver Berliner and I knew, because of the enormous expense of the stagehands and the cost of the 21-piece orchestra, that if we went one minute into overtime, even with a full house, we'd lose our tails. The show was running a little long and then Harry Blackstone Sr. took the stage. He was great and finished his act with the floating light bulb.

Harry Blackstone Sr.

As luck would have it, the light bulb malfunctioned. Blackstone Sr. recovered beautifully, went off stage and came out to re-perform the routine correctly. At that point Ollie and I were in the back of the auditorium watching the clock. If we could get the last note of the band out by eleven o'clock it was the difference of several thousand dollars. We knew there was no way in God's little green earth that we were going to get out of there by eleven o'clock. Unlike lesser acts, where we actually closed the curtain on the entertainment, you could not close the curtain on Harry Blackstone Sr. on his final performance of his career. That was the one and only time we played "It's Magic!" at the Pasadena Civic Center.

PASADENA CIVIC AUD.

1 Nite Only FRI. OCT. 21

Larsen & Berliner present the 5th Annual All–Magic Revue

IT'S MAGIC!

America's Greatest Magical Event

FEATURING INTERNATIONAL KNOWN STARS OF MAGIC

SEE – ON STAGE – IN PERSON

ART BAKER Your Host
Star of TV and Motion Pictures

FRAKSON
Perfection in Manipulation

CLIFFORD GUEST
Ed Sullivan's Favorite Ventriloquist

THE KEENERS
Miracles in Modern Magic

"SKIPPER FRANK"
Popular KTLA Personality

BOXLEY & MARIE
Spectacular Wonders

and Starring the World's Most Famous Magician

THE GREAT

BLACKSTONE

IVAN DITMARS and his ORCHESTRA

ALL SEATS RESERVED $3.75, 3.00, 2.50, 2.00, 1.50 Federal Tax Included
Mail Orders Accepted Now! Box Office Opens Mon. Oct 17, If Ordering by Mail Send Remittance with Stamped Self-Addressed Envelope to:

IT'S MAGIC! 1350 N. HIGHLAND AVE., HOLLYWOOD 28, CALIF.
For Information Call WEbster 9-3939 if no Answer HOllywood 6-1331

Bill's most elaborate illusion show was his 1969 appearance which included *Aerial Fishing* in a barnyard scene with Irene dressed as Daisy Mae, a magic shop scene borrowed from Dante's *Magician's Rehearsal*, a *Floating and Vanishing Piano* and a *Sub-Trunk* which climaxed with a guest celebrity appearing from the box, followed by a spot hitting Bill, leading the band in the orchestra pit. The opening number featured large playing cards in an Alice in Wonderland scene. NBC had just finished Alice in Wonderland as a TV special. We were able to get the costumes and scenery from the show, thanks to John Shrum.

Alice in Wonderland costumes

Bill Larsen Jr. as "Dante"

Although all the "It's Magic!" shows were well supported by the fans of magic, they were never what you would call profitable. The high cost of production against the relatively low potential gross meant the show would just about break even or lose money each year. This was acceptable because it was building a greater interest in magic which would benefit Bill's Genii magazine and my other dream, The Magic Castle. I was making good money as a writer and to lose a little on seeing the type of magic I wanted to see seemed a good investment in the future. Ollie Berliner had become more and more involved in his own radio stations and recording businesses over the years and didn't quite share my passion for magic. After ten years, with regrets, Ollie would no longer continue as co-producer of the shows.

At the end of 1959 famed Broadway producer Leonard Sillman expressed an interest in using a couple of Sherman and Larsen comedy songs for a new edition of his "New Faces of 1962" review. One of my favorite revues of all time was Sillman's "New Faces of 1952" which introduced new faces like Eartha Kitt, Paul Lynde, Alice Ghostley,

Leonard Sillman

Carol Lawrence and Robert Clary. Just the idea of meeting him was a major compliment. I assumed I would meet him in a Broadway office building but his home and office was in a Manhattan townhouse. When I arrived for my appointment I was impressed by a marble lobby with a few chairs and a desk that looked like it came from a palace in France. A grand chandelier hung in front of a two-story circular staircase. I was welcomed by a young gentleman who announced that Mr. Sillman was expecting me. He pressed an intercom button. Leonard Sillman, complete with a velvet-tufted robe and a cigarette in a 1930's holder, appeared at the top of the stairs and wafted down. All that was missing was the MGM orchestra. "Hello Milton, I've been excited about meeting you. I love your songs."

That was exactly what a 29-year old songwriter wanted to hear. We went into a lavish drawing room and talked about "Smash Flops." He asked if there were any shows I would like to see while in the City and suggested a new musical called "The Fantasticks." It was a small show in a small theater but he predicted a long run. He arranged a comp ticket. He was right. The show's original off-Broadway production ran a total of forty-two years with 17,162 performances—making it the world's longest-running musical.

Our "Smash Flops" never made it to "New Faces of 1962" but Mr. Sillman made my trip to New York a total experience.

The '50's were going well. Oliver and I had produced full-scale magic shows. I was on the writing staff of American's number one fun show and spent time building a cabin on five acres of desert land I had homesteaded earlier. I even bought a little bungalow near the beach in Balboa, California. I was using my carpenter skills that I had acquired from my grandfather and Floyd Thayer. I was writing songs with Dick Sherman in his pre-Disney days, and thanks to "It's Magic!" my side-tracked train was back on track.

ALL ABOARD FOR
THE SIXTIES

In 1961 my train was heading nicely down the track—but I had started to think there was more I could be doing with my life! After all, I had just turned thirty! Life was passing me by!

It was back to the Wilshire Ebell in 1961 where "It's Magic!" would remain for the next fifteen years. The show played one night in 1961 and 1962, and then in 1963, started playing two nights with one matinee. This was also the year the Magic Castle opened and the interest in magic seemed to be growing. Due to the availability of the illusionist Jack Gwynne, a special mid-season production was offered on March 13th and 14th of 1964, which was billed as the 9th Annual Edition. It was followed in November of the same year with the 10th Annual Edition. Two years later NBC Art Director John Shrum became associated with the show. His artistic talents added a very special class to "It's Magic!" and continued to delight audiences for the remainder of his life.

In 1961 John Daniel and Irene had a son, Dante, named after the great magician Dante. But by

Wilshire Ebell Theatre

late 1962 they decided to get divorced. They remained amicable and good friends throughout the years. Irene was born in Germany's Black Forest near the Swiss border the same month and year William Larsen Sr. founded Genii magazine. The Stolz family moved to Austria before Irene was even one year old, but was forced to move back to Germany when the Russian troops invaded Austria in World War II. Irene's family traveled frequently as the German police mandated that her father, then a customs agent, could not form any friendships that would/could compromise their position.

I had the rare good fortune of writing the show "Truth or Consequences" continuously for eighteen years. Bill was at CBS as an Associate Producer so we were both employed in the television industry. I got to know a fellow by the name of Don Gotschall, a friend of Bill's from CBS. He wasn't a magician; he was an entrepreneur. I guess the fifty-eight feet of bars I had built at The Brookledge and the fact that Don was basically a writer who wanted to hang out at someone's bar led us to become good friends. Don Gotschall and I made a very wonderful deal on a three-hundred-foot ferryboat in Oakland. We didn't have the money to buy it so we optioned the ferryboat. It was our intention to bring it down to the newly developed Marina del Rey and turn it into a showboat-type operation, which at that time would have been totally unique. We got as far as optioning a lease in Marina del Rey.

If you remember a bit of history, when the Marina del Rey opened in 1962, it was an absolute disaster. The former salt-marsh, fed by freshwater from Ballona Creek, had been developed into a small craft harbor. There was no breakwater and there had been a couple of rising water floods they hadn't anticipated. A winter storm caused millions of dollars in damages to property and boats. Everyone said the Marina would never make it. So we gave up our option on a little point in the Marina and tried the idea down in Newport Beach until we found out that complications regarding the sewage and insurance were well beyond our financial means.

It was about that time, from my office at "Truth or Consequences" on the 9th floor of the thirteen-story building at Highland and Hollywood Boulevard, that I noticed this old Victorian era house. The rest is the

Early days of the Marina del Rey

Magic Castle history, the famous handshake that began a wonderful relationship with Tom Glover and years of hammering and sawing. Since I had neither money nor credit enough to finance the Magic Castle project, I convinced Don Gotschall to be my partner. (Sometimes I can be very charming and very convincing.)

During the next year we renovated the Gothic Chateau building. Tom Glover displayed an enormous faith in my idea and watched as Don Gotschall, Don Culp and I stripped the zolatone from the entire interior of the house. The exterior was a challenge that we left for the last. The paint on the stucco building was faded and spotty, window and door frames were peeling and the finials atop the roof turrets had darkened to a grimy battleship grey. Bids to repaint the exterior were ranging upwards of four thousand dollars, which would have stretched the already limited resources past the breaking point.

Shortly before we opened, a friend of Don Culp's, Tony Barillaro, agreed to paint the entire exterior of the building including gilding the finials with silver paint, for a grand sum of one thousand, five-hundred dollars. Tony was an excellent painter and a hard, quick worker but his Italian bravado made the use of a safety harness unacceptable to him. Don and I watched in horror one afternoon as Tony, applying silver paint to the

finial on the topmost turret, slipped and fell from the roof. He landed on the second floor balcony, barely avoiding falling all the way to the pavement below. He shook his head, gathered his breath and stood up, unhurt and climbed back up to the roof to finish!

When the Biltmore Hotel in downtown Los Angeles was renovated, I was able to buy enough of the old red plush carpeting to cover the first floor of the Magic Castle. George Bardossas, a Greek immigrant, was simultaneously holding down several different jobs, including being a restaurant waiter and a building maintenance man. I hired him to install our newly acquired carpeting. George picked up the rolls of carpet in his truck and brought them back to the Magic Castle where he unrolled them on the pavement outside the entrance. George measured, cut the pieces and carried them inside. The day we opened, 2nd of January 1963, the last piece of carpeting was laid in place.

John Shrum was NBC's staff art director assigned to "Truth or Consequences" as well as many other shows. Even though I had not yet met him, I had admired his work. When "Truth or Consequences" required a Victorian drawing room set I met John. I took one look at his set and realized I needed his expertise at the Magic Castle. I introduced John to the wonderful world of rye Old-fashioneds at Nickodell's after a taping and was quite happy this shy and almost invisible man accepted. I brought him by the Magic Castle—then a construction disaster—half-stripped woodwork, paint cans everywhere, sawdust and sawhorses in every room. It was a scene guaranteed to terrify the average fastidious art director but didn't seem to ruffle his feathers. That began a relationship that lasted until his untimely passing. John was wonderfully intolerant of anything shoddy and became totally devoted to the Magic Castle, protecting me from my own enthusiasm. There is an homage to me in the reception area of the Castle displaying my tacky red velvet wallpaper I had installed… John felt we should keep it as a reminder that **he** should be left alone to design the magical mansion.

John was a colorful character. He always wore elaborate vests with matching bow ties. He would bring his parrot into the NBC office and put the bird on an apple box to be closer to the air conditioning vent. He would turn on either the television or the radio and leave the office, shutting the door. The parrot would serenade Fred de Cordova's "Tonight Show" production office, next door, through the air conditioning vents—except that same vent traveled in the opposite direction, several offices removed, into Milt Altman and Gino Conte's office. They could hear the serenade as well… however, faintly. When John would close the door and leave… I would go into John's office to check on the bird… and eventually, Shrum put me off limits to the bird nanny duties… telling me that my visits were disrupting Ditto's scales and singing, interrupting the continuity of his melodious serenade. Ditto was messy with the sunflower seeds, spitting the shells all over the back perch counter and office floor. John told me that when Ditto rode into NBC in the morning and then when returning home after the taping, Ditto would sing and cackle with laughter. It took some time but eventually Milt Altman asked John to leave Ditto, the parrot, at home.

Thanks to John and Fred de Cordova, John had a special production number: Shrum 1000. When he used that number to build a set or make a prop—everyone knew not to dispose of it but truck it to the Magic Castle after filming. John was never a partner and was never paid for his efforts as the official Magic Castle Art Director. He simply loved the concept of the club. Once I was determined to proceed with a project, John would move heaven and earth to see my project realized. He used the talented creations of the NBC scenic artists and the workshop time and again to benefit the Magic Castle.

John had wonderful rococo stencils made and, after we painted the Castle walls a deep burgundy, he supervised the dabbing of gold paint throughout the stencils to create wall patterns that are still part of the Castle today. The NBC scenic artists were quite creative painting cherubs, Dante's inferno, Mucha's maiden and much more. Did we need concrete blocks with a unique design to line our walkways? John would have a mold made. Did President Kennedy sit in a special rocking chair? John could have a set made exactly like it and place them upstairs on our portico where members were invited to relax and sip authentic Mint Juleps.

Dante dining room construction with Milt

119

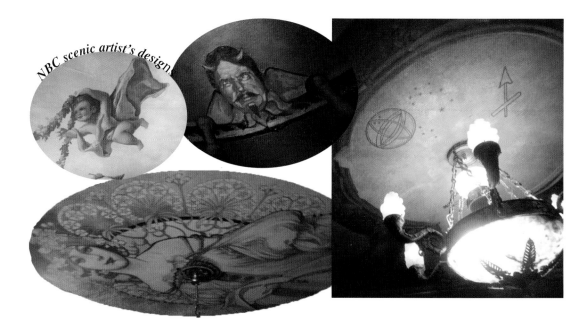

NBC scenic artist's design

We grew the mint plants in front by the fountain so our bartender would have fresh mint leaves daily. We all thought John as godlike and infallible in his artistic judgments, but he was capable of error. John had an inspiration; he wanted bubbles to cascade down from the fountain in front of the entry so he added liquid soap to the water. It worked, but it also covered the mint plants and everything else below with soap, almost ending our sitting-in-rocking-chairs-drinking-Mint Julep evenings.

Ghosts? Well, I don't really believe in ghosts but then again... In the early days of renovating the Castle, I would often stay overnight, sleeping on the couch in my office in the tower. In those days the house was still very Charles Addams-ish... very creaky, very spooky. It was a dark and stormy night when I was awakened by a crash of thunder and lightning that lit up the tower like someone had thrown a match in a lifetime supply of *Flash Paper*. It was pre-dawn and pouring rain as if Rollin B. Lane wanted to correct the drought of the early 1900's that wiped out his dream for an

orange grove in Hollywood. I flipped on the light switch and discovered that the power was out. Looking out of my tower window I could see there was a power outage in our part of Hollywood. Other than the torrential rain there was nothing unusual except for the fact that I heard someone playing the piano downstairs. I had locked the Castle at closing and I knew I was alone in the house. Dai Vernon hadn't started taking piano lessons yet. Who was playing the piano?

I always kept a few precision tools around so I grabbed a wrecker's bar and a flashlight and figured I'd surprise a musically-talented burglar. The piano was still playing as I reached the level where the mezzanine bar now stands. As I approached the stairway landing, the music stopped… I went into Irma's Room—no one was there. All the doors were locked. I doused my flashlight and flipped on the light switch. There was no power down here either—the storm had knocked out all the electricity. The explanation? There was no electricity… no one was there… not even Invisible Irma. There was no explanation? I was either crazy or I had to start believing in ghosts…

Everybody thought Walt Disney was crazy opening an amusement park in the outskirts of nowhere. The freeway didn't even go that far East. People called Disneyland "Walt's Folly," after all, Pacific Ocean Park had just gone belly-up! Walt was a visionary, a dreamer that made dreams come true. He surrounded himself with incredible talents that believed in him and proved that imagination has no limits. If I had a role model, it would have to be Walt Disney. I was fortunate to have been at the opening of Disneyland in 1955.

Walt & Roy Disney

Like Walt and Roy, Bill and I made a great team. I knew how to work the typewriter and hammer; Bill knew how to manage the adding machine, magicians and a cash register. The Disney Brothers had their Magic Kingdom and the Larsen Brothers had their Magic Castle. I was very touched when former President Robert Lamoureux presented me with a train whistle and an engineer's cap. He had remembered a story about my role model Walt Disney and my observation of him as he drove off in his locomotive at the opening of Anaheim's Disneyland.

Robert expressed eloquently in a few words what the Magic Castle has meant to him and what the Magic Castle has meant to the Larsen family… and it was Robert who spearheaded the movement to have the Larsen Brothers honored with a star on the Hollywood Walk of Fame.

Bill & Milt Larsen

In the early days, I surrounded myself with incredible talents that helped me make the Magic Castle what it is today: Bill and Irene Larsen, John Shrum, Don Gotschall, Don Culp, Tom Heric, Bob Barker, Gerald Singer, Ralph Edwards and all our friends in magic.

If you crack open your encyclopedia on Popular Music and Jazz you will find a rather extensive biography for Sid Weiss. Sid was a magician and his white goatee wasn't even gray when he joined the Magic Castle. His main claim to fame, however, was as a musician. He was born in 1914 and played bass with many of the biggest swing bands of the '30's and '40's. You can hear him swingin' that bass on some of the greatest record hits of all time by Benny Goodman, Artie Shaw and Tommy Dorsey.

Back in the '60's, Sid found working for a bank was a little more steady than touring with swing bands. At the time the Magic Castle was having some communication problems with our bank. The Security First National Bank was very old-fashioned. They still believed in the ancient concept that people should put as much money into the bank as they draw out. Sid explained that he was working for a much more progressive bank that had just opened an office in Hollywood. He introduced us to Bruce Fane, the Vice-President of the new branch, and we started a very nice relationship with the Manufacturers Bank. A young financial wizard by the name of Lewis P. Horwitz set up the entertainment division for the bank and that's how we met Lew, who also headed a film finance company: The Lewis P. Horwitz Organization.

When the Castle first opened in 1963, we drew our first members from three sources. First, of course, there were the magician friends Bill and I knew. Very few of these good friends really thought the Magic Castle would become a reality but what the hell, wouldn't it be great to have a full-time hangout? The cost of the bet-on-this-dream was only $35, so—why not? We realized that magicians alone could never support the club so we *put the arm* on our non-magician friends to become associate members. The pitch went something like this: "Give me twenty-five dollars." "What for?" "We're starting a new club… you'll love it." "Well, I dunno." "We'll have a great bar." "Okay, here's your twenty-five bucks." Most of our friends and new members were Bill's buddies at CBS and my gang at NBC.

After six weeks of being open, the Academy of Magical Arts' membership rose to 180—100 magicians, 80 associate members. By June, six months later, the membership had risen to 350, and by July 480. Bill and I had only one regret—that Dad hadn't lived to see his dream come to fruition.

Brother Bill met Irene when The Daniels visited the Thayer's Magic Shop. Bill fell in love with her instantly, smitten. In the June 1963 edition of Genii, Bill shared with Genii readers throughout the world that he had finally convinced Irene Daniel to marry him. They were married November of that same year.

The entire history of the Magic Castle and the Academy of Magical Arts is well recorded through a diary that has been kept for generations. The diary is in the form of the newsletters that date back to 1962 in which my Brother Bill took pride in writing in the style of his personal letter to the membership of the Academy. He used the same style in writing his editorial, Genii Speaks, in Genii every month. Through the newsletters and Genii, the world of magic knew all about Bill, The Magic Castle, Irene, the kids, their dogs, cats, his old station wagon and even his stuffed bear. Bill started writing the Genii editorials in 1953 after the passing of our father. Irene appeared in the Genii credits in 1965.

Irene and Bill

Irene has greeted magicians from all over the world for over forty years at the Magic Castle, traveled with Bill Jr. around the globe as ambassadors of good will for magic, Genii and the Magic Castle. She learned close-up magic from the first Magic Castle host, Jay Ose, and would entertain patrons at the Magic Castle with her warmth, infectious laugh and a four aces trick she learned from Leo Behnke.

Bill was absolutely crucial to the success of the Castle. It was Bill who had the respect of the magic community, whose imperturbable demeanor could calm the angriest of members, and whose relationship with magicians from around the world was vital to the growing interest and support of the Magic Castle.

Jay Ose was our Resident Magician, truly so. He lived in a room on the second floor, now the Dante dining room. In the afternoons he would entertain other magician friends playing endless games of Clobyosh, a rather complicated thirty-two card game of one-upmanship that Jay once tried unsuccessfully to teach me. Jay was one of the last of that dying breed—a Gentleman. He was shy, kindly, soft-spoken and had a gentle sardonic sense of humor. Jay was a recovered alcoholic and a chain smoker, selfless in his appreciation of other magicians. Jay absolutely revered Dai Vernon and it was Jay who suggested we send for Al Goshman, one of the best close-up magicians he had ever seen.

Seated L-R: Johnny Platt, Dai Vernon, Carl Ballantine, Jay Ose, Standing: Jack Walsh, Snag Werris

Al Goshman was The Baker Who's a Fakir. He was rumpled, unkempt and uncouth. Our first call to Al was to a pay phone in Brooklyn that Al had somehow rigged to send and accept calls for free. When Al arrived at the Magic Castle in a dirty T-shirt, I assigned Don Culp to take Al immediately to Dorman's Mens' Store on La Cienega and buy him his first suit. The donut baker from New York had a more aggressive personality than Jay and was able to use the Magic Castle as a springboard for a career in traveling industrial shows.

Albert Goshman

Dai Vernon was reserved, gentlemanly and composed. He was admired and held in awe by everyone. Dai came to stay with Jay Ose at the Castle and, after Jay's death, became our Magician in Residence. Having Dai Vernon at the Castle was a major coup.

Dai Vernon

Dai may have been largely unknown to the public but to magicians, he was one step this side of being a god. Jay mentioned that Dai once had quit magic to please his wife and worked as an architect but he fell off a roof and broke both wrists. Even with his old injuries, Dai could still out-manipulate any close-up magician in the world.

124

Channing Pollack was tall, handsome, elegant, sophisticated, charismatic and an absolutely flawless stage magician. Since our manager, Don Culp, was totally inept at magic, Channing felt this was unacceptable and taught Don a rope trick, which, to this day, is the only magic trick Don knows. Channing had a very successful career in the movies and always visited the Magic Castle when he returned from his travels abroad.

Channing Pollack

At one time, Harry Blackstone was arguably the most famous magician in the world. He was electrifying and his appearance in town was a major event. One of his memorable effects was utilizing a red devil appearing from a trunk. When he became a regular at the Magic Castle he was elderly and frail, moving carefully with the aid of a cane. His wife drove him in a tired Chevrolet Corvair, which barely made it up the steep entrance hill. He still had his famous shock of pure-white hair but he seemed just another old man, until one afternoon when a visitor was touring the Magic Castle with his small daughter. Harry had been upstairs visiting with Jay Ose and was coming down the main staircase, slowly and very carefully. As he took the final turn on the stairs he caught sight of the little girl. Back went his shoulders, up shot his head, and Blackstone strode down the rest of the stairs in splendor and strength to greet his little fan.

Harry Blackstone Sr.

The Magic Castle was definitely Bill Bixby's sort of place. He first came to the Castle with Ray Walston while they were casting a CBS female lead in "My Favorite Martian." Bill's method of casting for the part was to arrive at the Magic Castle in the late afternoon with a gorgeous girl in tow, spend a short time sitting in John Shrum's Kennedy rocking chairs on the porch, entertain her, then vanish with her and return later that night with a different gorgeous girl. He had learned that there were perquisites to stardom.

Bill Bixby

In the early '60's, stereo radio was new, especially in cars. Once "My Favorite Martian" was a hit, Bill immediately had a full stereo system installed in his new car and drove to the Castle, parked in front and invited us all to come and hear his new toy. Bill became a great fan of magic and even starred in a television series, "The Magician" in which he performed his own magic and frequently filmed at the Castle.

125

Cary Grant's first visit to the Castle was as a guest of a member. Later he returned as my guest and brought a small group for dinner and signed the tab (who was going to refuse Cary Grant?) A few days later our daytime receptionist and bookkeeper, Eleanor St. Germain, received a telephone call. "Will you speak to Mr. Cary Grant?" a woman asked. At first Eleanor thought it was a gag but then she was not about to say "no" to Cary Grant. Soon she heard an unmistakable voice say, "This is Cary Grant. My guests and I had dinner at your establishment a few evenings ago. There's something I do not understand and I'd like to go over the bill with you, if I may?" Eleanor gulped in semi-horror that she had somehow made a mistake on Cary Grant's bill. Cary began to list each item on the bill and its price as Eleanor hastily used her adding machine. "Well, I just don't understand. I had a wonderful meal for eight people and the bill was $89.48. Are you sure that is correct?" When Eleanor verified the total amount was indeed correct, Cary replied, "Well I don't think you charged me enough."

The next visit Cary made to the Magic Castle he pulled me aside and said that while we had some interesting wines, he felt there were a lot of California wines far superior and less costly. He asked me if I would mind if he came over some afternoon and helped me with the wine list. He offered his expertise and the Magic Castle wine list came to be officially designed by Cary Grant!

One November morning in 1963 I called Don Culp, our manager. He was still in bed. "Shall we open the Castle tonight?" Don hadn't yet turned on the television and hadn't heard what my concern was about. "Kennedy has been assassinated." I was worried that opening might seem disrespectful and perhaps we should call the help and not open that evening. Don felt our members might want a quiet place, an oasis in the middle of insanity, to sit and talk. He voted for opening and we did. It was a disaster. Less than a dozen people showed and the gloomy talk centered on whether Castro and the Communists had had a part in the assassination and what the consequences might be if they had. We closed and sent everyone home by 9 p.m. John Shrum removed the

Kennedy rocking chairs from the Castle porch, never to return.

Parking at the Magic Castle, especially in the early days, could be an adventure. We had hired a very nice, if not terribly bright, young man to be our uniformed parking attendant. He had to drive the cars to a lot in the back of the building, park them and then dash to the front again. The Magic Castle closed at 2 a.m. but frequently members would linger after the bar had closed. On those nights the parking attendant would bring the remaining cars to the entrance area, hand the keys to the appropriate members, receive his tip and go home.

John Daniel drove a white Cadillac convertible. One night several of us stayed to chat and the attendant brought in the keys and left. Soon John left but only a few moments later he was on the telephone. He had stopped at an all-night market and pushed the power door lock button to lock the car. Then he went into the market and when he returned, the keys would not open the door. Don drove to the market and picked up John, leaving the Cadillac where it was parked. The next morning we discovered that there had been two identical white Cadillac convertibles at the Magic Castle that night. The attendant had accidentally given the wrong keys to both John and the lady who owned the other Cadillac. The ignition keys were similar enough to work in either car, but the door keys were not. An exchange of cars settled the matter amicably. It was soon after that Bill and I hired a professional parking service.

We paid our magicians then, and still do, a minimum salary, far less than they could earn working in clubs or theaters. Aside from the very honor of performing at the Magic Castle, there was an added benefit. Film and television actors, producers, directors and casting agents regularly frequented our nightclub. Within a year of our opening, Jay Ose had landed jobs in feature films working with George C. Scott and James Coburn. He tutored Karl Malden for his role as a card shark in "The Cincinnati Kid" and easily developed friendships with many celebrities. He performed with Paul

Steve McQueen, Karl Malden in "The Cincinatti Kid"

Lukas and Hoagy Carmichael in CBS' "The Man Who Bought Paradise," as well as

Karl Malden and Jay Ose

on "The Alfred Hitchcock Hour," "Truth or Consequences," "The Steve Allen Show" and "Mr. Ed." People like Cary Grant would bring their friends to see this wonderful close-up magician. Jay had the rare ability of recalling names. If he remembered that someone had seen an effect on a previous visit he would surprise him by switching methods in the middle of the routine. He was always one step ahead of his audience. The ups and downs, the hoofing, the stock companies, the burlesque, the vaudeville, you name it and Jay had done it. Jay was our Resident Magician until his untimely passing in 1967.

Life Member Karl Malden was one of our first celebrity members. He loved to watch Jay perform his legendary close-up magic in what is now the Irma Room. He loved magic and was a great audience. He visited the Castle often and introduced other major celebrities to the club. Karl and his wife, Mona, had a lovely second home in Montecito, not too far from our former beach home. Our house was right on the water and our beach was often just hundreds of rocks after the sand went out for a swim. One foggy, winter morning about seven o'clock, I was having my morning coffee, reading the paper and watching the ocean when I heard a strange noise—clink—clink—clink. I opened our little beach gate to see a couple of workers loading rocks into a wheelbarrow. Standing with his back to me overseeing the work outside our gate was a man in a trench coat with a turned-up collar and a beat-up hat. I recognized Karl Malden.

Not being one to resist a gag, I called out to him, "Hey you! Those are my rocks you're stealing! Put them back!" For a moment he obviously didn't want to turn around but when he turned to face his accuser… "Milt! What the hell are you doing here?" I explained it was our home and he was welcome to take as many rocks as he wanted. I suggested he let the workers gather the rocks and he come join me for a nice hot cup of coffee. It was the first of many visits over the years. He was a frequent visitor to the Magic Castle and he loved to spend the evening with Irma.

Leo Behnke was tall, slim with scholarly good looks. He had a shyness and reserve that seemed to make him unsuited for a professional magician, preferring to design magic productions instead of performing. Leo moved to Las Vegas where he spent several years as curator of magician David Copperfield's museum of magic effects and paraphernalia. Leo followed Jay Ose as one of our first resident magicians.

Leo Behnke and receptionist

The tower in the Magic Castle used to be an unfinished storage area. In my King of the Mountain–Tree House days I transformed the storage area into a rather grand executive office. The problem was that I was never the office type. My real office was wherever the latest project happened to be. My desk was always a couple of sawhorses with a sheet of plywood on top. At one point I converted the tower office into a new Houdini Séance room. We used to use a *Dr. Q Spirit Hand* in the old séance. For the non-magicians, this was a carved hand on a wooden board that would answer questions. The original prop was lost some years ago—it is probably on display in someone's magic collection. I decided to include this neat effect in the new séance and re-created the board but I couldn't find a proper carved hand. A week later, I was making a telephone call and noticed a wonderful gay '90's high-buttoned shoe on the shelf above the phone. As you know, my wife, Arlene, was a studio costume designer and the shoe was simply one more objets d'arte that adorned our house at the beach. I got a great idea: why not use the shoe instead of the hand. It could be passed off as the shoe of Bessie Houdini when she used to be a dancer. I grabbed the shoe and ran down to my shop. It worked perfectly!

My magic library in Santa Barbara consists of only a dozen books or so. My favorite is Hopkins "Magic." Another well-worn book is "The Trick Brain" by Daniel Fitzkee, a wonderful treasure trove of magical ideas published back in 1944. I was writing some lines for the special menu for our Awards Banquet at the Beverly Wilshire Hotel. I had used every synonym for magic I could think of and needed another word or two. I cracked open Fitzkee's "The Trick Brain." In glancing through the index I found a strange reference: *Bill Larsen's Slipper*, Chapter XX, page 179. There it was: Fitzkee referred to a variation of the *Dr. Q Spirit Hand* published in a Sphinx Magazine: "…he substituted a small high-heeled slipper for the hand. The slipper, once the property of a dancer who had passed on, quite consistently tapped out answers." What I had thought was my own brand new original brilliant idea was something our dad had thought of half a century ago!

Señor Ortega worked as Harry Houdini's principal assistant. He lived at a large ranch down in the Irvine area. He loved magic and used to entertain the ranch hands and the kids in the community. Judging from his props he must have been very good. He bought most of his stuff from Thayers in the '20's. Later he also worked for Harry Blackstone Sr. His grandson, Dennis Magnusen, was moving to Hawaii and had some trunks of his grandfather's props. He wanted to find some place that would appreciate their magical value. In asking around he found two places that might be interested: Newport's Magic Island and the Magic Castle. Since they lived in Orange County, Dennis called Magic Island first—who already had lots of old magic. Then he called the Magic Castle and spoke to Dick Mentzer who put Dennis in touch with me. This wonderful collection is now part of the Academy of Magical Arts museum archives. For all we know, the very old Metamorphosis Trunk that came with the collection might *Thayer's Dr. "Q" Spirit Hand* have been Houdini's. I had been looking for a Thayer Dr. Q Spirit Hand for our new séance and there it was, in perfect condition.

Thayer's Dr. "Q" Spirit Hand

Thayer's Dr. "Q" Spirit Hand

Still Tops 'Em All!

And Still a Fifty Dollar Trick

THAYER MFG. CO.

Howard Thurston was the successor to The Great Kellar. Kellar was a world-famous stage magician and had the largest traveling vaudeville magic show at the time, requiring more than eight entire train cars to transport his props across the country. He was famous for

Thurston

his work with playing cards and called himself the King of Cards. One of his most famous effects was the *Rising Card*. In 1908 Harry Kellar bid farewell to the stage with Howard Thurston at his side. With his retirement, Kellar began the tradition of the Royal Dynasty of Magic by passing the mantle of magic to Howard Thurston. It is said that Kellar considered only Thurston to be worthy of succeeding him. Kellar retired and lived in Hollywood until his passing in 1922. Visitors to his study often admired the stuffed owl perched over his desk. The owl found a new home at the Magic Castle in the Owl Bar and has displayed a rare ability to answer any question that can be answered with a yes or no. Thurston died twenty-seven years later in 1936 and passed the mantle of magic to Dante. In 1955 Dante passed the mantle of magic to Lee Grabel and in 1994 Lee passed the mantle to Lance Burton.

Kellar

Lance Burton

Dante

Peter Pit didn't have an accent until he came to America in 1964 to appear on the Ed Sullivan Show where, according to Charles Champlin's review in the Los Angeles Times, "Peter Pit moves with the dancing cane like he is the Fred Astaire of Magic." We brought him back the following year to emcee the 11th Annual "It's Magic!" Peter stayed in Los Angeles and immediately became a member of the Academy of Magical Arts. He rolled up his sleeves and got involved. He worked very closely with Brother Bill as the Secretary of the Academy. He instigated the first swap meet in 1971, served twenty-two years on the Board of Directors, eighteen years booking our talent when the Palace of Mystery opened in 1976, fifteen years of co-producing our award shows, five years of appearing on "It's Magic!" and thirty years of being one of our best Master of Ceremonies in the Palace of Mystery. He won the Stage Magician of the Year Award in 1978. For the next twenty years Peter could be found writing, directing and performing. He was the emcee of seven FISM shows in multi-languages, booked cruise ship's talent and was one of the sponsors of the Academy of Magical Arts Junior program.

Peter Pit

William Read Woodfield was a brilliant writer and magician who brought the *magazine within a magazine* Magicana to the pages of Genii in 1964. He collaborated with fellow magical genius Charlie Miller until the late '60's at which time Charlie continued Magicana on his own. Bill was the producer and writer for television's "Mission Impossible" which I always considered to be the longest running magic show on television. All the early scripts that Bill Woodfield devised were based on his knowledge of magical effects.

Bill's preface to the first Genii issue of Magicana, November 1964 read: "Without question, the most practical, the most sophisticated, the cleanest, the most deceptive, the most MAGICAL magic history of the art is being performed night after night at the Magic Castle in Hollywood, California. There, every night is convention night where the best magic minds of our times meet, perform, discuss and exchange ideas. The tricks are all miracles—brilliant in conception, flawlessly executed. The tips and pointers are then will-o'-the-wisp technical niceties that experts Charlie Miller, Ed Marlo, Faucett Ross and Dai Vernon have devoted their lives to studying. Now, all these great technicians and performers are, so to speak, under one canvas. Miller and Vernon are practically residents. (Actually Jay Ose is the official Resident Magician and the best magical agent the Larsen boys could have found.) Ross, Marlo and every legendary name in magic, if not actually at the Castle, are in regular correspondence with Castle regulars Leo Behnke, Larry Jennings, Al Goshman, Harry Mendoza, Dick Zimmerman, Ross Bertram, Bob Gwodz and Bill Chaudet... to name only a few. Thus the opportunity to see magic, to develop magical thinking and to learn is unlimited. The editors of this little *magazine within a magazine* each month will select one or two of the miracles they have seen at the Castle and pass them along, in words and pictures, to the readers of Genii in the Magicana section.

It is a cliché in magic that if a magician desires to keep a secret, he should publish it. Cynics interpret this to mean that no one reads what others write. But we know better and hope that Magicana becomes a storehouse wherein today's magical greats keep their secrets, certain in the knowledge that their inventions will not only be read but will be performed."

A side thought about Charlie Miller: Charlie was a charming stage performer and appeared on "It's Magic!" back in the late '60's. As a card expert, he was in that class that included Dai Vernon, Nate Leipzig, Max Malini and other legends in magic. Although my entire life has been magic, I was also fascinated with the variety arts in vaudeville. Since I felt I was put on this earth to revive vaudeville, I started collecting anything and everything about vaudeville as a kid. You name it: records, films, scripts, photos—and I also got to meet the old vaudevillians that loved to share their memories with me. Charles had mastered the art of juggling and could accomplish a back flip in his later years even though he was a portly man. Quite a feat!

The younger magicians that were devotees of sleight of hand were often surprised and envious to see me with the great Charlie Miller, deep in conversation at the end of the Magic Castle bar. Was he imparting the great secrets of magic or some new Charlie Miller move? No! Charlie loved to talk about the comedy and novelty acts in vaudeville. We'd reminisce about Willie, West and McGinty, Professor Lamberti, Fink's Mules and the great comedy magic acts of the past... never about in-jogs or out-jogs.

"Mary Poppins" opened in 1964, a year after we opened the Magic Castle. Thanks to Dick Sherman, my then fiancé Barbara Logan and I had tickets to the lavish premiere at Grauman's Chinese Theater. The sportswear manufacturer, Phil Rose, offered his Rolls Royce limousine and chauffeur so we would arrive in style. As we waited to pull up in front of the red carpet the fans peered in the window of our limo and we could hear them yelling, "Ah—That's nobody... That's nobody!" Barbara Stuckey went under the professional name of Barbara Logan. She was a very bright public relations person. One of her clients was Tiffany's Jewelers when they opened their store in Beverly Hills. She became the head of public relations for one of American's most successful garment manufacturers, Phil Rose of California. I knew Barbara was a somebody!

Grauman's Chinese Theatre

In 1965 I produced "It's Magic!" as a solo venture for three nights, November 4th, 5th and 6th. This show marked the beginning of the team that became well-associated with "It's Magic!" Brother Bill was getting more and more involved as Associate Producer, Dick Zimmerman directed, John Shrum created the settings and Shirley Carroll carried on the publicity for her late husband.

Jay Ose, Bill, Leo Behnke, Geri, Art Baker and Milt singing with Irma.

TV City had an opening and posted all the available jobs. By that time, Bill belonged to the union and applied for an entry-level position in the cost control department just to move along. Again Jack Forman, the head of the studio, and Bill talked about magic after the interview and Bill landed the job. When Bill was the head of the cost control department he would go to production meetings and sit with the third floor programming executives. One of Bill's jobs was to cost out the live shows that were currently running, "Life With Father," "Climax," and "Playhouse 90." Bill was very good at accurately pinpointing the cost of the shows. The producers decided to move the production supervisors from "Climax" and put them on "Playhouse 90" which created an opening on "Climax." And once again, Bill and the executives started talking about magic. That very day, they plucked Bill out of the cost control department and moved him up to the third floor.

That was Bill's big break: he became Production Supervisor for "Climax," later Production Supervisor for "Playhouse 90" and Associate Producer for "Playhouse 90," "The Clear Horizon," "This Is Your Verdict," and "The Brighter Day." He did a lot of summer shows and retains, to this day, the distinction of being the only one who was ever kept on payroll as an Associate Producer at CBS then, now or ever since. Even if there was no show, Bill had a job. That was the happiest four years of his life. Bill had the pleasure of working with Frank Sinatra on a couple of his specials. At the time he was working with producers Saul Ilson and Ernie Chambers, both members of the Magic Castle. One night Frank and his entourage descended on the Castle for dinner. It was a great evening for Invisible Irma who found herself accompanying Ol' Blue Eyes.

Brother Bill always kidded me about being the reincarnation of Mrs. Winchester. She was the eccentric lady in San Jose who was told by a psychic that she would die if she ever finished the house where she lived. She built an incredible house with more than one hundred rooms and stairways that led nowhere. She never stopped building. Bill was probably right because the Magic Castle is still not finished. I've always loved that comparison and it's true. As long as I'm alive, I hope I go down in magical history as the guy who gave magicians a nice, if somewhat elaborate home. Until the Magic Castle there was no place in the world magicians could hang out and exchange in-jogs

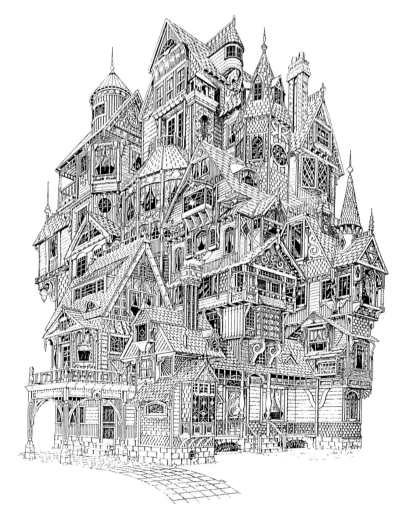

and out-jogs seven days a week. Most clubs and restaurants get old and uninteresting after a decade or so. Many have tried to imitate the Magic Castle but without success because it took a Larsen family, not only to conceive the project, but also to keep it working and improving year after year. Most people thought it was a pipe dream in the beginning but the Larsens had faith.

There were times, however, when I simply ran out of room. Bill also kidded that it might be a good idea to send me off to Europe and look at old castles for a while. The Magic Castle needed time to catch up to the improvements. In 1965 I was still writing "Truth or Consequences" and our "It's Magic! was very successful. I needed another outlet for my energy. I'm not a great believer in horoscopes and astrology but you'll find me in the good book of Aries… to a tee! Aries people, it seems, love to be creative and start things going. Once the Aries sees that the idea works he's off to another challenge.

I had found a good deal on a great old bank building on Melrose Avenue. John Shrum and I got together and drew some plans on the back of a cocktail napkin. I wanted to build a new theater and bar. It would be called: "The Wooden Nickel Music Hall." This would be an intimate little theatre where variety acts could perform. I didn't have enough money for the down payment but I was able to borrow enough to make the deal. The deal was contingent upon my ability to get a liquor license for the building. We found there were a number of problems, including the fact that the building was too close to a church. I dropped my option on the building.

Bob Muir happened to be at the Castle visiting with his buddies and, in particular, Dai Vernon. Bob had just completed a deal to build a high-rise medical building at the corner of LaBrea and Hollywood Boulevard. I happened to mention losing the deal on the bank building and Bob said if I wanted a theatre I could have his. He was referring to the Music Box Theatre, which happened to be on the LaBrea and Hollywood Blvd. property. Originally it was a theater for the Hollywood Women's Club, was briefly called El Patio Theatre, and then a fellow by the name of Ed Sartu had it for a while before it finally became the Music Box Theatre. The theatre had seemed to have a curse on it. No show was ever successfully produced there. I didn't know that at the time and wonder if it would have made any difference if I had.

The Music Box Theatre was scheduled for demolition but that wouldn't be for many months. Rent? Bob said to take care of the utilities, insurance and any expenses. To me that spelled "free." Wrong again! I decided to produce a show called "They Called It Vaudeville." Once again, the team of Larsen and Shrum went into action. John was able to get some great scenery from NBC and we put together a really great production team.

The Music Box was a nice old 900-seat theatre. We moved the Brunswick Gay Nineties bar that is now in the Owl Bar of the Magic Castle into the lobby of the theatre. I installed my sixteen-foot wide *Fotoplayer* pipe organ in the orchestra pit and surrounded the pit with some fabulous wrought iron railing we had just liberated from an old mansion next to the Wilshire Ebell Theatre. The Fotoplayer was a giant player pipe organ device designed for silent movie houses. The one brought for the occasion was totally restored by the late John Daniel and is in operation at John's private theatre in South Pasadena. John Shrum created the feeling of a grand old vaudeville house

through his special kind of magic. One of the reviewers commented on the fact that they had never noticed what an ornate theatre the Music Box was.

"They Called It Vaudeville" opened the evening of Christmas Day 1965. It was a really good show and opened to excellent reviews. My stepfather, Art Baker, was the emcee. The acts included the illusions of Alan Wakeling & Company, Marvyn Roy as "Mr. Electric," The Juggling Volantes, Ventriloquist Russ Lewis and the Marquis Chimps among others. Professor David E. Bourne opened the second half playing the sixteen foot wide Fotoplayer, accompanying Laurel and Hardy's "Big Business." Spencer Quinn played the banjo and led the orchestra. After the opening two weeks we thought we'd extend it, hopefully for a long run. Our ticket prices were very low and our weekly nut was very high, still we might have made it… if only… !!!

Nature dealt us a lousy hand in January of 1966. One of Los Angeles' rare but impressive floods not only slowed down business but the sump pumps at the theatre didn't work. We came in the morning after the huge torrent to find my prized Fotoplayer floating in an orchestra pit full of water. By the time the show closed I had lost the money I had borrowed to buy the bank building. It took me about a year to repay the loan and I swore I would never try to revive vaudeville again. Of course, I lied! If I had only known and paid attention to the alleged curse!

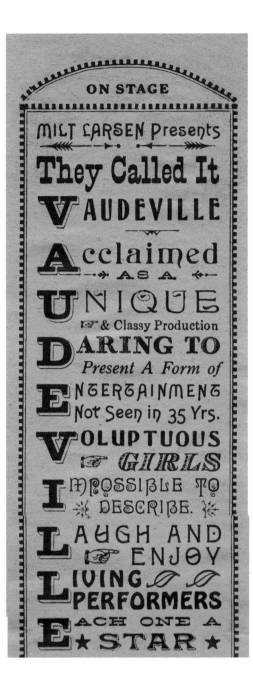

ON STAGE

MILT LARSEN Presents

They Called It
VAUDEVILLE

Acclaimed AS A

UNIQUE ☞ & Classy Production

DARING TO Present A Form of

ENTERTAINMENT Not Seen in 35 Yrs.

VOLUPTUOUS ☞ GIRLS

IMPOSSIBLE TO DESCRIBE. ✲

LAUGH AND ☞ ENJOY

LIVING ✍ ✍ PERFORMERS

EACH ONE A ★ STAR ★

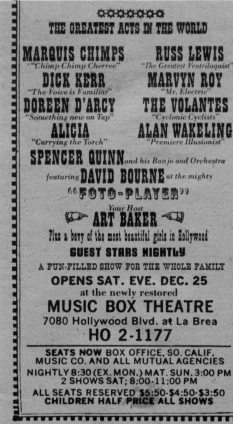

THE GREATEST ACTS IN THE WORLD

MARQUIS CHIMPS
"Chimp Chimp Cherree"

RUSS LEWIS
"The Greatest Ventriloquist"

DICK KERR
"The Voice is Familiar"

MARVYN ROY
"Mr. Electric"

DOREEN D'ARCY
"Something new on Tap"

THE VOLANTES
"Cyclonic Cyclists"

ALICIA
"Carrying the Torch"

ALAN WAKELING
"Premiere Illusionist"

SPENCER QUINN and his Banjo and Orchestra
featuring DAVID BOURNE at the mighty
"FOTO-PLAYER"

Your Host
☞ ART BAKER ☜

Plus a bevy of the most beautiful girls in Hollywood

GUEST STARS NIGHTLY

A FUN-FILLED SHOW FOR THE WHOLE FAMILY

OPENS SAT. EVE. DEC. 25
at the newly restored

MUSIC BOX THEATRE
7080 Hollywood Blvd. at La Brea
HO 2-1177

SEATS NOW BOX OFFICE, SO. CALIF.
MUSIC CO. AND ALL MUTUAL AGENCIES
NIGHTLY 8:30 (EX. MON.) MAT. SUN. 3:00 PM
2 SHOWS SAT; 8:00-11:00 PM
ALL SEATS RESERVED $5.50-$4.50-$3.50
CHILDREN HALF PRICE ALL SHOWS

Your early support of this production
will insure the return of big-time
VAUDEVILLE IN LOS ANGELES
Don't hesitate . . . buy your tickets

Both Bill and I appreciated the ten years Art Baker and Mother had together before Art's sudden passing August 26, 1966. Bill and Irene were traveling extensively in Europe in 1966. Art Baker died leaving Mother single again. Irene gave birth to a daughter, Heidi. And I was more interested in writing jokes and building Magic Castles than I was in getting married and having a family. There would be time for that later.

I was dating a wonderful lady for about eight years and she was there for the opening of the Magic Castle in 1963. She was also at my side sloshing through the flooded orchestra pit at the Music Box Theater. Phil Rose, often called the Jack Benny of the Rag Business, inspired an LP recorded with a full orchestra at our Brookledge studio. We produced the LP, "One Dozen Phil Rose's—Ballads of the Garment Belt." Phil paid for all 5,000 copies that were pressed to send to his very close friends and clients as Christmas presents. Barbara and I wrote parodies on classic songs: "Frankie and Johnny" became "Marvin and Myron," "Hava Nagila" became "I Am a Tailor," etc. Phil Rose was California's most famous designer of women's sportswear and gained international renown for his daring innovations in fashion. In addition to writing some of the lyrics for the album, the album was directed by Barbara. She edited "Twenty Years Less 8%" a satirical book published by Phil Rose in 1960 and had produced many unique musical fashion shows. Barbara was very independent and so was I. We were destined to get married and have a child just before the Magic Castle opened but we elected to postpone such an event until we were more settled, a decision made tragically sad by the events that followed.

On March 5, 1966 I drove Barbara to the airport to fly with all the executives of the Phil Rose Company to Tokyo, Japan. We decided to set the date and announce our wedding upon her return. The crash of their jet into Mt. Fuji took the lives of Barbara, her boss Phil and many of the good friends I had grown to know. Her loss was a shock and I felt very guilty that we had not made the earlier decision that might have meant she wouldn't have been on that plane. But life goes on and my friends at the Castle and Mother, Art Baker, Bill and his family helped me through a very difficult time.

After Barbara's death, Eleanor St. Germain became a very important lady in my life. She was slightly older and a helluva lot wiser. She had been widowed and was raising two teenage sons. When we needed someone to be our entire office force, Don Culp suggested Eleanor. She was our one-lady office when we first opened the Magic Castle. She helped guide the good ship Magic Castle through many troubled waters back in those early days. I met her through Don Culp who was our very first manager. Don drove

Milt and Eleanor St. Germain

an ice cream truck so Bill and I assumed he knew a lot about the food and beverage business. Don is doing well today as one of the head honchos of Executive Car Leasing. Bill and I both leased our cars from him. Don was interested in the Al Jolson Fan Club and Eleanor was a 100% dyed-in-the-wool Jolson fan. I had a huge Al Jolson record and film collection and that's how we all got to know each other.

In the very early days Brother Bill handled most of the Academy business from his plush executive office at CBS. Eleanor worked with Don on the day-to-day operations at the Castle. At that point, her business office was in a former bathroom adjacent to what is now our Dante dining room. For years there was a motto written on a file card over her desk: "Bumble Bees Can't Fly!" I had cited as a proven fact that is it aerodynamically impossible for the mass of a bumblebee's body to be supported by its tiny wings. When things were rough I would merely point out that bumblebees do fly—nothing is impossible!

When we opened the Mayfair Music Hall Eleanor became the office manager and my Assistant-Everything. She took over the very difficult job of becoming assistant to the President when we tackled the huge Variety Arts Center project. She was not exactly my second fiancé but we shared a deep love for each other. When her kids, Bernie and Phillip, became

140

grown men Eleanor decided that I would never grow up and moved to New York City where she pursued a career as a playwright. Unfortunately, she too passed away much too soon in life.

A tall, distinguished-looking English gentleman, Ted Salter, was active in the Magic Castle until moving to Hillsboro, Ohio in 1989. He had operated his own commercial art business in Los Angeles for many years, but performing arts and the Magic Castle were always quite dear to him. Puppetry and variety arts performances with his wife, Eileen, occupied much of his spare time. He demonstrated his *Back Painting Act* as a guest on "Truth or Consequences" and also on the "Steve Allen Show." Nearly six-hundred caricatures decorate the walls of the Magic Castle, including those of Orson Welles, The Great Tomsoni, Johnny Carson, David Copperfield, Doug Henning and Harry Blackstone, Jr. and bear his signature.

Ted once said that his caricature of Jay Ose was the first and started the Magic Castle collection. Ted was awarded a lifetime membership in the Academy of Magical Arts. Nielsen Magic published a book containing five hundred, fifty-one of the caricatures in 1988. Ted was a regular columnist for the LaughMakers variety magazine, contributing articles pertaining to puppetry, puppet stages and effects.

Although "It's Magic!" dates back to 1956, the idea of artistic posters can be credited to Shirley Carroll, our publicist, and her relationship with a young poster artist, later to go on to fame, Earl Newman. His first poster for "It's Magic!" was done in 1966. People said it was Jay Ose… or was it Stan Laurel… Or… well, whoever it might have been it was an immediate winner. Earl Newman did the next three years of posters and, by 1970, he was the Rembrandt of poster artists. Robert LaPlaine was a professional sign painter from the days when sign painting was an art. He contributed his talent to many of our "It's Magic!" posters in the collection on display in the Parlour of Prestidigitation at the Magic Castle. Each of Bob's posters was hand silk-screened. No two were exactly alike. He used real gold leaf in his gold lettering. Only 200 posters were made for each production and that's why they bring big prices in the magic collectors' market today. Bob always donated his talents for the love of magic. He donated his scrapbooks on magic to the Academy of Magical Art's Library.

IT'S MAGIC!
WILSHIRE EBELL Theatre NOV. 2~6 1966 ✳

143

144

Jay Marshall, a giant among magicians, was one of the funniest men that ever walked the planet, and he was also a vent! It seemed to me that Jay attended every magic convention ever held anywhere. Jay graced our "It's Magic!" stages several times. His first appearance was at the Wilshire Ebell in 1967 emceeing a bill that included John Daniels, Bob Haskell and Tony Slydini. His "Lefty" gloved hand puppet was legendary and was performed fourteen times on the "Ed Sullivan Show." Jay, as Jasper, opened for Frank Sinatra, Milton Berle and Liberace. Jasper was a one-of-a-kind entertainer and a true gentleman in the world of magic. He and his wife, Frances Ireland, owned, operated and published books for Ireland Magic Company, which later became Magic Inc. in Chicago.

Gary Edwards, Ralph's son, and his lovely wife, Suzanne, are devoted historians of "Truth or Consequences" and lifetime members of the Magic Castle. Gary recently found some old tapes of "Truth or Consequences" with segments with my favorite "Truth or Consequences" bit player—me! I played an eccentric airline pilot, an Indian Fakir on a bed of nails, a wacky magician and I always found ways of weaving our Magic Castle magicians into the shows. Acts included Jay Ose, Albert Goshman, Harry Blackstone Jr., Leo Behnke, Kuda Bux and many others.

Milt as a "Truth or Consequences" bit player, Indian Fakir

In 1967, after nine years with "Truth or Consequences" on NBC, I told Ralph that I had to make the hardest decision in my life. I realized that we had to give the Magic Castle our full attention if we wanted it to succeed. I asked Ralph to replace me on "Truth or Consequences." I told him it was probably the best job I would ever have in my life but I had to follow my heart and move on.

Ralph wished me well and said at one time in his life he was a staff radio announcer in Chicago. He felt there was more opportunity in Hollywood so he and his wife, Barbara, packed up all their belongings and headed west for the biggest gamble of his life. In trying to get a job, he ad-libbed an idea for a game show based on an old parlour game. The idea became America's number one game show on radio and then on TV, "Truth or Consequences." He made a decision and took a chance in 1940 that launched a production empire. I could only hope to follow in his footsteps when I made the similar decision to leave "Truth or Consequences." Ralph graciously accepted my resignation but said I could come back at any time. As it worked out, I worked for the show on and off for the next nine years.

Bill had become Associate Producer for Danny Kaye and Jonathan Winters for a year and did six specials for Nelson Chambers that made Bill more money than he ever dreamt was possible. But that was the end of Bill's television career. He had come to the point, while working with Jonathan Winters, that he realized he could not keep going on. The Castle used to take a few hours a week to sign checks but now the Castle was really a full-time job, Genii was a full-time job and television was a full-time job. He only wanted two full-time jobs, not three, so he chose to quit television in 1968. Bill quit his executive job at CBS-TV after fifteen years.

That was a momentous year. 1968 was the year the Academy of Magical Arts held their first Awards Banquet at the Century Plaza Hotel. Bob Barker presided as the emcee. Jules Lenier, who had relocated from New York a few years prior to help with Genii, produced the first show. Later Peter Pit and Dick Zimmerman produced the Awards Banquets until Mark Nelson and Dale Hindman took over. Bill had quit television to devote his full attention to Genii and the Magic Castle, and in June, Erika was born.

Bill was the soul of the organization, Academy of Magical Arts. He worked tirelessly, organizing the ever-growing membership, running the Magic Castle and using his CBS cost controlling skills to make it financially viable while, at the same time, publishing and editing Genii magazine. Bill was elected as the first President of the Academy of Magical Arts and remained in that position until his untimely passing in 1993.

As the fame of the Magic Castle grew, Bill and Irene traveled to magical events all over the world. Bill was made honorary member of every major magical society through his travels. As devoted ambassadors of magic, Bill and Irene introduced international magicians to the Magic Castle and "It's Magic!" Many magicians attest their success came from the first break given to them by the Magic Castle, "It's Magic!" and Bill Larsen more than by any other single force. Bill loved magic and always felt that magic effort, no matter how meager, should be encouraged, never dissuaded; elevated, never denigrated. My brother had no hobbies. He had two loves in his life, his family and magic. We never once had an argument. We had discussions, sometimes we didn't agree. But we never had an argument. For two brothers in business together that's something of a miracle in itself. We had a mutual love and respect for each other. Bill was selflessly generous.

Remember vinyl LP's? Oliver Berliner and I started producing albums under the name of Pacific International Productions, PIP. While Tom Edison was credited with the invention of the talking machine Oliver's grandfather figured out that most folks would rather have flat disk records than those pesky wax cylinders. He started a company called the Victor Talking Machine Company and bought a painting of a little dog by the name of Nipper listening to a tin horn and dubbed it *His Master's Voice*. Emil

Berliner also invented a gadget called the microphone. Oliver was very involved in the Latin music scene and owned a small FM radio station.

Our first PIP LP was Sherman and Larsen's "Smash Flops." We produced a few other LP's under the PIP label. Dick and I were pressed to write another series of comedic songs like "Smash Flops." We decided to take a slightly different tack and address headlines nobody talks about saying them in the most impolite way possible. We came up with the idea of "Sing A Song of Sickness," "What Goes Around Comes Around," later called "Banned Barbershop Ballads." One of our songs was a classic "Watch World War III on Pay TV." The amazing thing was back in the early '60's, obviously we thought there could never, ever be another world war, nor would pay TV ever work.

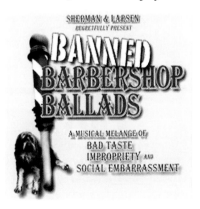

The networks would never, ever allow pay TV to take a stronghold. Here's a song that would be so out of place, so completely wrong, that it would be funny—or so we thought. The performances were by a great Pasadena Barbershop group *The Crown City Four* and produced by Oliver Berliner under the PIP label.

There were so many of the types of headlines that had a bite still in them: "At The Annual Get-Together of the KKK and the NAACP." That is really frightening. We are still waiting for that to happen. "It's Fun To Be Hazed" was based on a headline about a hazing that took place in some college where several people were hurt; so what goes 'round, comes 'round. There was another headline about a disgruntled fellow singing about "Sending The Girls Over There" to Vietnam. Now, we have lots and lots of women in the service, under fire and doing all kinds of heroic things, but back in the '60's you'd never think, or dream, of khaki and lace underwear in the service. Dick and I share a sense of humor that has intertwined our lives with lots of fun—great fun.

One day in the late '60's, we were surprised to find out that a new label had made its appearance on the record shelves: PIP Records. It was part of a major company, Pickwick International Productions. When we complained about their use of our label they apologized, offered us some nice money and suggested we change the name of

our company. Putting their check in the bank, we came up with a great name for our little company: The Electric Lemon Record Company. We figured most of our LP's were offbeat comedy and music and could be classified as Lemons—The Beatles had just formed Apple Records. The Apple label had a full apple on one side and an open half apple on the other. Our label has a full lemon on one side, and a half lemon on the other. We appreciated the similarities.

L-R: Milt Larsen, Boris Karloff, Forrest Ackerman, Verne Langdon

One of the most memorable people I have ever had the pleasure to meet was the original Frankenstein monster, Boris Karloff. Verne Langdon and I became partners in the Electric Lemon Record Company when we recorded mainly specialty LP's like Verne's pipe organ albums, "Poe with Pipes" with the great John Carradine, "Smash Flops," "Circus Calliope" and others. I was even elected as Governor in the Academy of Recording Arts and Sciences for two terms. One day Verne came up with the idea of making an audio collection of all the monster movies from the Universal Film vaults. Verne was working with Universal at the time and talked to them about getting the rights to use the tracks. They agreed and Verne and I started listening to the monster films. One of my hobbies was film projection and we actually sat in our little theatre at Brookledge and ran the films with the projection lamp turned off! We decided that we had a good product but we needed a quality name associated with the films to narrate. The obvious choice was Boris Karloff, with every pun intended, a monster name in the monster business.

Verne contacted his agent and to our surprise Boris said it sounded like an interesting project. We brought in the amazing Gothic horror historian Forrest Ackerman to write words for Mr. Karloff to speak and the master was cut. Boris was an actor of such caliber that the narration was done in one take. The engineers at Gold Star Recording Studios in Hollywood couldn't believe it. He was a true professional actor. We shipped the LP around and it was finally released as a Decca Record. It was an extremely rare record because Decca dropped it from its catalog after a couple of years. Although they said it was because of legal problems with some of the rights, I always secretly thought that it was because they were probably ticked off at the fact that we sold them the same rights they sold us. You see, Universal was owned by MCA who also owned Decca. Later my "Truth or Consequences" boss Ralph Edwards, and his wife Barbara, invited me to an occasional dinner party at their lovely home in Beverly Hills. I was a bachelor and filled the boy/girl requirement of their exquisite table. The lady they always placed me with was Mrs. Boris Karloff who told me Boris always treasured our production of "Boris Karloff and His Friends."

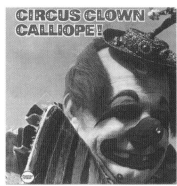

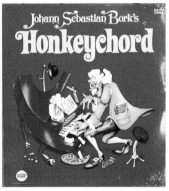

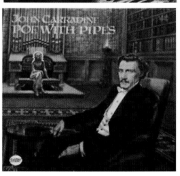

Verne Langdon frequently went by the name of Johann Sebastian Bork—a 90 year old wizard of the raggedy harpsichord who surrounded himself with some of the cheapest acts in showbiz. Bork is one of the wildest cats to come along since the early days of Victor Borge. He did a great spot on the Dinah Shore show on CBS.

Verne Langdon used to run Slammers Wrestling Gym in the San Fernando Valley. He had showcases created for his wrestling museum but they were too close to the ring and were in danger of being destroyed by an occasional flying body, thus he donated them to us. I had wheels attached so the cases could be easily moved around for various activities. They now house the ventriloquial collections, donated by Mrs. Edgar Bergen and Paul Winchell.

Edgar was a very active member of the Magic Castle and used to come in quite often. He was born in Chicago, Illinois to a Swedish family but grew up in Decatur, Michigan. At the young age of eleven, he taught himself the art of ventriloquism simply from reading a pamphlet. At age sixteen Bergen moved back to Chicago where he commissioned a Chicago woodcarver, Theodore Mack, to sculpt the likeness of a rascally Irish newspaper boy he knew into a puppet named Charlie McCarthy—who became Bergen's lifelong sidekick. Bergen's first performances were in vaudeville and one-reel movie shorts, but his real success was on the radio. He and Charlie were seen at a Hollywood party thrown by Noel Coward, who recommended them for an appearance on Rudy Vallee's program. The appearance was so successful the next year they were given their own show. Under various sponsors they were on the air from December 17, 1937 to July 1, 1956, nineteen years! For the radio program, Bergen developed other characters, notably the slow-witted Mortimer Snerd and the man-hungry Effie Klinker.

The star, however, was Charlie, who was always presented as a child (albeit in top hat, cape and monocle)—debonair, girl-crazy, child-about-town. As a child, and a wooden one at that, Charlie could get away with double-entendres that adult humans could not under the broadcast standards of the day. Bergen was still performing at the age of seventy-five and passed away suddenly three days into a two-week engagement as a *Farewell to Show Business* at the Caesar's Palace Hotel in Las Vegas in 1978.

L-R: Effie Klinker, Edgar Bergen, Charlie McCarthy and Mortimer Snerd

Paul Winchell donated the Jerry Mahoney figure, which is the first of the original reproductions being produced in very limited numbers by ventriloquist Jerry Layne. Paul also donated Jerry's first suit, made by hand by Winchell's father, who happened to be a tailor.

One day I was driving back to the Magic Castle from Home Depot on Sunset. I passed Columbia Square and Brittingham's Restaurant. On the left was Earl Carroll's Theater Restaurant with its autographed plaques. As I waited for a stoplight in front of NBC's Radio City Studios observing the kids across the street coming out of Wallach's

Music City, something strange happened—I saw Richard Himber. There he was, standing on the corner waiting to cross the street. He nodded hello as the light changed and I continued on my journey, perplexed. Since Dick Himber had passed away in the mid-'60's, I can only assume this man was an imposter—an amazing look-alike. Magicians know Himber because of the many tricks he invented and marketed: *The Himber Rings, The Himber Milk Pitcher, The Himber Billfold* and on and on. Richard had to be one of the greatest characters I had ever met. He made his fame in the '30's as a bandleader. His many Victor Records billed him as Richard Himber and his Ritz-Carlton Orchestra or as Richard Himber and his Essex House Orchestra. He was a great friend of my dad's and absolutely loved magic. Any visit to the Big Apple had to include a visit to Dick's apartment at the Essex House for lunch. The only problem was that Himber had a sense of humor that drove normal people up the wall. The usually rude waiters at Lindy's would run for cover when Dick entered the room. He was rude, pushy, abrasive, and obnoxious and everybody in New York knew him. He was also kind, generous and a delightful person to know. When you went to breakfast with Dick, you knew you would end up seeing the *Card-in-the-Omelet* and lunch meant you would find your chosen card in the mustard of a pastrami sandwich.

I started writing the Magic Castle Friday lunch menus on December 6, 1968. We were out of our fancy menus and the printer hadn't delivered the new ones. Instant printing had just arrived on the scene and they could print a hundred copies while you enjoyed a cup of complimentary coffee. That day, December 5th, I had fun writing a silly menu. I threw in a few names of people I knew were always at the Castle for Friday lunch. The next week we still didn't have the printed lunch menus and I threw in a few more names. A few members asked, "If I tell you who is coming in on Friday will you write something about them in the menu?" Any writer will tell you that you always need something to write about. Names... schames... fill up the space! The new pretty printed menus finally came in but the members wanted the silly Postal Instant Press nonsense. The idea of the *personal menu* had caught on and has continued ever since. My first poem was actually a Christmas poem written especially for the Magic Castle lunch menu.

T'WAS THE NIGHT BEFORE CHRISTMAS

By Milt Larsen
T'was the night before Christmas
And all through the Castle
Not a cocktail was stirring
Like who needs the hassle?
The rabbit was safe in his hat by the stair,
No magic tonight, for the little white hare.
Then all of a sudden we heard such a noise
T'was Invisible Irma and some of the boys.
There was Dante and Blackstone,
Houdini and Kellar –
Bill Sr., Jay Ose – all down in the cellar
Each ghost did a trick and showed a new sleight
Merry Christmas to all, and to all a good night.

Dec 1969

The original Houdini Séance at the Magic Castle officially opened February 27, 1969. Member Tom Heric had the initial idea and added his electronic expertise to my mechanical madness to create the first *dark séance*. E. Raymond Carlyle was our first séance medium. Later my writing partner and electronic wizard, James Williams, added his knowledge (and a few parts handed down by his father, Gordon Williams, creator of the Tiki Room and Lincoln animatronics for Disney) and the séance got more sophisticated. A big breakthrough happened when I found a company called Gilderfluke who made exactly what we had been trying to invent. The Gilderfluke brain and brick, Dennis Hebert, brought the séance into the 20th century.

In 1969, Dick Sherman wrote a new song called "With a Flair" for a Disney feature film called "Bedknobs and Broomsticks." He brought the writer-producer Bill Walsh to the Magic Castle for lunch one Friday and Irma allowed Dick to play the new song on her piano. The song would introduce British actor David Tomlinson as a sidewalk magician pitching spells and magical potions. Dick had pitched me as a technical consultant because David really was an inept, bumbling magician. Who else would be better qualified to teach tricks that fail than Milt Larsen? I was hired by Bill Walsh to create a comedy magic act for the film. For seven weeks I taught David Tomlinson a few tricks for his street scene. I had a small uncredited cameo appearance as David's stooge who gets a hatful of goop dumped on his head. I ended up on the editing room floor on the first release but was fortunately restored for the later DVD version.

Milt Larsen getting prepped by the prop men for the goop drop.

Milt Larsen as David Tomlinson's stooge.

L-R: Robert Sherman, Angela Landsbury, David Tomlinson, Richard M. Sherman

That's gold in them there vaults! One of the members of the Magic Castle, Maurice Lowe, had been trying to track down some 8mm films he gave to the Castle library many years ago. He brought in a half dozen reels of film and put them on Bill's desk. Our staff remembered those reels being moved from one end of Bill's office to the other. Maurice's request led us on a scavenger hunt, which resulted in our finding some fabulously rare films in our archives as well as Maurice's lost films. I transferred a 16mm film that I didn't know existed. It starts off with Bill and Irene Larsen doing a plug for the 15th Annual "It's Magic!" show at the Wilshire-Ebell on the Lohman and Barkley Show on television. That dates the Kinescope to November 1969. Bill was on the "It's Magic!" that year and he was in great form. On the same reel was Dr. Giovanni doing close-up magic, a magic bit from a vintage movie and a bunch of other treasures.

Bill Larsen in "Aerial Fishing" with Daisy Mae (Irene)

In 1969-70, Bobby Lauher and I wrote for the game show, "It's Takes Two" hosted by Vin Scully. Vin was the voice of the Los Angeles Dodgers. As an announcer he was a legend in the world of baseball. Hosting a game show was a new experience for him and he did a great job. It was a weekday game show where three couples gave numerical answers to questions to make a single averaged answer. An audience contestant would have to guess which of the three answers was correct or closest to being correct. When we were taping the show we would usually go out to lunch with Vin. One day one of the stagehands on the show asked

Vin Scully, "It Takes Two"

him why he would always go to lunch with the writers? Did they give him jokes? Vin replied that any time he ever went out socially the conversation would always focus on *the great American pastime*. Milt Larsen and Bobby Lauher were sports morons—they knew absolutely nothing about baseball!

I was kind of out of the TV writing business in 1969-70. Bobby Lauher and I both left Vin Scully's "It Takes Two" show after the first season to pursue other interests. My *tiger by the tail* was the Magic Castle and Bobby was still writing "Truth or Consequences." We were both working on the book for "Victory Canteen."

Bobby and I also produced and wrote a little epic at KTLA called "The We'll-Get-You-To-Bed-By-Midnight Movie." It was a funny concept: a couple watched the movie in bed, making comments and all the TV audience saw were the two slippered feet and the television set. The gags were kind of Ernie Kovacs-ian electronic sight gags coupled with crazy lines provided by the off-camera voices of Daws Butler and June Foray.

As a side note–the director of that show, a very talented guy, had some financial problems after the show ended and I lent him a thousand dollars. Like so many soft touch deals I never heard back from him… until about seven years later when he called and said he'd like to sport me for lunch. I figured "here it comes again" but, what the hell, curiosity and a free lunch? Who could resist? He told me his sad tale but now he was doing okay. He apologized for taking so long and gave me a cashier's check for the full amount plus generous interest.

In this story about my life one name keeps constantly coming up: Richard M. Sherman. Dick and I go back to the days that we had both just gotten out of school. He graduated from Bard College in New York and I was summer '49 at Los Angeles High School. We got together because of our mutual interests. His father was Al Sherman, a

Dick Sherman and Mickey Mouse on Main Street, Disneyland

great popular songwriter. I was a collector of personality records. I wanted to be a TV comedy writer and Dick was an aspiring songwriter. We have both done well over the years in our respective goals.

Aside from being the closest of friends for over a half a century I have had the pleasure of collaborating on songs with Dick I don't really consider myself a songwriter but when songs were needed for our Mayfair Music Hall shows I teamed with Gene Casey and often Verne Langdon writing special material. The joy of my life has been my collaboration with Dick. We have written over two hundred songs together. That's a just a drop in the bucket when you consider the classics that Dick and his brother Robert have written.

Although all our songs are *music and lyrics* by Richard M. Sherman and Milt Larsen obviously I'm more of a lyricist and idea man working with one of the most brilliant composers in the business. However when we sit down together to create a song the words and the music enter both of our minds at the same time and musical magic happens.

Both the Larsen Brothers and the Sherman Brothers have stars of Hollywood Boulevard's Walk of Fame and we have both won our fair share of honors and awards albeit Dick has a lot more than I do. One in particular stands out: On March 11, 2010 the Sherman Brothers were honored with a door window on Main Street, Disneyland. A window dedication is the highest honor anyone can receive at Disneyland. We were all on hand for the celebration. Castle Art Director, the late Joe Hoffman, thought Sherman and Larsen should have their own door at the Magic Castle.

MAIN TRACK: MAGIC CASTLE – THE SEVENTIES

VICTORY CANTEEN – ALL ABOARD!

By the early '70's we had utilized every inch of the Magic Castle. The small open porch on the south side had become the Terrace Dining Room, the old furnace room had become the Palace of Mystery, and the basement was now the Hat N' Hare Pub. The attic and servants quarters had become the offices and magicians library. There was simply no more expansion room in the grand old mansion. Bobby Lauher and I were doing a lot of TV writing and I was producing a number of nostalgia-type stage shows.

After ten years of marriage, Geri became a widow a second time when Art Baker passed away in 1966. By then she was in her late '60's and didn't expect to marry again. Yet, as chance would have it, she met Rubin Jaffe. They clicked. Rubin Jaffe, Geri's third husband, was a candy maker. They lived in his beachfront home in Montecito after their marriage in 1970. My mother went through life believing nothing is impossible.

L-R: Milt, Rubin Jaffe, Geri Jaffe, Bill

And if things were going wrong, you just had to sprinkle a little woofle dust on it and everything would be all right. They were married seven years before Rubin passed away in 1977.

In 1970, thanks to publicist Shirley Carroll, we had three entries in the Hollywood Christmas parade: a double-decker bus plugging the show Dick Zimmerman and I produced for several editions, "Where It Was" which introduced the world of ragtime music and Eubie Black to Los Angeles audiences long before Marvin Hamlisch introduced it in the film, "The Sting"; a vintage electric streetcar, Red Car, complete with an all-star Dixieland band plugging "The Legends of Jazz" and, of course, a Venice Beach Boardwalk tram featuring the magicians of the Magic Castle with a dozen tuxedoed magicians jumping on and off the tram to perform walk-around magic to the crowds.

In addition, we did a show called "The Sounds of Silents" which brought a series of silent movies to the Wilshire Ebell Theater. The unusual part of the show was a full thirteen-piece orchestra that accompanied the movies, along with a pipe organ and a Spike Jones sound effects man, Joe Siracusa. Joe was known as The Good Humor Man because he provided joy through his wacky music and sound effects. The first half was devoted to silent comedies and the second half featured the orchestra and Lon Chaney in "The Phantom of the Opera." The Wilshire Ebell had a Morton pipe organ that hadn't been used in years. When Lon Chaney turned to face the audience in his famous scene, the pipe organ blasted forth played by Verne Langdon. Later we produced another "Sounds of Silents" silent film concert with Rudolph Valentino in his classic "Son of the Sheik" and played the show in some colleges in the Southern California area.

I produced several concerts with the legendary ragtime composer Eubie Blake who lived to be one hundred years old. One day I drove Eubie to a television interview.

Eubie was admiring some of the hookers decorating the streets of Hollywood. At that time Eubie was celebrating his 90th birthday. I mentioned that I was 45 years old and I pondered the fact that he was exactly twice as old as me. I felt I had accomplished a lot in my forty-five years on earth but, if I died that day and was born again, I would have another entire lifetime of forty-five years. Eubie stopped looking at the girls for a moment and said, "Boss, if you spend time thinking about stuff like that why hang around for another forty-five years?"

Although the Magic Castle, "It's Magic!" and "Truth or Consequences" were doing well, my train ride was going off on another track. I loved producing

Eubie Blake, seated;
Dick Sherman and Milt standing

and I loved the living theater. In 1970, Bobby Lauher and I finished the book for a musical play, "Victory Canteen;" a hilarious send-up of every 1940's wartime movie and we asked our friends Dick. and Robert B. Sherman to create the score. We had such a great time working together we decided to produce the show ourselves. We raised the backing, put together an amazing cast and rented the five-hundred-seat Ivar Theater.

The Ivar was a neat legitimate theater in the heart of Hollywood. It had been the home of many hit plays and revues. Stan Seiden was the owner and a very nice guy but I learned a lot about the pitfalls of producing from him. He had produced shows like "Pajama Tops," which proved you don't have to be classy to make money. When I told Stan his modern coin operated ice cream machine was not right for a 1944 musical he said there would be no problem in taking it out of the lobby for the run of the show—as long as we paid him for his weekly loss of income from the machine!

One time during the run, Stan called to say that we might be hearing about a fire that had started in his upstairs office. Not to worry—the fire was put out quickly and had only destroyed some old financial records. Hmmmm… After a seven-month run I told Stan we were going to have to close the show. He was surprised. He asked, "Why? You are making money, aren't you?" I replied, "No, the cast is too big and the theater is too

VICTORY CANTEEN IS A BALL.
VICTORY CANTEEN IN A GROUP IS A BALL AND A BARGAIN.

VICTORY CANTEEN

THE NEW HIT MUSICAL OF THE FRANTIC 40's

THE VICTORY CANTEEN

small. We're losing money." Stan looked at me quizzically. "But YOU?… You're doing okay aren't you?" Then he rubbed his fingers together as if counting money. I got the message. He thought I was doing what any respectable producer would do—skimming money off the top. I told him I was brought up in a diffcrent world. I could never be dishonest. He looked at me like a father whose son had just admitted to some great sin. In a great sense I admired Stan. He later became the head of the Nederlander Organization on the West Coast. He was a pro. Stan's partner at the time was Lee Witten who also owned the hamburger stand next to the then prestigious Huntington Hartford Theater on Vine Street. Lee died in a light plane crash trying to land on the Hollywood Freeway. The most unusual thing about the accident was that the freeway was littered with thousands of small unmarked bills.

"Victory Canteen" opened at the Ivar Theatre in Hollywood, January 27, 1971. The show starred Patty Andrews of The Andrews Sisters. It had opened a few weeks before the Sylmar quake to excellent reviews. John Shrum had created a two-story set that was very top heavy and had a complex tri-vision sign forming the back wall. The earthquake had not changed anything at the Magic Castle; the pictures were as crooked as before the shake. After checking out the Magic Castle for earthquake damage, I decided to drive over to see if the Ivar Theater and/or set were still standing. Hollywood Boulevard looked more like a war zone disaster area; broken glass, water pouring out from some of the buildings—surely the Ivar must be a pile of rubble! To my surprise nothing was damaged. Later in the day we called a meeting of the cast and crew to see whether or not we would attempt to do the show that night. The unanimous vote was the show must go on.

Top-Bottom: Milt Larsen, Dick Sherman, Patty Andrews, Bobby Lauher, Robert B. Sherman

The director of the show was Jack Baker. Jack had fired one of our cast members, Teri Garr, because "she couldn't sing, dance or act." We loved Teri but the director's word was law. Teri, of course, went on to be a superstar in films and television and Jack is now in the real estate business in the Valley. That's show biz! Jack didn't believe in follow spotlights so the show had a very complicated lighting design where special spotlights provided pools of lights. Although we had checked out the safety of the building and the scenery, nobody had thought to check out the lights.

The earthquake had re-adjusted every spotlight in the theater. When Patty made her entrance out of the grease pit trap in the floor, the special spot that was supposed to hit our star actually lit up a patron in the first row. The earthquake was a disaster and so was that evening's production of "Victory Canteen." Despite its shaky start the musical got great reviews and went on for a reasonably long run.

Other youngsters in "Victory Canteen" became major stars: Anson Williams, Marsha Cramer and Lorene Yarnell. Anson became one of the stars of television's "Happy Days," Marsha went on to play Wendy in "Peter Pan" on Broadway for years. Lorene was only in the show the first few weeks. She got great reviews and burned up the stage with her sensational tap dancing. She clearly stole the spotlight from the star and Patty Andrews said: "Either she goes or I go!" Unfortunately Patty was the name over the title—the star of the show. Lorene joined forces with a mime partner and became one part of the very well-known team of Shields and Yarnell.

Lorene Yarnell and Patty Andrews tap dancing for Victory Canteen

Patty Andrews was a total professional and never missed a performance. On the opening night, Patti's sister Maxine joined her onstage for a well-deserved standing ovation encore. It was a great hit and Maxine agreed to do it often. The only problem was that Patty and Maxine were anything but good pals. She would come in at the end of the show and the two would knock 'em dead with "Apple Blossom Time" and "Boogie Woogie Bugle Boy." Then Maxine would leave the theater. On the nights Maxine would appear, our company manager Bill Schneider and I would meet Maxine at the bar across the street and hoist a few. We would check the time and rush her across the street for the encore.

Directly behind the Ivar Theater was a gay bar. Not just a gay bar, it was a very gay bar: whips, chains, leather, bare bodies. It just wasn't the image of the innocence of World War II. The owner and patrons were good businessmen and their customers were happy to play our game. Every night at our intermission the bartenders put on '40's coats and all the gay guys retreated to the back rooms. The music changed to Glenn Miller and our ticket buyers loved it. The bar made money and the minute our show resumed so did the action in the bar.

After the show closed I wrote a letter to one hundred and two New York producers. Waissman and Fox were very successful Broadway producers who responded with an interest. They had just produced "Grease," one of the season's biggest hits. They liked the concept of the show but they said the book needed more of a book. Bobby Lauher and I were offered the job of going to New York and working with another writer to create a new version of the musical. The business deal was unacceptable to us plus the fact that Bobby and I didn't like the idea of moving for any length of time to New York. In addition to the Magic Castle, I had just leased a theater in Santa Monica that would become the Mayfair Music Hall. That seemed like a lot more fun.

The Sherman Brothers, with our blessing, wrote an entirelt new score for a new World War II home-front musical, "Over Here" which starred Patty and Maxine Andrews. It was a hit and ran for two years on Broadway. Despite the fact the show was a hit, the Sherman Brothers and the producers had to defend a nasty lawsuit by Patty Andrews' husband. The producers didn't need the aggravation and canceled the National Tour of the musical. We had turned our backs on the chance of a Broadway musical but it just wasn't in the cards.

Several years later I totally rewrote the stage play as a screenplay called "Wings Over Kansas." The musical film is a comedy about the home front in 1944. No sex, no violence, no vulgar words, no flaming car crashes—no wonder it may not sell in today's world but what the hell. I'll give it a try. I honestly think it's one of the Sherman Brothers best scores.

During World War II the tobacco industry were heroes letting "Lucky Strike Green Goes Off To War" by sending troops free cigarettes. One of the songs from the score, written by the Sherman Brothers, literally stopped the stage show every night: "Smoke 'em Up"! The lyrics: "Fifty million thanks, we're winging to you yanks, smoke 'em up, smoke 'em up, smoke 'em up!" explained how America was thanking our troops by providing cigarettes.

Bobby Lauher and I were pretty hotshot writers back in the late '60's and early '70's. In addition to our standard gig of writing "Truth or Consequences" we wrote a summer replacement show on NBC called "The Mickey Finn Show." Fred "Mickey" Finn was a Dixieland jazz veteran. The show started as kind of a Ricky-Tick Lawrence Welk Hour and wasn't doing too well. The network decided it needed comedy and hired Bobby and myself as writers. They turned over the direction to Bill Foster, a really talented and inventive comedy director. Under his direction we changed the show into a cross between Hellzapoppin' and Spike Jones where no one was safe. We dropped stars through trap doors and supered cartoon-style thought balloons over the heads of innocent people. It was

"The Mickey Finn Show"

a television first at that time; a smorgasbord of sight gags. The ratings went up but not soon enough to save the show.

Later Bobby and I received two calls in the same week and had to make a decision. Bill Foster called to say he was going to direct a comedy special for NBC and would like us to join the writing staff. At the same time our agent called to say ABC needed writers for a new summer show starring Ricky Nelson. It was a sixteen-episode job! Obviously we couldn't do both shows and, obviously, sixteen half-hours were better than one one-hour special. The show we accepted was "Malibu U." based on Petersen Publishing's Teen Magazine. Pop star Ricky Nelson starred as the dean of a fictional college where the biggest music stars of the '50's performed once a week. How could it miss? It was a memorable bomb and was cancelled after airing only seven episodes. The one memorable thing about the show was Leonard Nimoy's performance of a novelty song, "The Ballad of Bilbo Baggins." The show we turned down was the American sketch show "Rowan and Martin's Laugh-In Special" that went on to become a series that aired 140 episodes—and that's the truth!

Rowan & Martin's Laugh-In

In 1971 we were busily at work writing a new revue called "The Big Show of 1928" which was scheduled to open December 27, 1971 at the Huntington Hartford Theater. For business and artistic reasons Bobby and I quit the show before the opening and asked that our names be removed from the credits. The show opened, was a big success and played for about five years on the road. We kept our artistic pride but lost one helluva lot of royalties. If you'll remember these are the same two writers that turned down that one time special, "Laugh-in" in lieu of a sixteen week series. Smart, eh?

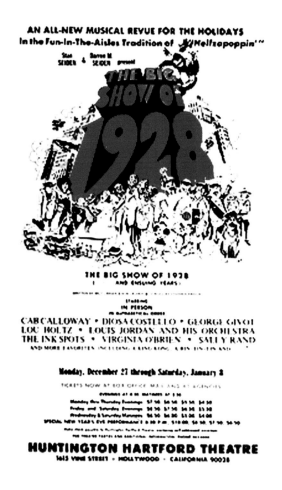

Bobby and I worked on many projects. Because of our extensive credits on "Truth or Consequences" we were called in on a number of game show meetings and pilots as *show doctors*. Sometimes we were hired and sometimes just called in to make suggestions for our friends in the business. Usually talks would start with a show concept. Invariably the question would come up: "Who's going to host the show?" They were always looking for a new face. How do you find a box office star that nobody has ever seen before? Ralph Edwards had pulled off a miracle like that when he found Bob Barker but it doesn't happen very often.

One day we received a call from Bill Burch, the former writer/producer of "Truth or Consequences." He was now one of the big executives at Universal. He asked us to work on an idea for a game show pilot starring Don Adams. The first day I arrived at the studio before Bobby, I was delighted that the guard knew my name and directed me to a bungalow office on the lot. Reserved parking lot signs were marked Mr. Larsen and Mr. Lauher. Entering the office I found a lovely secretary who said she was assigned to our project. She asked if we preferred two offices or one. I said we always worked as a team; one office would be fine. She was there to give us anything we wanted. When Bobby arrived he was duly impressed. Wow! This was the big time. The secretary gave us a brief outline and a nice note from Bill saying our contract was for three weeks with a first draft due date. It was an enjoyable three weeks. No one ever met with us and we wrote what we thought was a very serviceable and funny script. As we neared the end of our contract we called Bill and said we had finished our first draft. He asked if we were happy with it? We said, "Yes." "Great—have your secretary send it upstairs."

Don Adams

The next day we arrived at the studio and noted the guard commented that our names were not on the list. Then we noticed our names were no longer on our parking spaces or the office door. Two other writers were now at our desks and the secretary told us she heard we had done a great job. She said Mr. Burch wanted us to call him. We did. Did he want a meeting? "No... your checks will be in the mail. Thanks." That was it. Bobby and I drove off the lot and that was the last we ever heard about the project. Well, that's show-biz!

"Mr. Television" proved radio could be more entertaining with pictures. Many people were not aware that "Uncle Milty," Milton Berle, was an excellent magician and a charter member of the Magic Castle. When he would bring guests to the club you could always count on his doing an impromptu close-up performance—to the delight of our

Milton Berle

other guests. He used to hang out at Martinka's Magic Shop in New York with his good pal and teacher Nate Leipzig. He was a friend of our dad's who knew him because of his magic interest. When I first introduced myself to the legendary star I said, "Hi Uncle Milty, my name is Milt Larsen." He quickly replied, "My name is Milton and your name is Milton—according to the Webster Dictionary milt is a spleen of a fish." From that day on it was always, "Hello Milton—This is Milton."

My first professional experience with Berle was back in the '70's. Bobby Lauher and I were hired to write the Patsy (animal) Awards. The host was Milton Berle and it was taped at Universal City. I wrote a version of the old burlesque sketch "Stand In." That's the sketch where the straight man is playing a scene with a girl and the comic is the stand-in. The director calls for the stand-in who gets belted with a huge powder puff. I got a call from the producer that an unhappy Milton Berle wanted to see me in the make-up room. When I came in he waved the script at me and quietly bellowed, "Who wrote this SH*T!?" I admitted I was the culprit. Then I explained I had just tried to remember how it went for the benefit of the tech people. I told him I knew it was one of his classic bits and assumed he would remember it and not need a full script. Then he complemented me on being a young writer that understood comedy sketches, threw the script in the wastebasket and performed it without missing a beat.

Bobby Lauher was a great friend and a great writing partner. He was also an excellent actor and worked with the comedy legend Ernie Kovacs as the "second banana" on his game shows and also on his ABC TV Specials. When Bobby Lauher passed away suddenly in 1973 I temporarily gave up TV comedy writing. (I came out of TV retirement in 1977 to write for the Jim Nabors Variety Show.)

One day in 1972 I received a call from the Goodson-Todman office. Would I like to appear on the "To Tell The Truth" show, as a magician and co-founder of the world-famous Magic Castle? It was a good chance to fly to New York City at someone else's expense. It was a fun experience. The show was a huge success running from 1956 until 1981. The game involved a panel of four celebrities attempting to identify a contestant with an unusual occupation or experience. Two imposters are allowed to lie but the central character is sworn *to tell the truth*. The panel would try to determine which one was the *real* person. A great idea—I wish I had thought of it! It was one of the longest running shows on television. Pre-show I was interviewed by two actors who would claim to be me. They did a great job—I was almost fooled. We have a video of the program in our Academy of Magical Arts Video archives. Watching me is rather scary.

"What is your name, please?"

My name is Milt Larsen.

Will the real Milt Larsen please stand up?

Milt Larsen performing Serpent Silk.

After more than four decades, I watched it and saw a dark-haired young guy claiming to be Milt Larsen answering questions from a panel consisting of Bill Cullen, Kitty Carlisle, Gene Rayburn and Peggy Cass, with Gary Moore as host. Kitty Carlisle correctly figured out that I was the real me. Then I performed a very short version of the *Serpent Silk* to prove I was a real magician. Kitty explained she nailed me because she was in a show at the Huntington Hartford Theater across the street from the Ivar Theater where "Victory Canteen" had been playing.

In 1973 the Magic Castle had been open for ten years and was doing well. Unfortunately I had run out of space to expand. I had used every nook, cranny and broom closet. For ten years I had pushed out porches, utilized steamer trunk storage space in the attic for the library, dug out the floor in the basement to make our first Palace of Mystery where the pub museum is now. More expansion for the Castle? No way! We were actually parking cars in the parking garage because the surface lot where we were parking cars now was a twenty-nine-unit apartment house. Charles Manson's friend Tex Watson lived there and a hippie couple used to have matinees on their open porch to the delight of our lunch patrons. Under Bill's direction and his constant plugging the Magic Castle in Genii—plus Bill and Irene's promoting the Castle and Academy of Magical Arts at every magic convention, the club was now well-known as the new Mecca of Magic. We were compared to Maskelyne and Devant's Egyptian Hall in London. The "It's Magic!" shows were now an annual event at the Wilshire Ebell Theater. I also produced a number of stage shows but I really needed a new project. My Mrs. Winchester need to continue building was not being satisfied.

I approached Castle property owner Tom Glover with a modest idea: build a restaurant on the hill between the Magic Castle and the Yamashiro. I wanted to seat patrons in a couple European turn-of-the-century compartment railroad cars. The cars would shake and the feeling of traveling through the countryside would be accomplished via a form of video rear-projections. The place would be called the Orient Express and the staff would all be Mata Hari-type spies. I thought it was great idea and even bought two railroad cars at the legendary MGM auction in anticipation. I wanted to build a half doughnut-shaped restaurant lounge between Yamashiro and the Magic Castle. The inside of the circle would have a view of a fifty-foot cascading waterfall and the outside would be a spectacular view of Hollywood. Tom wasn't exactly excited about the idea so I looked for another project.

Visions of "Larsenland" by Hubbell Braden

John Shrum and fellow Art Director Hubbell Braden used to delight in giving visionary sketches of the Glover's Hollywood Hill. Mr. Glover was very patient with me. He was a classy gentleman but he didn't really want me to turn his eleven acres of Hollywood into "Larsenland."

SIDETRACK –
THE MAYFAIR MUSIC HALL

My good friend, Dr. Thomas Heric, was a very successful neurologist and head of St. John's Hospital in Santa Monica. He was a major Gilbert and Sullivan fan and collector and we both loved the British Music Halls.

What about a British Music Hall? That piqued Dr. Tom's interest. We both thought the idea merited further investigation—a British Variety Theater. We scouted a few buildings in Hollywood but they were all encumbered with problems. About that time I often took a daily lunch tanning session at Will Rogers beach. One day on the way home from one of those sessions I had to take a traffic detour that brought me to Santa Monica Blvd. For the first time I noticed the Mayfair Theater, saw the fly loft and realized at one time this theater was a legitimate stage theater. Of more importance was a small sign on the second floor window advertising it was for rent. The rent sign was for the upstairs offices but the theater lease was about to run out. Dr. Tom and I negotiated a ten-year lease and one helluva challenge.

Mayfair Theatre

John Shrum, Tom Heric and I formed Old London Music Hall, Inc. Brother Bill elected to pass on the project to devote himself full time to the Magic Castle and Genii magazine although he was one of our greatest fans and supporters.

When we took over the Mayfair Theater in Santa Monica it had been modernized. What charm it may have had when it was built in 1911 as the Santa

Monica Opera House had been sacrificed to the Great God of Plastic and tacky curtain cover-up. The stage had been removed years before and the cinema screen was placed in front of the huge vintage Altec-Lansing Voice of the Theater speakers. It had been renamed the Majestic Theatre and had seating for about six hundred people. When we leased the theatre in 1973 we cut the seating down to three hundred. The three partners, Dr. Tom Heric, John Shrum and myself, sat in the back of the theater and pondered the best way to turn this swell old barn into a place where we could put on a show.

As always the solution came from *Mr. Junk*, our old friend Ernie Evans who ran Scavenger's Paradise and saved architectural artifacts one step ahead of the wrecking ball. Ernie called and said they were about to demolish the Belmont Theater and we might be able to use some of the stage hardware.

The Belmont Theatre had been one of Los Angeles' fine old movie palaces. It stood at 1st and Vermont and had been built in the early '20's. Anyone remember the Bimini Baths and the Palomar Ballroom? The Bimini Baths were once an oil field with a natural mineral springs supplying crystal-pure hot water to a huge swimming pool larger than most people have ever seen. The Palomar Ballroom, built in 1925 of Moorish design, boasted of being the largest and most famous dance hall in the West Coast. They were neighbors to the Belmont Theatre. Strategically located, 1st and Vermont was easily accessible by the big electric trolleys and was considered a resort on the west side of town.

Belmont Theatre exterior

Belmont Theatre interior

John and I went to meet Ernie and his son, Rick, at the Belmont Theatre. There it was, everything we needed! Gold-leaf boxes, marvelous gold-leafed carved pillars of Hannibal's army, paneling—it was a Victorian theater *do-it-yourself-kit*. Forget the stage hardware, we wanted the entire theater interior! Ernie made his deal with the owner and soon his trucks were dropping off staff plaster, columns, boxes and unique treasures from the Belmont Theater to the new British Music Hall on Santa Monica Blvd.

Belmont Theatre interior installation at Mayfair Music Hall

It took quite a lot of finessing to obtain the special permit from the Santa Monica Building and Safety Department to install the Belmont Theatre interior to the bare walls of the Mayfair Theater. It was a magic trick of its own, but when we were finished, patrons marveled at the fact we had uncovered a lost Victorian Music Hall. Local Santa

Mayfair Music Hall completed conversion using the Belmont Theatre interior

Monica schools conducted tours of the theatre showing students the only authentic British Music Hall in Southern California. It wasn't an authentic British Music Hall—it was the Belmont Theatre. But if they wanted to believe, let them believe…

Bernard Fox

"A Night in the Old London Music Hall" opened at The Mayfair Music Hall in Santa Monica on October 16, 1973 and ran successfully until 1981 with twenty-one different editions. The Mayfair shows were great fun. When we were casting for our first show we were having a difficult time finding a believable typical British Music Hall Chairman. In the olden days of the Victorian Halls a dashing and dignified manager acted as compeer and kept order in the often rowdy music halls of the era. We interviewed just about every British actor in town and were about to give up. On the last day of auditions, the perfect Chairman entered from the back of the theatre: "Good evening ladies and gentlemen—coming to you at eeeeeenormous expense… !"

178

We knew we had found our chairman. Bernard Fox became our consummate Chairman and continued in most of our many editions of the show. Bernard's father was a music hall chairman and Bernard knew his art well.

Bernard Fox was a very popular actor in films and TV, well-known for his characters on "Bewitched" and "Hogan's Heroes." He lucked out when he got a part in the film, "Titanic." The part was important but not huge however the mega-million dollar epic took months to make and our own, our very own Bernard Fox was on the payroll long enough to pay for his new home in the Valley.

The original Majestic theater that we turned into the Mayfair Music Hall did not have boxes on each side of the stage. We created two very authentic Victorian looking boxes using the staff plaster elements of the Belmont theater. When we opened the stage left box was the stage for our Chairman. The stage right box housed our four piece orchestra.

A couple of years later we expanded the stage and uncovered the original orchestra pit. About that time Ernie Evans called to ask if we had any use for a pipe organ console that had been in a fire. The two manual keyboards and all the stops looked pretty but the console was irreparable and was going to be junked. The price, as usual with Ernie, was free. Naturally I accepted his kind offer and thought of a cool idea.

I went to the local carpet store and asked them to save cardboard tubes. We painted them gold and covered the back wall of the old ventilator shaft with the *pipes*.

Arlene provided white tie and tails for the top half of a mannequin dummy and found a bushy white wig. I made a track out of some lumber and made a trolley that would bring the dummy in and out. I loved using Sears & Roebuck's cable garage door openers to move effects. When completed it looked as if an old gentleman would enter the box, be seated at the organ and delight our pre-show audience. We used Verne Langdon's Pipe organ LP's for the music.

In the program we called him Professor Otto Matton, (Automaton) the Mayfair Music Hall organist. Our audiences loved Otto and would often ask about his health. Years after the Mayfair closed I would still get inquires about that neat old man that used to play the pipe organ at the Mayfair Music Hall.

When possible we booked old-time vaudeville acts on the bill. A great favorite was Mousie Garner who was one of the later Three Stooges and a regular at the Mayfair Music Hall. The venerable Mousie enjoyed one of the longest running performing careers in the history of entertainment, stretching from vaudeville to virtual reality. Mousie made his stage debut as a child in 1913 singing, dancing and imitating Al Jolson in a family musical-comedy act developed by his father. Mousie played the piano with his nose. We had a Tom Thumb upright piano in the Mayfair lobby and Mousie would entertain during the intermission and after the show. One night Jack Lemmon took over his piano and played while his pal Ray Bolger danced the soft shoe in the lobby. Chaz Chase got a million laughs

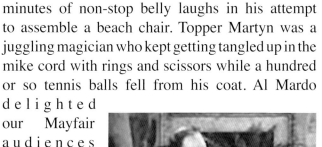

by simply eating his costume. Joe Roth got nine minutes of non-stop belly laughs in his attempt to assemble a beach chair. Topper Martyn was a juggling magician who kept getting tangled up in the mike cord with rings and scissors while a hundred or so tennis balls fell from his coat. Al Mardo delighted our Mayfair audiences with the act he sold to Bob Williams and Red Dust. He

Topper Martyn

Al Mardo and Flash

was billed as "Al Mardo and Flash." Flash was the limp dog that would do tricks. I loved the slapstick, physical humor that was very popular in the old vaudeville days.

One of the funniest acts we ever booked at the Mayfair was an act called "The California Seals." We usually hired the animal acts sight unseen and they were always pure gold. In this case a Beverly Hills psychiatrist wanted to be in show biz and bought the act from the original trainer. The seals were fully trained and would go through their tricks in rotation. All you had to do was start them going, they'd do a trick and you'd give them a fish. Easy? Even a doctor and his beautiful brunette, leggy wife couldn't fail. Or could they?

The act looked great; four happy little seals flapping about on stage. The doctor looked fantastic in his flamboyant ringmaster's costume, complete with the hip-hamper filled with sardines. His wife was appropriately dressed in her revealing costume. The

"The California Seals"

only problem was that the doctor kept forgetting to reward the seals after each trick. Try to picture four seals finishing a balancing trick and then stopping cold to glare at the trainer. The wife would coach him: "Give them a fish—give them a fish!" The doctor would finally remember, toss them each a sardine and the seals would go on to their next trick. The audience thought it was the funniest act they had ever seen. The doctor and his wife didn't appreciate the laughs—after all, this was a serious seal act! I understand the doctor pursued his show business career but he traded his seal act for a trained lion act. I hope he remembers to feed the lion.

Gene Bell used to open for the great French singer and dancer, Josephine Baker with an incredible tap dancing routine. The first time I saw Baker and Bell was at the old RKO Hillstreet Theater in downtown Los Angeles. I had a few of her old 78's made in the late 20's and 30's. I was a mere youth and she was an old lady. Actually she was probably pushing sixty but when you are a mere youth… When we opened the Mayfair Music Hall in 1973 I remembered seeing the show-stopper tap dancer extraordinaire by the name of Gene Bell. If only we could get an act like that! I was told to call him; his number was listed in the telephone book. It was the beginning of a long and very happy relationship. Gene performed often at the Mayfair Music Hall and later at the Variety Arts. His wife Lupe became the librarian for the Society for the Preservation of Variety Arts.

Gene Bell

One night Jimmy Cagney attended one of our Mayfair Music Hall shows. The great tap dancer Gene Bell was on the bill and he had a bit where he danced up and down the aisle of the theatre. Jimmy joined Gene for an unforgettable impromptu soft-shoe on the aisle carpets that looked like they had been rehearsing for years!

The formula for our shows at the Mayfair was a combination of staged musical and comedy numbers by a cast of seven plus two variety acts. We staged a different revue every three months. Our orchestra consisted of a piano, primarily played by the late Gene Casey, who also wrote original songs and was our musical director, Joe Tenny on drums and Art Levin who had the ability to make his single tuba sound like a big brass band.

Much of the credit for the success of the Mayfair shows should go to Arlene Zamiara. I met Arlene when she was the costume designer and wardrobe lady on "Truth or Consequences." She saw the opportunity to work like hell for little or no money, utilizing her great talents for creating period costumes. She subsequently created the wardrobe for all our original shows. Perhaps she also could see into the future when she would become Mrs. Milt Larsen.

Arlene Zamiara

The only room we could find in our little theater for the costume department was the former movie projection booth. It was a nice room but only accessible via a vertical ladder. The heavy costumes had to be hoisted through a trap door by a series of block and tackle ropes. We changed the revue every three months with new material and new costumes. Arlene designed and made all the costumes for the shows while she was still working as a full-time TV costumer.

Although I had left the main track on my magical journey, I never lost track of magic and magicians. We always put magicians in the line-up as well as vaudeville acts. Even though he was not a partner in the new enterprise, Brother Bill loved the Mayfair and constantly supported us in the pages of Genii magazine and the Magic Castle newsletters. The Music Hall featured guest stars like Billy McComb, Terry Seabrooke, Marvin Roy (Mr. Electric) and many others. Other non-magic veteran acts also appeared as guest stars: Nick Lucas, Gene Bell, Jack Spoons and others. The Castle's landlord, Thomas Glover, was a very talented musician and delighted in being the very welcomed guest horn player in the orchestra pit. I found magic was still very much in everything I was able to accomplish. The Mayfair was a great opportunity to try magic ideas in another format.

One of our funniest numbers at the Mayfair was a black art bit with our resident soprano Maria Weber singing the classic "With Her Head Tucked Underneath Her Arm" as she walked the bloody Tower Green in reference to the beheading of Anne Boleyn, wife of King Henry VIII. As she sang, Maria would take off her head and juggle it. Maria Weber was our Lucille Ball. She was a brilliant soprano and also a very funny comedienne. As a running gag in every edition of the revue we had at least one number *trying to get* the soprano. During a beautiful song she might be swept away by a windstorm or a blizzard. In another song we had the set fall apart behind her. One of my favorite gags had her singing in a hoop skirt that kept elevating until her head reached the stage borders. It was a credit to Miss Weber and to the clever ingenuity of Arlene Zamiara. In a reverse of that gag we had Maria in a hoop skirt singing as we slowly dropped her down through a trap in the stage until she disappeared. The stage manager picked up an empty hoop skirt. That was magic!

The Mayfair Music Hall had a small six-foot deep stage but the theatre was so beautifully designed by John Shrum that no one realized how short the stage actually was. People assumed the theatre had a deep stage and we just never opened the back curtain. We did everything *in one* in front of scenery. We often would rent the theatre for film shoots. The Mayfair was a Bavarian Opera House in "Young Frankenstein" for the hilarious musical number "Puttin' on the Ritz," with Peter Boyle as the Frankenstein monster. Two hundred dressed extras were in the audience for the scene.

The first day's shooting was ruined because of the sound of the Santa Monica Municipal trash trucks collecting refuse in the adjacent alley. The entire scene had to be re-scheduled another day at (as our Chairman would say) eeeenormous expense! Mel Brooks tried unsuccessfully to get the city to cancel their trash trucks until after the shooting. They refused. That day Mel took things into his own hands, walked a block up the street and lay down in the alley, blocking the trucks. The police didn't think it was so funny but the filming went on without a hitch and one of the funniest scenes in the history of movies took place in our own, our very own Mayfair Music Hall.

Mel Brooks

183

The feature film "Harry and Walter Go to New York" was looking for an elegant music hall theatre. The creative producers scouted the Mayfair Music Hall and looked at the theatre. It was perfect but it wouldn't work for them because of the depth of the stage. They returned a week later with the director, producers and the art director.

The theatre was absolutely what they wanted but the shot they needed was from the back of the stage looking out past the performers into the audience. It was crucial to the plot. They couldn't get around it.

I offered a solution. "How much is it going to cost to build the set in a studio? And how much to take out the brick wall at the rear of the building?" We had more unused area behind a brick wall at the back of the stage. It was a solution they pondered. Engineers and their construction coordinator were consulted. In 1976 taking out a portion of the rear brick wall would cost $32,000, a far cry cheaper than building an entire music hall theater set themselves. So Harry and Walter gave us a twelve-foot opening with two pillars at each side and a new backstage. For all the shows after that, John Shrum had to design two Roman columns or two pieces of scenery to cover the new columns but we enjoyed having a deeper stage.

We put local talent in British songs, in British costumes with British staging so we instantly had become British. I found myself speaking with a British accent when I was in the Mayfair. I loved the Mayfair and so did many of the celebrities who frequented the place.

James Caan, Lesley Ann Warren and Elliott Gould

The $32,000 music hall set

Mae West had a beach house near the Mayfair and loved our shows. She was always the star. When Mae wanted to visit, her secretary would call and say Miss West would like her usual seats in what we called the Management's Box. It was in the back of the theater where she could be private and unnoticed. Of course, she always arrived in a chauffeur-driven vintage limousine accompanied by some of her boys. She would be wearing a flowing white gown. Somehow her presence was noticed. Bernard Fox would politely ask if she wouldn't mind being introduced. She relished her bows to her standing audiences like a true queen of the theater. Mae was quite a lady.

Mae West

Rock star Rod Stewart was a frequent visitor to the Mayfair. His family had been performers in the British music halls and he loved the era. Another British chap who frequented the Mayfair was a former stilt walker and acrobat from Britain, Archibald Leech. He later changed his name to Cary Grant. One night Cary invited me to join him for dinner at a favorite Italian restaurant across the street from the Mayfair. We got to talking about an English entertainer by the name of Stanley Holloway. In the '20's Holloway developed the characters of Sam Small, Albert and the Ramsbottoms family. His most famous monologue was "The Lion and Albert" where he pontificated about the time the family took young Albert to the zoo where the lion 'swallow'd him 'ole.' Cary surprised me by reciting the routine word for word with a thick British brogue over our antipasto:

There's a famous seaside place called Blackpool.
That's noted for fresh air and fun
And Mr. & Mrs. Ramsbottom
Went there with young Albert, their son…

After dinner we went back to the Mayfair and our Chairman Bernard Fox announced we had a special added performer… a young man by the name of Archibald Leech. Cary came on stage and flawlessly performed "The Lion and Albert" for our very surprised audience. I offered to give him a permanent spot on the bill but he said he was rather busy.

One time Bernard Fox said there was a newcomer to the States who loved music hall and might direct some of our future shows. He was a name in England but not well-known over here. I met the man and he seemed just a bit wild-eyed and strange. No matter, we had a director for the current edition and I said I would keep him in mind. His name was Marty Feldman. Mel Brooks recognized Marty's immense comedy talents and cast him as Eye-gore in the film "Young Frankenstein." He became a major comedy star, sadly dying of a heart attack at the age of 48 in Mexico City during the making of "Yellowbeard." I reminded him about his offer to direct the Mayfair shows. He said he would still love to since he loved music hall entertainment but he had become rather busy.

We opened the Mayfair Music Hall in Santa Monica in 1973. In 1975 we decided to turn the upper balcony and offices of the old 1911 theatre into a restaurant. That meant losing several rows of seating. In the construction process we found many wonderful reminders of days gone by when the theater was called "The Majestic." There were vintage gum and candy wrappers, combs, keys, and empty containers of items for sanitary precaution. All old theaters had under the seat ventilators or holes to the old air plenums.

Among the discarded treasures we found was a wallet. It was intact with a couple of dollars and identification showing that it had belonged to a young serviceman in World War II. The address on his drivers license was a Santa Monica address. We made a phone call and I spoke with the kid's father. We found his son had made it through the war and was still living with his wife in Southern California.

I asked the father not to tell his son about our find and outlined a fun plan. As writer for Bob Barker's "Truth or Consequences" I had to make this a special occasion. One of our favorite variety acts we booked from time to time at the Mayfair was Mardoni and Louise. They were a mind-reading act but Clayton Mardoni also did a pickpocket act. It was the perfect set-up. The parents told their son they had gotten tickets to a show at the Mayfair Music Hall. During Mardoni's act he would pick the son to help him on stage. Stage pickpockets usually secretly steal items from their victim's pockets—pens, a wristwatch, a belt and always the wallet.

When it came time to return the items Mardoni said, "And don't go home without your wallet," and handed him his lost-for-30-years wallet. At first, he said it wasn't his wallet, but upon closer examination, it dawned on him that it

Mardoni & Louise

was his and his reaction was priceless. It even made the local papers.

A passing thought: If the kid was twenty in 1944, he would have been born in 1924 and would be eighty-eight years old today. I hope he's still around. Maybe we can find him and invite him to the Magic Castle.

I had had a wonderful relationship with Carl Tegner, the property owner of the Mayfair theater. His father had originally built the theater as the Santa Monica Opera House and Carl loved the idea that we restored it. He even had a 1910 electric car stored in the adjacent warehouse. When Carl passed away his nephew took over the theatre with no appreciation of the theatre or how we had improved the building. His only concern was to raise the rent by 100% at the end of our lease.

We offered to buy the property and the adjacent commercial building but the owner simply wouldn't budge. The Mayfair shows had a great run with its British Music Hall format for eight years but the end of the Mayfair Music Hall was in sight. The Mayfair had been everything an eccentric writer/producer could want. We could write, produce and direct our own special type of variety shows. Our cast was like a family and every performance was a fun experience for everyone involved. But all good things may come to an end and we started thinking about another venue. (Note: The theater was closed after one of our famous California earthquakes and was finally gutted and demolished in 2011, leaving only a façade to satisfy the demands of historic preservationists.)

In 1975 the Magic Castle was prospering, and so was the Mayfair Music Hall, at least until the lease ended. I was getting a little bored. Time was slipping by and I wasn't building anything. That lull in my life ended abruptly when the Los Angeles Fire Department noticed we didn't have adequate fire sprinklers in our old landmark mansion in the Hollywood Hills. The Castle had simply grown too big for the original old home. That was when we turned an adjacent parking structure into a new theater annex.

Our landlord, Thomas O. Glover, saw the commercial need and constructed a new building between the Castle and the parking garage to provide new service areas, bathrooms and a passageway to join the two buildings. John Shrum designed the new theaters, the Palace of Mystery and the Parlour of Prestidigitation. He made them look like they were part of the original mansion. Later we would be able to describe the Castle as three times larger on the inside than it is on the outside—a magical illusion!

It was a giant job once again to create our old world ambience by using parts of old mansions and buildings. By utilizing the upper floor of the parking structure we increased the square footage of the Castle almost 100%. When that project was completed in 1976 it seemed like my entrepreneurial train had stopped once again. I started thinking about my dream of creating a home for the Society for the Preservation of Variety Arts.

The new Palace of Mystery

I had spent my life collecting theater books, posters, records, and films—anything that pertained to the Variety Theater. Those collections I had picked up as a kid had grown to enormous proportions. I purchased whole estates at sales and auctions. I had acquired thousands of items from the estates of entertainers and legendary theatrical names like Eddie Cantor, Ed Wynn and showman Earl Carroll.

I started thinking about sharing my collections with other people, aka the public. I contacted a number of universities, libraries and other institutions only to find out they weren't nearly as interested in my passion as I was. So I thought it would be a cool idea to start our own museum for the Variety Arts. Hell, if Getty, Norris and that guy Guggenheim could do it—why not me? We started by displaying some of my Ed Wynn collection at the Mayfair Music Hall.

In 1975 John Shrum, Dr. Thomas Heric, Bill Larsen Jr, Dick Sherman and I formed the Society for the Preservation of Variety Arts. Gerald M. Singer volunteered the legal work to make it a non-profit 501c3 organization. Our goal was to find a home for the collections and establish a place where we could bring the same kind of awareness to variety arts that we had created for the art of magic.

L-R: Dr. Tom Heric, Dick Sherman, Milt Larsen, John Shrum, Bill Larsen

Since the Magic Castle was prospering, the Mayfair Music Hall was running very successfully—at least until the lease expired, I was writing comedy for television shows and I was still a moderately young man, I needed something more. I started looking around for a place that could house my collections and those collections that I felt we might acquire if we had the space. It would take two years before my quest was fulfilled.

I received a call from TV Producer Carolyn Raskin. Her huge credits included "Rowan & Martin's Laugh-In." She had read an article about my activities and my long association with "Truth or Consequences." They were about to produce a new daytime variety show starring Jim Nabors. They were looking for a writer to handle the game segment of the show. I met with Carolyn and explained I was really too busy to take on a full-time writing job. It was probably the first time a producer heard of a writer who said he didn't want a job. She went on to explain that I would only have to be responsible for one segment and knew I could do a great job. What would it take for me to change my mind?

I laid out my terms: I would not have an office or office hours. I would go to the production meetings, if required. I would be present for tapings, in case of changes. I would receive WGAw overscale. (I thought the terms would kill any chance of a deal.) Carolyn asked who represented me. At the time I didn't have an agent but Army Grant and I had recently finished a magic special and one of Hollywood's top agents, Harold Cohen, had acted as our agent. I said my agent was Harold Cohen. She knew Harold as he had been her agent on some deals previously. She would call him and see if a deal could be made.

I left her high-rise Century City office and made a beeline for the pay phone in the lobby to see if I could call Harold before Carolyn could talk to him. Luckily Harold was in his office. I told him of my meeting and the fact I had said he was my agent. I also told him about my terms. He said he doubted very much they would accept my terms but he would be happy to give it a try. By the way, did I have any idea of what scale was for five one-hour shows a week? I admitted I didn't have a clue. He said I might be surprised.

Later that day Harold called and told me I had the job. 100 shows! They met all my outlandish terms. Harold apologized for taking 10% of a deal he didn't make. He was right about the money. I would have been happy with much less—but what did I know? It was a fun job and Jim Nabors was a delight to work with.

I was contacted by some people interested in my project to preserve the Variety Arts who suggested the historic Pasadena Playhouse might be the perfect home for a variety theater museum. I had many meetings with the city and the management from the

Playhouse—people on well-intentioned committees who, in my opinion, tripped over each other and got nothing done. The blue-haired society ladies in Pasadena wanted to do something but they couldn't agree on a straight course of action. They obviously were more interested in devoting the future of the playhouse to very legitimate dramas, ballet, opera, etc. and were not terribly thrilled with my lofty goals to honor the vaudeville, burlesque, circus and the gut-bucket theater. I was getting more and more frustrated. There's nothing worse than an energetic person dealing with several lethargic tennis-shoed committee women dragging their Gucci-covered feet.

One day, as I drove away from a disappointing lunch meeting at the Pasadena Playhouse I noticed a *For Sale* sign on the top floor of the Friday Morning Club building, downtown Los Angeles. That's interesting. How could the Friday Morning Club be for sale? Caroline Severance built the Friday Morning Club as a ladies club for a social and political organization for women, founded in 1891. I remember when we were touring the Larsen family of Magic act we played that theatre quite often. Mae Norton, a lecture agent, would hold auditions once a year at the Friday Morning Club. Mae would bring in bookers from resort hotels and theatres across United States to preview acts. So once a year the Larsen family would go to the Friday Morning Club to audition our act.

Friday Morning Club

As a kid of ten or twelve years, I loved that theatre. The dressing rooms were upstairs with windows that overlooked the stage. You could watch everything that was going on below. I knew the property, knew it had a large ballroom upstairs and a little theatre as well as the larger theatre and a full kitchen. I made a few phone calls and inquired about its availability. Yes, the ladies of the Friday Morning Club had decided to sell the building and move to more modern quarters in a Wilshire Boulevard high-rise. They were asking $700,000. The real estate agent asked if we wanted to make an offer. I said, "Try $650,000." To my surprise, he called back and said we had a deal. They liked the fact that we were planning to use the building as a non-profit club devoted to theatre.

The Italian Renaissance-style building was among downtown's most historically and architecturally noteworthy structures. The simply grey façade sheltered an elegant interior with golf-leafed, coffered ceilings, faux-marble columns and wood-paneled walls. Throughout the 1930's the Variety Arts Center attracted prominent speakers like Eleanor Roosevelt and hosted live radio shows with Al Jolson and Eddie Cantor. Frequent guests included Charlie Chaplin and Cecil B. DeMille. It was perfect for the Society for the Preservation of Variety Arts!

Bill and I had started the Magic Castle with no business plan and no capital. Bill was a really good businessman and a great administrator. He loved the concept of re-creating our Dad's dream for the Academy of Magical Arts. I was a Dreamer like my dad with no business skills whatsoever. I was a whiz with a hammer and a saw. Somehow it worked, mainly due to the fact that we surrounded ourselves with friends and associates that believed in our visions of the future. We started the Mayfair Music Hall with no business plan, no capital and just started building another dream. Dr. Tom Heric understood business. John Shrum designed an incredible facsimile of an Old London Music Hall and I found bits and pieces of old buildings and physically make it work. What a fabulous opportunity! Brother Bill, John Shrum, Dr. Tom Heric and Dick Sherman shared my vision of another institution that might rival the success of the Magic Castle, and preserve my life-long ambition, vaudeville!

It was a crazy idea but it just might work!

Once again, I had no business plan, no capital and no real idea of what I was doing. I had simply made an offer to purchase a 66,000 square foot building in downtown LA and surprisingly The Friday Morning Club accepted the offer: $650,000 with $150,000 down. Of course, we didn't have the $150,000 but we'd figure out some way to get it.

As published in Genii 1977, written by Bill Larsen: "The biggest news of all for Milt and me is that we have found a home for the Society for the Preservation of Variety Arts, Inc. This is a two-year old non-profit corporation that Milt and a few of us founded two years ago with the idea of doing for the other variety artists what the

Academy of Magical Arts has done for magic. We have been working with the City of Pasadena to refurbish the Pasadena Playhouse but there have been so many delays that we turned our attention elsewhere and came up with the Friday Morning Club on Figueroa in downtown Los Angeles, just between the new Bunker Hill redevelopment and the new Convention Center. "

That was in 1977. This book is meant to be about my life in magic. The Variety Arts represented a decade of my life that taught me a lot about the world of business and politics. There were triumphs and failures. It was a fabulous experience and I have no regrets but that will all be part of another book at another time.

We ended up moving the Society for the Preservation of Variety Arts, dedicated to the preservation of vaudeville, into this unique space. Our intention was to buy the property and try to do with it what we had done with the Magic Castle. The basement was a huge lounge, shops and maintenance areas. Half the square footage of the basement was a two-stall gentleman's lounge with one sink and the huge ladies' eighteen stall marble lounge, dressing room, steam room and a makeup room. After all, it was originally a ladies club!

Variety Arts Center Ladies Room

The first floor was the 1,158-seat theatre with a twenty-eight foot stage and a full fly gallery, balcony and perfect acoustics. The second floor up on the mezzanine floor was the offices and more balconies. The third floor was a very large, beautifully paneled library behind the balcony and museum. It included collections of playbills, gag files, memorabilia and videotapes of all performers and interviews with famed personalities who had appeared at the Variety Arts Center. The fourth floor was a meeting room that we turned into another little theatre. We originally called it The Grasshopper Street Theatre because that is the name the city had originally called Figueroa Street. We found a small amount of amusement naming the theatre that but it seemed too confusing so we finally changed the name to the Tin Pan Alley Theatre. We put in a nice-sized stage and one hundred fifty cabaret-style seats for revue performances.

Tin Pan Alley Theatre

The fifth floor was the ballroom, seating three hundred in a banquet style arrangement. It had tables, mezzanines, a large kitchen; a beautifully designed nightclub area with an orchestra stage for Vince Houser's Art Deco and His Society Orchestra. This floor also had the WC Fields Bar and the Earl Carroll Lounge. The sixth floor was the clubroom.

Variety Arts Theatre Auditorium

*Vincent Houser aka Art Deco &
His Society Orchestra*

WC Fields' Bar

Variety Arts Ballroom

The most controversial item in the Variety Arts Center was a 52-foot scale model of the Italian luxury liner, Contessa diConte, built by MGM in 1947 for the film "Luxury Liner" docked on the roof awaiting a more permanent berth. I purchased it at the MGM Studio auction and it is the only boat in the world that had spent more time on land and in the air than on the water! The Society for the Preservation of Variety Arts had more than three thousand members, every one of whom was a valuable asset in helping to preserve the past and build the future in variety entertainment.

A bit of Los Angeles trivia: In the early '30's, many of the downtown Los Angeles theatres were used for radio broadcasts. Prior to the building in Hollywood of NBC's Radio City and CBS' Columbia Square many of the theatres had radio hookups. The early stations were owned by car dealers, many of whom were on or near Figueroa Street. Don Lee Cadillac started the Don Lee Mutual Broadcasting Company. Earl C. Anthony Packard started KFI and KECA (ECA came from Earl C. Anthony). KFAC? (Franklin Auburn Cord, owner of the Franklin, Auburn, Cord & Duesenberg company). An early photo of downtown Los Angeles reveals many radio antenna towers. It was interesting to discover a room at my planned music hall at the Beaux Arts Theatre had a direct line to *radio central* that connected the theatres with transmitters. The Beaux Arts was at 7th and Bixel, Don Lee Cadillac was at 8th and Bixel. It somehow made sense.

In the late '30's, The Friday Morning Club's theatre played host to the "Hollywood Hotel" show starring Hedda Hopper, "The Burns & Allen Show" and many others.

After twenty continuous annual shows at the Wilshire Ebell in Los Angeles, "It's Magic!" moved to the Variety Arts Theater in 1977. That show featured Billy McComb, Ted Winkel, Ioni, Diana the Enchantress, Absolon and my brother, Bill Larsen, Jr., in "Memories of Dante." Bill loved Dante and accomplished a remarkable portrayal of "The Great Dante, the Magician." When Bill was a teenager he appeared as an illusionist in high school variety shows and magic conventions. He surrounded himself with dancers from the Red Skelton TV show and John Shrum wangled scenery and costumes from the NBC Special "Alice in Wonderland." Of course, Bill's co-star was his wife, the lovely Princess Irene.

Ted Winkel

Ioni

Diana, The Enchantress

Billy McComb

Absolon

Bill Larsen as Dante, with Irene

Most everyone will unhesitatingly agree that the creation of the Society was a fulfillment of a beautiful idea. The SPVA was unlike any other entertainers' group or club and had the potential for rescuing vaudeville and its performers from obscurity. The main purpose of the Society was to accomplish specifically what its name implied; to preserve all that may still exist of the old variety arts and artists and to implant as

The Society for the Preservation of Variety Arts WC Fields Bar

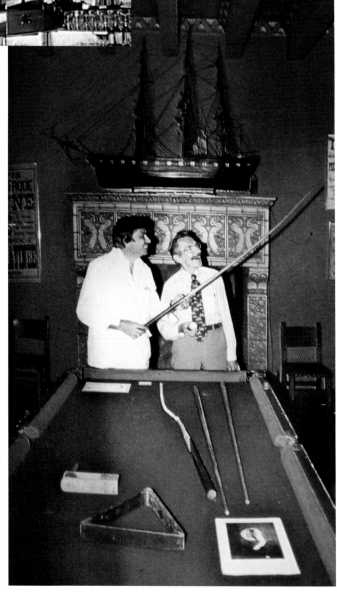

Dick Sherman and SPVA librarian Carl Fleming. In back is the massive Tiffany designed Batchelder tile fireplace, topped with the Eagle miniature ship from "Mutiny On the Bounty."

much of the magic and excitement of the old vaudeville era into the fledgling variety artists of today, as may improve the breed and the state of the art. I was keen on this adventure—I had been born to fulfill this ambition.

Imagine having Red Skelton lecture and demonstrate on the subjects of pantomime and pratfalls. How priceless it would be to have Bob Hope give some inside tips on comedy timing and emphasis. Who can better tutor on the subjects of the straight man than the indomitable George Burns? And is there anyone who could challenge George Burns as being the king of holding audiences on the tip of a cigar? What would we now give to have Jack Benny share some esoteric information in timing, gestures and his famous Benny look? Groucho could have added a wealth of material on the sunny side of sarcasm, cynicism and biting humor. These people belong to a class of true entertainment aristocracy. And they are a dwindling group. It is sad that we were not able to establish such a Society years ago. What an incalculable loss it was that no Society existed at a time when these artists were in their strides. But what a great place for them to finally find a home now.

Edgar Bergen lectured to SPVA students of the theater about comedy and his early days in vaudeville and radio. A video was made of this lecture and is now part of the priceless collection. Other lecturers that appeared in a series of seminars co-sponsored by U.S.C. included such great names as George Jessel, Buddy Ebsen, Jack Haley, Rose

L-R: George Jessel, Buddy Ebsen, Jack Haley, Rose Marie

Marie, Eddie Parks, Nick Lucas, Roberta Sherwood, Donald O'Connor, Benny Rubin and others.

L-R: Donald O'Connor, Roberta Sherwood, Nick Lucas, Charlie Chaplin

L-R: Al Jolson, Bob Hope, Eddie Cantor, Cecil B. DeMille

While we can still profit from the phonograph recordings and films of those who are no longer with us, we have forever lost the direct contact by which, through the learning process, much of their artistry could have been translated and passed on to future performers. As each day passes we lose someone who could have contributed some invaluable thought on this subject the day before. In this sense, SPVA had the ability to actually stop the clock and deny the grim reaper his claim against the talent and artistry as well as the life.

In addition to the educational aspects for the professionals, the Society offered the memorabilia and material which it gathered, stored and exhibited for the benefit of all, professional, enthusiast and the public. Phonograph records are being broken and lost every day. Films are deteriorating hour by hour. Papers are lost, destroyed and sequestered. Many items not recognized for the great treasures which they are, are destroyed or disposed of every single day. There was not one minute to lose. It was not just the function, but the sober and committed duty of the Society to seek out, find, appropriate and preserve every such item, to be cared for, revered and exhibited in its museum for all to look at and learn from.

Johnny Carson & Eddie

Johnny Carson started his career as a ventriloquist and magician. He loved magic. In 1943, Dunninger made his debut on network radio and was a spectacular success. For those of you too young to remember Joseph Dunninger, he was a mentalist who astounded radio audiences with his ability to read minds over the airwaves. One of my favorite bits in our variety arts archives is a take-off that Johnny Carson did on his 1955 CBS-TV show that preceded the "Tonight Show." It was a summer replacement show for Jack Benny. Dunninger had people stand in the audience and tell them things he could not possibly know. In Carson's version he had a guy stand up and Johnny started revealing things about him. As the cleverly written sketch unfolded, it revealed facts the audience learned that the guy was an international spy wanted by the FBI. It was great comedy. Joe Dunninger was married to Crystal Spencer, one of the most beautiful showgirls of the Ziegfield Follies.

When Johnny Carson moved from the East Coast to the West Coast in 1972, they assigned John Shrum as the "Tonight Show" art director. Johnny Carson was a member of the Magic Castle, loved magic and John Shrum's designs. Once in a while, John would design a set that would happen to fit into the Magic Castle, with Johnny's permission. They would paint it on canvas and use it as a piece of scenery for a while. When they were finished with it, they would take it down, roll it up and piece it into a ceiling at the

Milt on Johnny Carson set at Variety Arts Center

Magic Castle as a fresco. When NBC completely remodeled the "Tonight Show" set John asked if he could have the old one. So we utilized the backdrop of the Johnny Carson Show, Johnny's old striped curtain and many other pieces of Johnny's old set at the Variety Arts Center and the Magic Castle.

John often perched himself on his favorite bar stool in his *office* at the dining room Owl Bar at the Magic Castle. He had a great time complaining about the quality of the orange slices for the Old-fashioneds, the two burned out light bulbs and the fact that one of our waiters was not wearing his white gloves. He kidded his friends and talked about the wonders of the Huber Marionettes, which he had seen in the Palace of Mystery the night before. He would certainly tell Jim McCawley at NBC about them on Monday. One night he went home and went to sleep. He is still in that deepest of all sleeps. The Magic Castle will stand as a monument to the memory of the man who made pillars magically disappear and combined good taste with fun-filled function. He loved to say he hated magic. The opposite was true. He loved magic and magicians. John stayed with "The Tonight Show" until he passed away in 1988.

Johnny was a frequent visitor to the Magic Castle and very, very involved with the club. He was an excellent magician and started as a ventriloquist magician when he was a youngster and never lost it. Another celebrity and frequent visitor to the Castle was Cary Grant. He was on our Board of Directors for many, many years. When Cary

Johnny Carson

Cary Grant

retired, he hung up his gloves and never did one thing after that. He never appeared on television or made movies or made charity appearances. His attitude was he had had a great career, he wanted to go out on top and he certainly didn't need the money. Johnny Carson really admired Cary for his attitude. So when Johnny Carson retired from "The Tonight Show" he basically wouldn't go any place other than his boat. His one exception was traveling to Wimbledon for tennis matches once a year.

Penn & Teller

Penn and Teller, billed as the "Bad Boys of Magic" were knocking them dead at the Canon Theater in Beverly Hills. Due to another show previously booked to come in, they were looking for a new venue—fast. They checked with me about using the intimate Masquers Theater at the Variety Arts Center. I loved the idea but we had just signed an open-ended rental agreement with a guy who was going to do a musical version of Dracula. The imposing set was already under construction. Penn and Teller were able to get the Las Palmas Theater for the continuation of their run and were a phenomenal success. It turned out the Dracula set was the best thing about the musical which closed after two performances! Penn and Teller's show might have changed the fate of the Variety Arts Center.

Our first major show, "Red, Hot and Cole," was a musical revue celebrating the legendary songwriter, Cole Porter. It might have been a huge hit except for the fact that it opened the same week that the country *ran out of gas*. People panicked when

KAYE BALLARD GEORGE LEE ANDREWS
in
RED, HOT & COLE
A MUSICAL PARTY
MUSIC AND LYRICS BY
COLE PORTER
BOOK BY
RANDY STRAWDERMAN JAMES BIANCHI and MURIEL McAULEY
WITH
JONELLE ALLEN
CHOREOGRAPHY BY
LEO MULLER
DIRECTED BY
RANDY STRAWDERMAN

they thought the price of gas might reach one dollar a gallon! (Remember the year was 1977.) As they lined up for gas they were definitely not lining up to purchase theatre tickets downtown. It was a very expensive show and the producers decided to close it after a few weeks. Jack Smith, Los Angeles Times columnist, caught the show on the final weekend and devoted his column to it the following Monday. His *Cole With Gossamer Wings* review was written with sincerity and love. The column resulted in a flood of calls but it was too late to save the show. Had that first show become a hit it might also have changed the fate of the Variety Arts Center.

The Variety Arts Center was home of a lot of fun and excitement. A number of good things came out of our attempt to create a center for the variety arts in downtown Los Angeles. Harry Anderson, Lance Burton, and Victoria Jackson were just a few who got their first professional breaks there. Victoria played a cigarette girl who stood on her head and recited original poetry. Johnny Carson caught her act and her appearance on the "Tonight Show" propelled her to Saturday Night Live. Lance Burton came from Kentucky to do "It's Magic!" in the big theater and his appearances on the "Tonight Show" helped pave his way to super stardom in Las Vegas. Michael Feinstein used to play cocktail piano music in the Roof Garden lounge for tips because he liked the sound of our Steinway and couldn't afford one of his own. Two of our favorite Variety Arts family members were Ginni and Joey D'Auria. They did everything from running the elevators and manning the reception desk to performing in dozens of our original productions. Joey can be remembered on the "Tonight Show" doing his Mr. Flamo act—holding his hands over a row of burning candles

Joey D'Auria as Dr. Flameo

screaming in pain and in tune. Joey's big break was the chance to take over the role of Bozo the Clown, playing the legendary host for more than a decade in Chicago. Joey D'Auria was our first choice to portray Weber in our musical "Pazzazz!"

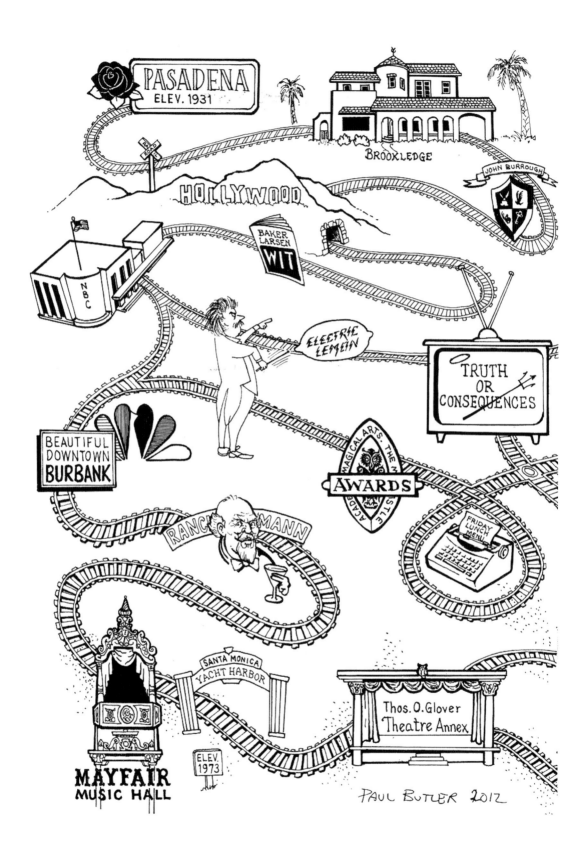

By the end of the '70's, I was very proud that I had created three attractions that were sketched on those tourist maps they sell on Hollywood Boulevard: The Magic Castle in Hollywood, The Mayfair Music Hall in Santa Monica and the Variety Arts Theatre and Center in downtown Los Angeles. The magical train was still on track. I asked Paul Butler—the super talented artist that used to do illustrations and cartoons for Genii magazine on the Magic Castle (and of course "The Great Hockmann" book) to come out of retirement to create a map so people will get a better idea of why I have likened the story of my life to a train ride where the main track is always magic. Carol Marie and I are very glad he clarified it. Thanks, Paul Butler.

Over the years, with the long run of "It's Magic!" and the Magic Castle, people have often asked who booked the acts? Up until 1993 and the passing of my brother, Bill Larsen Jr. booked all the talent, assisted by Peter Pit and others. Bill and Irene attended all the conventions and had a keen eye for talent. After Bill died, I took on the job for a short period of time. I found it time consuming and thankless so I turned the job over, as quickly as possible, to Peter Pit who marvelously booked all the acts for the Magic Castle. With the passing of Peter Pit in 1999 the entertainment director for the Castle became the former President and board member, the late Ron Wilson.

Bill, Ron Wilson, Peter Pit

The present director of entertainment of all the Magic Castle theatres is Jack Goldfinger. Goldfinger & Dove traveled the world with their award-winning act until settling down to take on the enormous challenge booking acts for the Academy of Magical Arts. When Jack was a very young man he and Dove had a great act and really wanted to be on our "It's Magic!" show. To magicians, playing "It's Magic!" was like *playing the Palace* in the golden days of vaudeville. It didn't happen until one day in 1976. We had an act drop out. Bill and I discussed a replacement in his office. Bill asked, "What about Goldfinger? He's here tonight." I went downstairs to ask Jack if he would be available. When I popped the question he responded with an explosion of glee and I will swear, to this day, that he actually levitated and literally flew around the room. He has never lost that electric enthusiasm and is a great asset to the Academy of Magic Arts.

THE EIGHTIES –
THE VARIETY ARTS CENTER

The Society for the Preservation of Variety Arts

We had in the Variety Arts collection just about everything Ed Wynn ever did, including playbills, scripts, posters, records and even his old breakaway piano. It *Ed Wynn* was a rather large collection of show business material. I had a large silent movie orchestrations collection and the largest collection of British Music Hall music, at least in the United States. I had offered the collection to a number of places including U.S.C. and the Huntington Library. I specially collected the early burlesque for the humor and vaudeville sketches. But it was not what the Huntington Library wanted. They were looking for donations that could be displayed next to a Gainsborough portrait. Huntington Hartford had Lawrence's Pinkie but I had Pinky Lee. They turned me down. When you are a collector you are a packrat, you can't throw anything away. My collection was getting enormous. There is a time when the collection starts collecting you.

So instead of getting rid of the collection, I got some other vaudevillians and collectors to loan us their ephemera to display at the Society for the Preservation of Variety Arts. Now we had room to do justice to the enormous variety arts collection.

I have the entire Earl Carroll collection—every scrapbook going back to the Earl Carroll Theatre in New York in 1922. He built his second theater, the first theatre in Los Angeles, in 1938 on Sunset Boulevard. Earl Carroll was a contemporary of Flo

Ziegfeld and George White, producing full stage extravaganzas annually. George White called his shows the "Scandals," Flo Ziegfeld had the "Ziegfeld Follies," Earl Carroll named his shows "Sketchbooks" and "Vanities." All three producers were in the business of glorifying the beautiful American woman. Earl Carroll was very, very successful in New York where he had a major theatre. He decided to move his operation to California where he built the Earl Carroll Theatre, now the Nickelodeon Theatre on Sunset Boulevard. A twenty foot tall neon portrait of Beryl Wallace adorned the theatre façade.

Beryl Wallace

In 1938 it was a tremendously successful nightclub. Earl was so innovative most showrooms in Las Vegas copied his art deco design of banquette seating, long cocktail tables, more banquette seating, another row of cocktail seating and more banquette seating. He designed two revolving stages one within the other with a revolving outer ring which could either operate as one full turntable or could go in the opposite direction so they could perform numbers like the old Busby Berkeley routines. There were two side stages about twelve feet in diameter that also revolved. In addition, there were two more stationary side stages. It was a brilliant design.

Earl Carroll had planned to build, and had the blueprints for, America's largest theatre designed for the property west of the Earl Carroll theatre on Sunset Blvd. It was to be a 5,000-seat theatre and house everything state-of-the-art. At the time when there were only radio studios on Sunset, Earl Carroll's plans included television studios for any network and a heliport on the roof. He was very much ahead of his time. In 1948 he was well on the way of realizing his dream and of obtaining the financial backing he needed to build the complex. He had a financial meeting in New York when on his return to Los Angeles, his plane crashed into Mt. Carmel in Pennsylvania.

Earl Carroll's publicity for his new motion picture theatre and broadcast studio

The question became a Lady and the Tiger-type story; no one seemed to know if Earl Carroll had sold the project or not. He died in the plane crash with his primary partner, showgirl Beryl Wallace and his theatre designer. It's interesting to ponder—if Earl Carroll had sold the idea, and he was the kind of person who could have sold the project had he lived, it would have changed the entire face of Hollywood. Most likely NBC wouldn't have moved to Burbank and CBS wouldn't have moved to Fairfax. Sunset and Vine could have been the film capital of Hollywood.

A lovely and talented lady, Jennifer Mosier, became fascinated with Earl Carroll's life and used our archives to complete a very in-depth Masters Degree paper on Carroll. It would make a great TV documentary. I also wanted to write a story that I called "The Last Memo." Mr. Carroll didn't waste time with long letters. His short memos were fascinating. The search for the last memo would make a great story. Some day when I have the time... Oh well, that's another story.

Earl Carroll started the tradition of having stars sign huge slabs of concrete in 1939. The first two blocks signed were those of his star showgirl Beryl Wallace and a young star of the day, Ronald Reagan. These two were displayed with a cement block which our Patron Member Cary Grant re-signed for us in 1980 to replace his original block stolen from the wall on Sunset Boulevard.

The original cement blocks were found in the basement of the old Earl Carroll Theatre Restaurant when the Music Center's Theatre Group purchased it. Gene Autry had bought the blocks from the Earl Carroll Theatre and then left them in the basement of the newly named Moulin Rouge Theatre. Harry Blackstone Jr. was working at the Moulin Rouge Theatre, which became the Aquarius theatre when "Hair" was presented there. Harry called and said they had heavy autograph blocks in the basement and offered them to me to make needed room in the basement for the theater. There must have been one hundred twenty of them. Some were broken, some had coke syrup dripping all over them; they were really in bad shape. But I took them all, restored the broken blocks, cleaned them up and put them into the Variety Arts Center basement.

Cary Grant resigning autograph block

I got a call from Gene Autry one day from Omaha. He said, "This is Gene Autry. You stole my blocks, the autograph blocks. Those are mine and you took them." I replied, "A., I didn't know they were yours and B. Are we talking about the Earl Carroll signature blocks? If you want them, come get them."

I quickly explained to him what had happened. The original blocks weighed about seventy-five pounds each, as heavy as a sack of concrete. What occurred to us is that you don't hang a block of concrete over the heads of the diners; one little earthquake — the liability could be horrendous. So we carefully made duplicates of each block out of Styrofoam. What we had on display at the Variety Arts Center were the Styrofoam duplicates.

Gene Autry thanked us for the restoration and storage of the blocks when he picked up the originals. He had purchased them for his Gene Autry Museum. When we closed the Variety Arts Center, we lent our collection to Debbie Reynolds for her museum.

Earl Carroll portrait surrounded by autograph blocks

In my earlier book, Hollywood Illusion: Magic Castle I mentioned our first meeting with the legendary George Burns. George became a very good friend of the Castle, dropping in quite frequently. He also loved the Variety Arts Center; after all it was a living museum and a tribute to the golden days of vaudeville and, if anybody knew anything about vaudeville, it was George Burns. One day I got a call from Irving Fine who was not only George Burn's lifelong manager for years but also he had been the manager for Jack Benny. Irving was a marvelous man and was also a legend in show business in his own right. He asked if he and George could bring a couple of people up for lunch at the Variety Arts Roof Garden. They were major cable TV executives and he had something he wanted to talk to them and to me about. The next afternoon George and Irving arrived and I met the two young network executives. Then we sat down and had lunch. George was charming, funny and delightful. Irving pitched a TV special he had in mind that George Burns would host. At that time George had starred in the "Oh, God!" movie and had, once again, become a major superstar at the top of the pack.

Irving and George outlined a TV special that would feature the world's greatest comedians. Many of the great comedians were still living and George could get these comics to appear on the special. He named a dozen or so of the greatest names in the history of TV: Milton Berle, Sid Caesar, Red Skelton, Phil Silvers, Jonathan Winters,

George Burns

Red Buttons, Jackie Gleason, Lucille Ball... an incredible list of stars. With George hosting, it was sure to be the comedy show of the century. The network executives listened and at the end of the pitch Irving asked what they thought. The executives adjourned to discuss the project privately. When they returned to the table one of them said: "Mr. Fine, we have a problem. We have discussed this and it sounds like a good idea, but neither of us have ever heard of some of these people you've been talking about." Irving bristled: "The greatest names in show business—the great comedians of all time and you don't know who they are?"

L-R: Lucille Ball, Red Buttons, Sid Caesar, Phil Silvers, Red Skelton

Their answer was: "Mr. Fine. We know they were big stars in their day but I'm afraid our newer, younger generation would not be interested in watching them. We will have to pass on your project." At that time the waiter brought over the lunch check and, as proper waiters are instructed to do, placed the check in the center of the table within reach of whomever would pay the bill. Irving Fine immediately picked up the check, stood up and said: "George and I have to go now. In

Milton Berle, Jackie Gleason

all the years that I've been a manager, lunching with some of the most important people in the world, I've been known as the guy who always picked up the check. Young man, I'm picking up the check and handing it to you!" Irving then said, "Let's go George." And George and Irving thanked me, went down and got into their waiting limousine and drove away. I went back to the table and one of the executives said: "I think we offended him." They were right.

I made a rare appearance as an actor in Hart To Hart's 1981 episode entitled "Murder Up Their Sleeve" where a magician and his brother, who has had surgery to look just like Jonathan, plan to replace him and hopefully gain control of the Hart empire. Other Magic Castle members in the episode were Harry Blackstone as the magician and Tony Giorgio as Cheshire.

On January 12, 1982 Bill wrote in his editorial "HERE'S BIG NEWS. For the first time in twenty-five years the 'It's Magic!' show will be staged away from Los Angeles. Our Midwest magicians will be able to see a special edition of the show through the auspices of Frank Pearson and the St. Louis Theatrical Company starting February 2nd. The run will be Feb 2-7, Taft Theater, Cincinnati, Ohio; Feb 9-14, State Theater, Columbus Ohio; Feb 16-21, American Theater, St. Louis, Missouri; Feb 23-28, Hanna Theater, Cleveland, Ohio and March 2-7 at the Stanley Theater in Pittsburgh, Pennsylvania.

L-R: Petrick & Mia, Dick and Diana Zimmerman, Kramien & Company, Shimada

The show will feature 'It's Magic!' stars such as SHIMADA from Japan, (six times on "It's Magic!—a record), KRAMIEN and COMPANY with his illusions, DICK and DIANA ZIMMERMAN, BOB and GINNI LEWIS, PETRICK AND MIA, AND DIANA, THE ENCHANTRESS. All produced by the Larsen Brothers in association with Kevin O'Connor. Special settings by John Shrum. Directed by Dick Zimmerman."

There was a lot more to that story than meets the eye—or the history books!

Kevin O'Connor, the son of Shirley and Norman Carroll, was very involved in Southern California theaters. For years he was the director of the La Mirada Civic Theater. He had dealings with Frank Pearson of the St. Louis Theatrical Company and worked out a deal to tour a road company of "It's Magic!" for their theaters in the Midwest. The tour was originally scheduled to play in October and November. For whatever reason, Frank and Kevin decided to move the dates to the spring. The shows opened February 1-9 at the Taft Theater in Cincinnati, Ohio. Kevin and I flew to the Midwest a week ahead of the show for the usual publicity promotions.

The shows were designed to fly rather than *bus and truck*. The acts were set and all was very cool. Let me rephrase that: It was very, very cool! Spring in the Midwest can be very pleasant. January-February 1982 went down in history as the coldest snowfall in seventy years. Kevin and I are California kids. But the theaters were booked, tickets sold and *the shows must go on*. Natives of the cities in the Midwest are used to heavy snows and blizzards—but not in February. At one of the theaters, the acts made it okay but the scenery, lighting equipment and large props were still grounded at the airport. The show was a financial disaster for the producers. Luckily (or thanks to Kevin's business sense) our contract was honored. It was quite an unforgettable experience. It was also our first and last road tour.

One of the high points of the tour happened when Kevin and I were doing our advance publicity junket. We had finished our work in St. Louis on January 23rd and Kevin noted that we had a few days off before our meetings in Cincinnati. We had an open invitation to see the Le Grand David show in Beverly, Massachusetts. I questioned Kevin—Boston didn't seem to be on the way from St. Louis to Cincinnati. But he replied that it was no problem and before I knew it, we were on our way to Boston. The cast of Cesareo's show would meet us. They were thrilled.

After hosing down the plane with hot water we took off for Boston. It was a nice and uneventful flight until we encoun-

tered rough weather on the East Coast. The flight crew offered the passengers complimentary drinks to calm down any jangled nerves. Kevin and I and the rest of the passengers were feeling no pain as we neared our destination. The plane landed safely, taxied down the runway and slid to a stop.

Remember that great scene

in the movie "Airplane" where the people in the waiting area panicked as the plane crashes into the window? Our airplane luckily did not replay that scene and was able to come to a complete stop inches away from the window. As they poured Kevin and me off the plane we didn't know anything was wrong until we entered the terminal to be greeted by Cesareo Pelaez, David Bull and a number of scared-stiff, ashen faces of other cast members. It was a really close call. Our plane landed safely but the next plane that landed after us had an accident. To emphasize the severity of the moment, here's a report:

"At 7:35 p.m. on January 23, 1982, a World Airways DC-10 overshot the runway while attempting to land at Logan Airport, and fell into the ocean. The DC-10 touched down 2,800 feet beyond the displaced threshold. Under normal circmstances such an incident would have been of minor importance and the plane would have had sufficient space to come to a full stop on the 10,000 feet long runway. However, the runway was covered in ice and the braking action was poor to nil. When it became apparent to the pilots that the aircraft was not able to stop on the runway, they steered the plane off the runway in order to avoid hitting approach lights beyond. The plane then skidded across a field and a taxiway before coming to rest in the 30 degree waters of the Boston Harbor."

By the way, we loved Le Grand David's show. For those who may not know, on February 20, 1977, Le Grand David and his own Spectacular Magic Company made its debut on the stage of the Cabot Street Cinema Theatre with a show that is still running. In 1985, the Le Grand David Company opened a second two-hour spectacle of magic, music, comedy and dance at Beverly's other antique playhouse, the Larcom Theatre. The two productions showcased over 1,000 costumes, 700 entrances and exits,

100 classic illusions, 45 backdrops, 35 years in a small town, 4 hours of stage magic in 2 antique theaters. The shows are produced, directed, designed and choreographed by Marco, the Magi. Marco, the Magi became a great friend (Cesareo Pelaez, Marco the Magi, was honored with a Masters Fellowship by the Academy of Magical Arts in 2002. Cesareo passed away March 24, 2012.)

We continued the Midwest tour through sleet and blizzards. Our last show was in the Hanna Theater, Cleveland. Pittsburgh was cancelled. During the Hanna run I walked across the street to discover an artist working on the restoration of the Palace Theater. The Palace is part of Playhouse Square: four magnificent theaters located on a *superblock*. In 1986 the Sherman Brothers/Milt Larsen's musical "Dawgs!" played the cabaret theater at the Cleveland Palace. The head of Playhouse Square was Larry Wilkins who later became the head of Kennedy Center in Washington D.C. We had serious discussions with Larry, the Mayor of Cleveland, and a number of power players about a Cleveland Magic Castle.

"Dawgs!" was actually born in 1983. One day I was talking to my old pal Dick Sherman and I commented on all the songs the Sherman Brothers had written about dogs over the years and many other dog songs for Disney films. I felt that dogs were being slighted in favor of the award-winning musical "Cats." After all, cats are notorious snobs and take themselves entirely too seriously. Dogs are fun, they love people, they love life—they are funny! I wrote the script for a stage revue; Bob and Dick Sherman provided songs from their various films which included "No Dogs Allowed" from "Snoopy Come Home" and "When You're Loved" from "The Magic of Lassie" which was nominated for an Academy Award for best song. "Dawgs!" also featured Sherman Brothers songs from many Disney films including title songs: "101 Dalmations" and "That Darned Cat." I had the pleasure of writing words and music with the Sherman Brothers on one song we wrote expressly for "Dawgs" called "The Bow Wow Ball."

Arlene, my wife, created the wonderful costumes out of dozens of human hair wigs. The costumes had to be shampooed every night after performance. One evening during the run of the show we thought it would be cool to invite the cast to bring their pet *dawgs*. The next few days we had a problem with fleas. Arlene won a Dramalogue Award in 1984 for her outstanding designs and execution of the designs. We performed "Dawgs!" at the Variety Arts Theatre downtown and then took the show to Playhouse Square in Cleveland and the Golden Opera House in Colorado. I always had hopes that some day we could play the show in a theatre across the street from "Cats." If it was a smashing success the reviews could say, "It's reigning Cats and Dawgs."

Bob Stivers produced celebrity television specials for all three networks. He produced the amazing "Circus of the Stars" for CBS in which celebrities performed circus-type acts. There were nineteen shows in total, the first being broadcast in 1977, the last in 1994. Over the years the series featured many leading movie and television stars. The cast read like a who's who of Hollywood. A number of friends worked on the show and I got a call in 1985 to help with an act. They needed something for legendary movie star Lana Turner to perform. I suggested a little illusion that Dad used from time to time in the Larsen Family of Magic show.

Lana Turner

It was a stage version of a small effect: a glass in a frame was displayed. A playing card was placed on each side of the glass and a knitting needle was pushed through the cards and the glass. It was a very pretty effect. Dad had the Owen Brothers manufacture a three-by-three foot sheet of glass in a frame.

After showing the glass Dad placed two jumbo playing cards on each side of the glass and pierced the cards and the glass with a fencing sword. I thought it would be a flashy and effective trick that I could teach anyone to do. It was one of those wonderful stage illusions where the assistants did all the work.

The producers loved the idea and asked the natural question, "Where is the prop?" Well, that could be a problem. There was only one ever made and that was forty years ago. I said I would check it out. I called around and no one had ever heard of it—it simply didn't exist. So I suggested that one of my magic builder/designer friends, Don Damaskin, could make the illlusion for the show. I ad-libbed a price of a few hundred dollars and the producers said, "Go for it." Don was my right-hand man at the Magic Castle and all my other enterprises. He was a jack-of-all-trades and a master of most. He was a carpenter, plumber, painter, electronic genius, artist… the only thing he couldn't figure out was how to build an oversized *Glass Penetration Illusion*.

Glass Penetration Ilusion

So I went down to the Variety Arts shop and made the prop. I remembered the one Dad had and it simply wasn't all that complicated. I met Lana Turner for the first time at her lavish apartment in a Century City. I showed her the props and she was a quick study. No problem. I assured the producers that Lana had no problem with performing the trick. The day of the taping at Caesars Palace, I was there and the prop was there. But Lana Turner was missing. They checked the airport and Lana had arrived. The Caesar's limousine had picked her up. The drive from Las Vegas' McCarran Airport was only a few minutes. Where was Lana Turner???

The mystery was solved when Lana finally arrived. She explained that in all her movie career she had never done a live performance. She had a severe case of *stage fright*. She had asked the limo driver to drive her around the streets of Las Vegas until she got up enough nerve to walk onto the stage. The happy ending to the story was that Lana did a great job of presenting Dad's old effect. I think that was Lana's first and last television appearance. It was Circus of the Stars' show #10 which aired in 1985.

Bob Stivers was a member of the Magic Castle and also the Society for the Preservation of Variety Arts. He gave me the Nickelodeon piano that is now at the Magic Castle in the Inner Circle. Bob loved Rolls Royce cars and owned several. One day he arrived at the Variety Arts Roof Garden for lunch in one of his impressive cars. On the way out I mentioned that I would love to have a limo to pick up VIPs. Without missing a beat he said, "How about a Bentley? I've got a 1939 Bentley that I don't like. It has the

chauffeur's compartment. I like driving my own cars. Want it?" I asked the price. He just told me to call his office in the morning. He would have his mechanic check the Bentley from front to rear. He was happy to donate it to the club. Bob was an amagingly generous man.

1939 Bentley

Dick Mentzer was a former drama critic who worked for years as an administrator for Actors Equity and the Actors Fund. He started working for me in the box office of the Variety Arts Theater for the "It's Magic!" show of 1981. I hired him for three weeks and he became my right-hand person for the next ten years.

Dick catalogued over two hundred fifty items for the Society for the Preservation of Variety Arts, ranging from small-framed photos to large lithographs. To give you an idea of the kinds of items in the collection, we had a fabulous Strohbridge lithograph of Miss Billie Burke in the comedy "The Runaway" which was produced by Charles Frohman in 1911. This may have been Frohman's last production since he made the mistake of booking passage on the maiden voyage of the new Titanic in 1912. Billie Burke, of course, was the good witch in MGM's "Wizard of Oz."

We also have a lithograph of David Montgomery in the part he originated on Broadway of the Tin Man from the "Wizard of Oz." It was autographed and worth a small fortune to collectors. Fred Stone played the part of the Straw Man. Montgomery and Stone were major stars of their day recording, back in 1912, "Travel, Travel Little Star." One of the lines: "He met a sailor with a wooden leg named Jim... But we didn't know what he called his other limb." Good stuff!

Richard Mentzer was always on time. He took the bus to work and walked into our office at precisely 7:30 a.m. One day he was ten minutes late. We could not and would not tolerate this type of inefficiency in our organization so I told him to clean out his desk. His services would not be required in the future! Actually his desk was already cleaned out since Dick had chosen to retire and move to Wichita, Kansas. Dick paddled our broken lifeboat through the stormy seas of downtown Los Angeles. We remember some great times, mixed in with all the problems. Being my assistant was a thankless job and I'm not sure I ever thanked him for his help and his loyalty. Therefore, thank you Dick Mentzer!!!!

Nearly a hundred years ago a baby came into the world. His name was Alston Roberts. As a kid he sold newspapers on the streets of San Francisco. In those days the newspaper vendors were prominently Italian and always wore black shirts. Alston didn't have enough money to buy a black shirt so he wore his white one. That's how he got his moniker "Whitey." In the annals of vaudeville there were some acts that were consummate entertainers. Names come to mind like Herman Timberg, James Barton and Joe Penner. These acts could sing, dance, tell jokes, act in scenes, do acrobatics—you name it. Whitey Roberts was one of those acts. His basic act involved a comedy routine in which he said, "I didn't come here to tell jokes." Then he would juggle, do magic, sing and dance.

Whitey had a great audience participation bit with ten people onstage—each with a musical school bell. They would shake the bell when Whitey pointed to them. Under his direction they would play "The Bells of St. Mary." His handling of the audience was simply hilarious. Whitey kept assuring the tenth player that he had a big part. He never got to ring his bell until the very end of the song when he rang his bell once. Funny? You had to be there.

Whitey's act included juggling three objects, one of which was a china plate. In the course of the routine he kept *accidentally* dropping the plate. Then he would continue with ever diminishing pieces of the plate until he got down to one pebble-sized piece. Again, funny stuff. Whitey could tap dance while jumping rope. After a few bars, he would purposely trip on the rope and go into another bit. This was a running gag. I produced a show to raise funds for the Los Angeles Conservancy at the Palace Theater on Broadway. Broadway, Los Angeles, that is. Whitey was about ninety at the time. He was great but some of the audience commented later that they were concerned that the old vaudevillian kept tripping on his jump rope.

Whitey Roberts

One of my pet peeves is that people never seemed to take the variety arts seriously. Opera, ballet and *the-a-tah* were there for the carriage trade. But if you didn't own a set of white tie and tails or sport a diamond tiara you were entertained by variety arts in the hundreds of vaudeville theaters that dotted the United States. Folk history of the country can be traced through the jokes of the vaudeville comedians who spread the word faster than those newfangled telly-phones! Circus, vaudeville, burlesque, magic, tent shows—were all part of our rich folk history.

Soap bubble magician Tom Noddy is very active in the resurgence of "New Vaudeville" in San Francisco. My pet theory, in the glory days of vaudeville, is there were no *old vaudevillians*. Kids found they could pick up a few extra pennies by performing on the streets. People wanted to see more and the kids moved

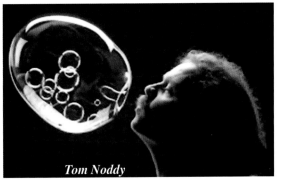

Tom Noddy

Harry Anderson

to amateur nights and then to the big stages in the vaudeville theaters found in every major city. The cornerstones of vaudeville were the small time variety acts. Headliners like Harry Houdini, Nora Bayes, Harry Lauder, Eva Tanguay and others were the big attractions but the audiences were totally entertained by the jugglers, acrobats, animal acts, tap dancers and those wonderful novelty acts who simply did amazing physical humor by eating their costume or dancing a rubber-legged dance. "Hats Off" starring Harry Anderson and a cast of street performers paid homage to vaudevillian entertainment at the Variety Arts Center.

Brother Bill had seen Lance Burton win the Grand Prix gold medal at the IBM Convention in the Midwest. I had the opportunity of meeting Lance Burton when I shared the stage with him at Tony Spina's "Tannen's Jubilee" in the Catskills. I was doing my crazy carpenter act. I shared Bill's enthusiasm for this fine young combination of Elvis and Dracula doing flawless magic so I booked him for the next edition of "It's Magic!" at the Variety Arts Theater. He was thrilled to be booked on the Johnny Carson "Tonight Show" to publicize "It's Magic!" and his rise to fame is legendary. At the time, Lance was under twenty-one so he had to wait to meet his fellow magicians at Sunday brunch at the Magic Castle! He has been a good friend and frequent visitor at the Castle throughout the years.

Writers can write anywhere, driving a car, sleeping, eating or just about doing anything. "Truth or Consequences" produced five shows a week for eighteen years. We had three different acts per show that included reunions, audience participation acts, star acts and practical jokes. For years after the show had gone off the air, an alarm would go off in my head and I would wake up Tuesday morning when we used to have writers meetings, thinking and writing "Truth or Consequences" jokes or stunts in my head; once a writer, always a writer, even if you're not getting paid!

In 1985 Geri Larsen Baker Jaffe started giving annual parties in Santa Barbara for the wheelchair confined and older people who couldn't get out very often. Mom was the life of the party. Arlene outdid herself preparing for the party weeks in advance and decorated everything patriotic: red, white and blue. She designed and dressed Erika's daughter Little Libby Larsen in a costume befitting a Broadway show, which was appropriate when Libby belted out a couple of songs in her Broadway Ethel Merman-style. I performed the old Larsen classics, the *Serpent Silk*, *Cut-and-Restored-Rope*, the *Blue Phantom*, and the *Die Box* complete with Dad's *Old Mother Hubbard* patter.

In the mid-'80's, Peter Pit worked with Steve Martin creating The Great Flydini act, produced eighteen Academy of Magical Arts Award shows with Dick Zimmerman, booked Penn and Teller at the Magic Castle, interviewed forty-eight magicians for the Academy archives, wrote a Genii column "Knights at the Castle" and wrote resumes for such Castle regulars as Monte Smith and Bob Jardine. He later developed his Pitstop program to analyze and help magic acts achieve advancement in the art of magic. He had the energy and drive of a ten-year-old kid.

Steve Martin's The Great Flydini

Buddy Ebsen played Davy Crockett's sidekick in a series of Walt Disney films in the mid-'50's. Buddy was very active at the Magic Castle and the Variety Arts Center. He had fun playing

MILT LARSEN & TERRY HILL PRESENT

THE 39TH ANNUAL EDITION OF

IT'S MAGIC!

AMERICA'S GREATEST ALL-STAR MAGIC REVUE!
OCTOBER 26TH THRU OCTOBER 29TH

ALEX
THEATRE
GLENDALE

the part of dads in the staged radio version of the Dick Sherman/Milt Larsen musical "Charlie Sent Me." Roger Rittner co-authored the book. Dick and I wrote the original

speakeasy era type songs back in 1957 for a show that never happened "Spangles of 1927." I ran across a ten-inch demo LP of the songs that we recorded with Rosy McHargue's band half a century ago. "Charlie Sent Me" was the first major musical comedy written especially for radio in the 1980's. It was the happy collaboration of Academy Award winning songwriter Richard M. Sherman, radio drama producer/director and preservationist Roger Rittner and myself, comedy writer and theatrical impresario, with a cast of seventeen talented musical comedy and radio actors. It was the first radio performance of Buddy Ebsen whose successful career had included every facet of

Buddy Ebsen and Milt

show business except radio. "Charlie Sent Me!" opened in the Roof Garden Restaurant of the Variety Arts Center in downtown Los Angeles in 1984 and was recorded for National Public radio two weeks later with Art Deco and his Society Orchestra.

When I met Arlene Zamiara on "Truth or Consequences," I asked her to do some of the costumes for our Mayfair Music Hall revues. She had a rare knack of making very expensive-looking costumes for next to nothing. She was my kind of gal. She still makes her own dresses and fancy gowns when we go to parties. Why spend $1,000 when you can make the same dress for $29.95? Later she headed the wardrobe department and ran the extensive gift shop at our Variety Arts Center downtown. We enjoyed working

together and playing together. Love had crept into my life.

History was made in 1989 when I gave up my more-than-half-a-century of bachelor-hood to marry the lovely Arlene Zamiara. It was a memorable occasion because no one attending the party at my home in Santa

Milt, Arlene and Dawg

You are invited to a beach party!
The Date: August 27, 1989
Sunday afternoon
The time: 1:30 pm
until darkness
The Place: Edgecliff
by the sea

The Hosts: Milt & Arlene

Barbara knew a wedding was going to take place. That included my brother and my

wife-to-be. Magician/minister John Booth officiated and we have been very happily married ever since.

Arlene was very independent before we got hitched so she doesn't seem to mind that I spend half my time at the Magic Castle, leaving her in Santa Barbara to care for our four-legged family. Arlene is the love of my life. August 27, 1989 we made that relationship official.

I got involved with the Los Angeles Conservancy by doing their premiere show in 1989. It was a vaudeville show in the old Palace Theatre. At that time the cinema screen was permanent. They had a beautiful stage but no one could see it and we couldn't use it. We had to do everything *in one*. I was the Master of Ceremonies. Gene Bell was on the bill with Whitey Roberts juggling. It was quite constraining to have to perform the entire show in front of the movie screen.

Back in the late '70's a bright young writer by the name of Michael Callie had succeeded in imitating Mitzi Shore's Comedy Store with a comedy club called "The Laugh Stop." Then he got an even better idea. He announced that he was going to give the world a really great magic club in fashionable Newport Beach, fifty miles south of Los Angeles. Bill and I never objected to anyone opening a magic club. The Academy of Magical Arts, as originally set up by our father, William Larsen Sr., was and is a "social order dedicated to the advancement of magic." Any venue that consistently offers employment to magicians and top quality magic to the audiences should be supported. Where the canker gnawed was that the promoter of the Magic Island made a very big point that while the Magic Castle was the Cadillac of magic clubs, his new club would be the Rolls Royce! While the members of the Castle had to settle for low paid amateurs, his new club would pay fabulous salaries and attract the biggest names in magic. While the common people might want to belong to a club like the Magic Castle, his new club would attract a much higher class who, of course, all lived in Orange County. While merrily ripping off our original ideas, he continually made negative remarks in advertising and the press about the Magic Castle. Thus we could never give the club any real support. Several of our very good friends lost a ton of money investing in Michael Callie's Magic Island. The club never seemed to work. In 1992 the Rolls Royce was sent to the junkyard. All fixtures and equipment of the Newport Magic Island was sold at auction. The Rolls Royce may have looked great on the outside but it didn't have an engine… or a heart.

In the olden days of "It's Magic!" it wasn't really important whether Brother Bill and I made money or not. Luckily we usually broke even. Sometimes we'd make a couple of dollars and sometimes we'd lose a couple. I've always felt that if there hadn't been an "It's Magic!" I don't think we would have started the Magic Castle. By producing these annual magic shows, and with the success of Genii magazine, we proved there was a very, very big interest in magic in Southern California. In the '50's when we first started these shows magic was pretty dead as an art form. It was just after World War II and it was unheard of for a marquee in Las Vegas to announce a magician, much less advertise a magic headliner. We had to bring magic out of the doldrums and the annual magic shows did just that. All of a sudden we were seeing first class magic on a first class stage.

"It's Magic!" started in 1956 with "Hocus Pocus '56" and hadn't changed that much until Terry Hill came aboard. He taught me how wonderful it is not to lose money. His business was producing shows. He would book the theater, we provided the talent, they gave us a check, we'd pay the acts and there'd be a profit for the producers! Wow!

Magic had been inbred into both Bill and I. Our father was probably the most enthusiastic magician the world has ever known. There was no way that Bill and I, and all our magician friends, would not want to see magic prosper. "It's Magic!" was the fuse that lit the skyrocket that started magic being popular again.

My associate Armand Grant and I had a number of meetings with Jeff Sagansky who, at that time, was the President of CBS Entertainment. Jeff liked the idea of doing a magic special, something like an award show but not really an award show. After a number of ideas were scuttled, we came up with the simple concept of "The Magicians Favorite Magicians." Army is somewhat of a living legend in the television world. He has been a programming executive in all three networks in the days when there were only three networks. Sagansky gave us the green light to move ahead but our original idea, which was to bring in magicians from all over the world, was simply too expensive to make sense to the network. My friend Army is something of a genius when it comes to budgets. We went back to Jeff and asked him to give us a maximum budget number. Army chiseled, hammered and squeezed, but the end result was a budget that we could all live with and the deal was set. Army Grant and I would co-produce the show for CBS; we brought in the skills of Bill Foster as line producer and director. Harry Anderson was the Host and we conducted a survey of the Academy of Magical Arts Award winners with the help of Erika, Irene Larsen and Genii magazine.

Shortly after we taped the special Jeff Sagansky left CBS. The new President was less than enthusiastic about our efforts. He found the show old-fashioned and unexciting. We had tried to present pure magic instead of pure sensationalism. I guess we should have tossed in more sex and violence. We were very proud of the end result of the show. We tried to maintain the integrity of presenting the best magicians in the eyes of their magical peers. We presented a fresh, simple, clean and very entertaining hour of sheer magic and most people, after seeing the show, agreed. But the show sat on the shelf for a year and a half. It was frustrating to Army and I because we could have been ahead of the pack instead of being compared to shows that were done later but aired long before ours.

The Pendragons

Falkenstein & Willard

John Carney

Norm Nielsen

Rudy Coby

Hans Moretti

Once again the regime changed at CBS and Leslie Moonves took over as the new President. Suddenly we had an air date! We assume Mr. Moonves waved his magic wand and we thank him. "The Magicians Favorite Magicians" featured performances by The Pendragons, Falkenstein and Willard, John Carney, Rudy Coby, Norm Nielsen, Hans Moretti and Helga.

Over the years I have kidded my wife, Arlene, about her obsession with earthquake preparedness. From the beginning of our marriage, our house was stocked with an outside bunker with food, water, tools, medical supplies, batteries—everything you are supposed to have in case of an earthquake. In addition, she prepared both of our cars with fully loaded knapsacks and emergency gear. When we lost power when the earthquake hit she had her act totally together. Out came the lanterns, the portable radios, etc. I love my wife because she has refrained from saying, "I told you so."

Jack Oakie was a very active member of the Magic Castle and Variety Arts Center. The world premiere of Mrs. Jack Oakie's musical "The Kid From Muskogee" was produced at the Variety Arts Roof Garden in 1989. At the Magic Castle it was always fun when Jack and his wife, Victoria Horne, would join Irma for a song or two. Victoria Horne was the wacky niece, Myrtle Mae, in Brother Bill's absolute favorite film, "Harvey." Jack would usually come in to the Castle after a Dodgers game with a baseball cap and turtleneck sweater. I named our comedy archives the Jack Oakie Comedy Collection in Jack's memory because of all the gag lines and comedy scripts from Snag Werris, Eddie Cantor, Jack Huston, Billy House, Earl Carroll and Whitey Roberts. Snag Werris' script collection included complete and original scripts of the "Colgate Comedy Hour" and "All-Star Revues" of the early '50's, the "Jackie Gleason" Shows, the "Ben Blue" shows, the "Frank Sinatra" shows, his personal gag files, carefully arranged by subject and bound with a donation from Beech Cameron.

The Eddie Cantor collection included a mammoth joke file and hundreds of letters, scripts, photos tapes, etc. There are complete scripts of all the Earl Carroll revues of the late '20's and '30's. Whitey Robert's gag files were assembled by the ultimate vaudevillian whose career started just after the turn of the century. Whitey danced with the ladies to the music of Glenn Miller.

From the early days of building the Magic Castle I recognized the value in saving anything I could get my hands on. Some day I might need it. I started gathering art glass windows, paneling, fancy molding, chandeliers, beamed ceilings and just about anything from the buildings that were being demolished at a rapid rate in the '60's and

The Musart Theatre as it looked in 1949.

'70's. I also had to store sets from our various stage and television shows. At one time I had three old movie theaters that I rented and used as warehouses. (Old theatres in the seedy parts of town could usually be rented on a month-to-month basis for very little money. Property owners always hoped someone would come along and agree to a long term lease but until then it was a good bet the month-to-month could be a long time.)

One of the theatres I rented in the '80's was the Egan Theatre, across from the convention center on Figueroa. It was built in 1913 as "The Little Theater." The name changed to the Musart in 1933 when it became part of FDR's depression WPA project. It was a beautiful intimate house with a very big stage. I always wanted to restore it but it was doomed to later demolition and, after all, I had other projects at the time.

One of our very supportive members of the SPVA was Ray Klemp, a real estate developer. He called to make an offer we couldn't refuse. His Klemp Company had just sold a twenty thousand square foot building in Santa Ana. It had been a costume and prop rental shop for years. The new owner wanted the building clean—that is—empty. Would we want the contents? We asked the price. Ray said ZERO!!! We could have everything in the building for free BUT there was a catch—the building had to be empty in thirty days. Naturally we took his offer sight unseen. Then we found we had inherited a two-story building filled to the rafters with hundreds of vintage costumes, stage props, draperies, lighting equipment, flags and, you name it. My technical right-hand man, Don Damaskin, put together a team of workers and tackled an enormous job. We filled a half dozen huge dumpsters with trash and a dozen large truckloads took our newfound treasures to the Variety Arts Theater. We literally filled our 1200-seat theater

with an incredible array of stuff. My future wife, Arlene, took charge and found we had
enough military band uniforms for two or three parades; she had a field day with over a
hundred naked mannequins; and there were hundreds of human hair toupees and wigs.
Those hair pieces would inspire Arlene to design and make all the costumes for a future
stage revue "Dawgs!" It was an amazing donation and one helluva challenge.

Back in the days when Howard Hughes was making headlines by giving his
fortune in his will to a guy he met whom had befriended Howard by giving him a ride

Milt and Howard Hughes (Michael Parrish Newman)

to Las Vegas, Howard Hughes came to the rescue of the Variety Arts. Shortly after hearing that the City of Los Angeles had foreclosed on their loan to the Society for the Preservation of Variety Arts, a non-profit museum of show business and entertainment center, eccentric billionaire Howard Hughes showed up at the historic building to present SPVA President (me) with a check for $1,100,000. The local bank, however, remembered that Howard was really an actor, Michael Parrish Newman, bearing a remarkable resemblance to the legendary billionaire who happened to be appearing in his one-man show "Howard Hughes Lives" at the Variety Arts Center. The Center was devoted to comedy but a million dollar foreclosure is no laughing matter. Wanted: a bank with a sense of humor! The whole thing turned out to be a hoax but, what the hell, it made the papers. We got a little of our own cheap publicity by sending out the photo of Howard Hughes handing me a personal check for $1,100,000. Obviously the check was as phony as the photo but it did make the second section of the throwaways.

Over the years I had a couple of alter egos. Back when I started writing the Friday lunch menu news I had fun relating stories about Professor Harry Hockmann. Harry claimed to be the *world's oldest vaudevillian and magician.*

Professor Hockmann exposing himself!

Since Harry would never divulge to anyone exactly how old he was, you had to believe him—even when he spoke of his friendships with Abe Lincoln and Julius Caesar. When the "Masked Magician" flagrantly exposed the secrets of magic on television, we published a book to retaliate: "The Great Hockmann Exposes Himself and Other Vaudevillians." Harry's stories were edited by Carol Marie and the book was illustrated by Paul Butler. It's on the "Happy Days Asylum"-seller list. Harry also appears as my guest on my CRN radio show "Hear Them Again (For the First Time)."

Brother Bill loved the 1950's film "Harvey." Jimmy Stewart played Elwood P. Dowd, a mild-mannered, pleasant man, who had an invisible friend resembling a six-foot tall (puka) rabbit. My other fictional friend is Hare E. Houdini. Hare E. lives in an apartment beneath the Grand Staircase of the Magic Castle. He is in charge of animal relations at the Castle. Watch for a new TV series featuring Hare E. Houdini and his friends. We haven't sold the series yet but watch for it anyway.

My wife Arlene was not my wife when we were operating the Variety Arts Center in the '70's and '80's. I asked her to share a few of her memories of those *good old days*:

Hare E. Houdini

"I loved the parties! At the New Year's Eve parties we dropped balloons from the forty foot ceiling in the Roof Garden Ballroom at midnight as finely dressed couples danced on the wonderful dance floor to Art Deco in his white tie and tails with his sixteen-piece orchestra. Then there was Milt's birthday party when we surprised him by decorating the entire outside of the six-story Variety Arts Center with banners and balloons. Bill Victor, his daughter and her Girl Scout Troop decorated from the top of the building to the street entrance. We had an army of volunteers that made centerpieces for special parties and holidays that helped decorate for the biggest, fanciest and best parties—on no money! Everyone helped to make them such a success."

"We had a party to honor Weber and Fields where I made over fifteen 1890's Mae West-type gowns and dressed the first fifteen ladies that walked through the door. (Arlene lucked out—the first ten ladies were models from downtown that came to the theatre for the first time.) We gave a big party for the Texaco grant and received five elevators full of flower arrangements for free!"

"I remember the day Sybil Brand, philanthropist and civil leader, came into my gift shop. She sat down with me and started telling me how she had always wanted to work in a gift shop. Her father would not let her because he said she would be taking a job away from someone who really needed it and they were too rich for her to work. I loved sitting at the bar all night long, laughing. One time Norris Baronian, who only had one leg, had happened to be drinking too much, fell off the bar stool and laughingly said, "I think I just broke my other leg." (You had to be there.)

Sybil Brand

"I enjoyed making centerpieces for Debra Winger and Timothy Hutton's wedding; loved the vintage elevators with two girls dressed as pageboys and meeting the vaudevillians like Nick Lucas, Gene & Lupe Bell, Whitey Roberts, the Wiere Brothers, Jack Spoons and other regulars. Best of all, when the Pope drove by in his security bubble, we had the best seats."

Then there was the flip side to the good memories: "Every time it rained the basement got flooded… and the basement was my gift shop and wardrobe room."

"The building had been overrun with feral cats—many of which we caught but several of them had hid in the fan room. So we were also overrun with feral fleas. Milt's shop had sawdust on the floor, a perfect place for fleas to hide. When Milt walked in with his white pants on, he came out with black pants… all from fleas. Whenever I needed to go into Milt's shop I wore rubber waders. It was quite funny when I was wearing a gown!"

"I had fixed up a little apartment on the rooftop of the building for Milt to sleep in when it was too late to go home. Everyone kept using the apartment so he never had a chance to use it very often. I kind of think maybe he didn't like it. It was very small and ugly, but it did have a bed."

"On occasion the Variety Arts rented out the big theater to rock bands and when they performed their sound checks, plaster dust would rain down on my costume racks. And I remember having to climb under the big fans into little rooms or walk across beams up in the attic to get to the decorations for the holidays. I also remember having to sell the best wardrobe collection I ever had because we needed the money."

"Good or bad, it was an exciting, wacky and unforgettable time—and it was fun!"

Milt & Arlene caricatures
by Al Rosson

The Variety Arts went on for about twelve years. It was a constant battle trying to get people to come to downtown Los Angeles. Downtown didn't have the right reputation for safety. We had started with absolutely no capital and the Center operated at a loss all the time. We finally had to file Chapter 11 and abandon the complex.

Noted comedy actor Harry Anderson was on the SPVA Board of Directors. He started as a street performer magician on the Venice Pier. He started performing at the Magic Castle and credits us for giving him his first real break when we booked him on the first "It's Magic!" show held at our new Variety Arts Theater in 1977.

Harry Anderson on "Night Court"

Harry became a TV star in the hit show "Night Court" (1984-1992). Harry was very serious about the preservation goals of the Variety Arts and made some very effective *sugar speech* pleas to the Community Redevelopment Agency but the Variety Arts Center had to finally close its door in 1990. The bankruptcy, tax problems, sale of the building, litigation could be the basis for a very interesting book. The good times outweighed the bad times but in the end we had to give up the dream.

When we closed the SPVA we had the problem of what to do with all the collections and materials that had filled our 66,000 square foot building. Harry came to our rescue and offered to pay the very hefty storage charges while we looked for a new home. I still have hopes that the concept will rise again in the future. In the meantime I thank Harry Anderson for his helping hand at a very difficult time.

My train ride through life was derailed but I jumped back on the main track, magic. The Magic Castle was doing quite well. Full steam ahead!

THE NINETIES

WIN SOME—LOSE SOME
BACK TO THE MAIN TRACK—
MAGIC!

I started collecting vaudeville-type things as a kid wanting to absorb as much as I could about show business, comedy and old theatres. The Music Museum came about because I was a frequent guest on the "Reminiscing with Rasputin" on Yesteryear U.S.A. Music Museum radio show is a half-hour show playing those 78 records from my collection of recordings by show business personalities, produced by Frank Bresee. It features yours truly and old friend and radio personality David E. Berger as Rasputin and began in 1993. The pre-1926 acoustical records were kept in an underground vault watched over by our old friend Professor Harry Hockmann who makes an appearance on every show.

The Paramount Theatre at 6th and Hill, Pantages, the Orpheum Theatre and Alex Theatre in Glendale were the theatres that continued to play vaudeville shows through the '50's. The Paramount Theatre was built in 1926 by Sid Grauman and was home to the likes of Fats Waller, Rochester and Kitty Murray. Vaudeville returned off and on until television came into the forefront in 1952. Fanchon and Marco were a brother and sister dancing team that moved into producing vaudevillian shows on the West Coast. They toured their shows throughout the Pacific Northwest. Almost all the theatres in Los Angeles offered Fanchon and Marco vaudeville "Ideas" shows at one time. The shows were structured like vaudeville with a big band on stage or in the pit, lavish production numbers and a main theme. The Alex Theatre in Glendale was a huge Fanchon and Marco theatre and maintains a pictorial museum of their shows in the lobby.

The flagship for the Fanchon and Marco was the Boulevard Theatre on Vermont and Washington. Charlie Skouras' penthouse was on top of that theater, the main offices for Fox Theatres, West Coast. Vermont was called Film Row, after all, the film distributors had offices there. At one time, Fox West Coast owned almost every theatre in town. I've got the mural from the Majestic Crest Theatre in Westwood depicting the Skouras brothers saving the world. It was done in the '40's when the Crest Theatre was built. It's quite a wonderful piece. Henry Fonda's second wife, Frances Seymour Fonda, who just happened to be Peter and Jane's mother, built The Crest Theatre.

Fanchon and Marco's Sunkist Beauties

In 1993 the City of Glendale asked producer Terry Hill to bring shows to its newly restored Alex Theatre. Terry, a longtime member of The Magic Castle, approached me with the idea of bringing back "It's Magic!" After losing the Variety Arts Theatre downtown, I had decided to devote my energies to the Magic Castle, television shows and other venues. After thirty years of continuous production, I had felt it was time to hang up the "It's Magic!" top hat, after all, we had the large Palace Theatre at the Magic Castle for the larger illusion shows now.

Terry pointed out that although magicians could be seen throughout the year at the private club, the Magic Castle, the public rarely had a chance to see these great performers. The Magic Castle had stage limitations and was restricted to audiences over twenty-one years of age. There was a real need for an exciting, full-evening family shows like "It's

Terry Hill

238

Magic!" I agreed and a new partnership was born. The Alex, with its Egyptian motif, proved to be the perfect setting. We produced "It's Magic!" for the next eight years at the Alex Theatre.

Steve Allen had volunteered to be with us at the Academy of Magical Arts Awards banquet. When Terry Hill and I were given the job of producing the Alex's Theatre 75th anniversary show in 1993, Steve Allen was our first choice for the emcee. Steve readily agreed. Steve's roots were in vaudeville and he loved talking about his vaudevillian mother, Belle Montrose. Red Baker and I met Steve when we were both teenagers. We were aspiring gag writers working for Ormond McGill... picking through the trash cans. Steve was very friendly and very helpful. We visited him often and found him to be a man who was very serious about his comedy. He was one of the nicest people I have ever met. He wasn't a magician but he was truly magical in everything he accomplished in life.

A diminutive giant in showbiz, Billy Barty was a good friend, an active member of the Magic Castle and a marvelous entertainer. Terry Hill and I produced a show called "Big Band Ballyhoo," in which Mark Nelson, a Magic Castle stage manager, received a pie in the face from Billy at the conclusion of the show. It took a lot of manipulation as Billy was riding a scooter and Mark towered over Billy with his 5'9" stocky frame. In another scene Billy went nuts at his junior drum set and his assistant had to carry him off stage, kicking and screaming— something the audiences always seemed to love when it happens to a little person. During the "Ballyhoo" show, featuring Johnny Thompson (The Great Tomsoni) as the emcee, Johnny (an original member of the Harmonicats) and Billy reminisced about working with Spike Jones in his traveling show. Spike used to love taking Billy to the red-light district in New York during the '40's and '50's and playing gags on the professional women of the era. Billy loved it all too.

*Johnny and Pam Thompson as
The Great Tomsonis*

I've been fond of the Los Angeles Conservancy not only for their love of historic theatres but also for their involvement in the South Park Task Force — a downtown LA redevelopment agency. I loved the old theatres and when we were doing the Variety Arts Theatre I was active in the South Park Task Force. Developing downtown Los Angeles

Orpheum Theater interior

was crucial to our success. The next show for the Los Angeles Conservancy in 1994 was the 100th anniversary of Orpheum vaudeville in Los Angeles. I had forgotten that the Orpheum was such a gorgeous theater. It's also in excellent condition all things considered. The theater was built in 1926. As part of the "Last Remaining Seats" series presented by the Los Angeles Conservancy once again I brought vaudeville back for one night only to help preserve and bring attention to Broadway's fabulous theatres being threatened by extinction because *nobody wants to go downtown syndrome*. I produced the show, hosted by Steve Allen.

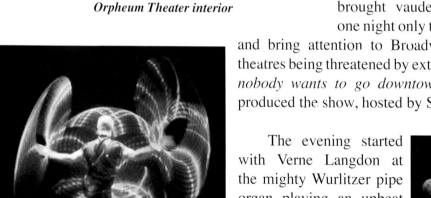

Mat Plendl

Chester Whitmore

The evening started with Verne Langdon at the mighty Wurlitzer pipe organ playing an upbeat medley of show tunes from "Paramount on Parade" to "Looney Tunes." At exactly 8 p.m. the giant organ console sunk majestically into the orchestra pit and the curtain opened on Art Deco and his Society Orchestra on stage. His big band sound filled the packed 2,200 seat Orpheum. The incomparable Steve Allen took over the stage. What a delightfully charming and very funny man. The first act, Mat Plendl, was an absolute show stopper, six dynamite minutes of gymnastics with dozens of flashy hula hoops. Nobody sleeps while Mat does his act! Then Steve brought on the Palm Springs Yacht Club, a funny musical trio. They were joined on stage by the tap dancing team of Chester Whitmore and Taps Mulligan (aka Rusty Frank). Steve Allen reminisced about being born in a trunk and about his vaudevillian mother, Belle Montrose, who had played the Orpheum many times. He treated the audience to a 1960 Kinescope film of his mother re-creating her comedy act with Steve as straight man on his "Tonight Show." I remember seeing Harry Blackstone Sr. and his big stage vaudeville revue at the Orpheum when I was a kid. Our own Harry Blackstone Jr. brought back wonderful memories

Belle Montrose & Steve Allen

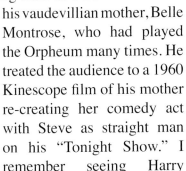

DeCastro Sisters

Harry Blackstone Jr.

as he wowed the audience with the Blackstone classics: the *Vanishing Birdcage* and *The Dancing Handkerchief*— receiving another great ovation.

Michael McGiveney donated his time to stop by on his way from Florida to Virginia to help Harry. Michael's Dad, Owen McGiveney, the quick change artiste, was an Orpheum circuit headliner. The three DeCastro Sisters showed us what showmanship is all about with a fast-moving medley of their hits from "Copacabana" to "Teach Me Tonight." The Chester Whitmore Dancers, about a dozen strong hoofers, brought the live part of the show to a palm-pounding finish.

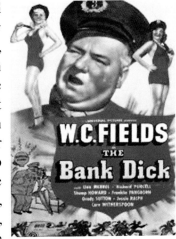

The second half featured a brand new print of the W.C. Fields classic "The Bank Dick," directed by Arthur Hiller. Bell Goren made my job as Producer very easy while Tommy O'Brien and Steve Markham made every act look great with special draperies and scenery. Steve Allen introduced a dozen or so celebrities in the audience but the one that got a double standing ovation was our own member Jonathan Winters who was there with some of the Magic Castle's Friday Lunch Bunch.

Jonathan Winters

LIVE ON STAGE

Crazy Words Crazy Tunes

A NEW MUSICAL MADNE
PRODUCED, WRITTEN AND DIRECTEI
BY MILT LARSEN AND
GENE CASEY

VO-DO-DE-O

DOES THE SPEARMINT LOSE
IT'S FLAVOR ON THE
BEDPOST OVERNIGHT

HUT SUT SONG

MAIRSY DOATS

YES, WE HAVE NO BANANA

STARRING
LON HUBER
DANIEL NANNI
AND
MARGARET TAYLOR
STAGED BY
KELLY WARD

OPENS JUNE 25, 1980
LIMITED RUN
TIN PAN ALLEY
CABARET
VARIETY ARTS CENTER
940 S. FIGUEROA STREET
LOS ANGELES

FEATURING
THE WACKIEST HIT SONGS OF THE 20's, 30's & 40's

Gene Casey-Milt Larsen musical revue "Crazy Words, Crazy Tunes" was listed in the coveted Critics Choice listing of the Sunday edition of the LA Times. It first played at the Variety Arts Theatre. Gene Casey dusted it off and brought it back to life years later at the Center Stage Theater in Woodland Hills in 1993. It enjoyed a record long run at two theatres in the Valley before it moved to the larger Westwood Playhouse for a two week run. Our good friend George Falcon put "Crazy Words, Crazy Tunes" on the cover of his Key Magazine. Another version of the same show opened in 1995 at the Palm Springs Convention Center starring Kaye Ballard, directed by Gene Casey.

Paramount Pictures contacted me in 1993 to perform my legendary tablecloth yank at the end of Gomez and Morticia's Tango dance in the "Addams Family Values." Peter Pit had given them my name to audition for my rare ability to yank a tablecloth. They had a table set up with three settings. It was a bit of a challenge since the table was round. As all champion tablecloth pullers know, it's a lot easier with a square table. Fearlessly I yanked the tablecloth and everything stayed in place. I got the job. Then came the filming day. I was at the studio bright and early and dressed in Gomez' costume. The table was set pretty much as the day before but this time with water in the goblets and ginger ale in the champagne glasses. Again, fearlessly, I yanked the cloth. While they were drying off the three actors playing *The Playboys* and the prop man replaced a couple of broken glasses, I regained my confidence to try again. At the end of the morning my score was three hits and four misses but they got their three or four seconds of footage. You can't recognize me but if you look closely you will see my back and hands that stand in for actor Raul Julia as Gomez Addams.

I also doubled for Rupert Everett in the 1996 film "Dunston Checks In" yanking a tablecloth for a five-place table setting without dropping one plate, even with four takes! It's a Faye Dunaway-Jason Alexander comedy. Lloyd Overstreet put me in touch with the prop man after he asked me if I knew anyone that does the old tablecloth gag. "Did I need anything special?" Yes… a square table! The day of the shoot came and I saw the props for the first time. You guessed it! A banquet-size round table with two tablecloths! By the way, I did it on the first take.

242

I take a lot of bows and love taking credit as the "creator and builder of The Magic Castle." That is true but the Castle might just be a grand old house if it wasn't for the concept of a club for magicians. When our fa-ther, William W. Larsen Sr. first announced the formation of the Academy of Magical Arts and Science in the pages of Genii in April of 1951 many people thought it was just a gimmick to sell sub-scriptions to the magazine. If you read his editorials you will know that he was serious about the need for an organization devoted to the advancement of the art of magic. Bill and I were very aware of Dad's devotion to the idea.

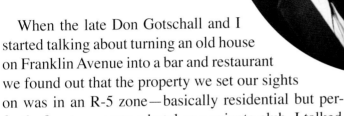

Bill and Milt

When the late Don Gotschall and I started talking about turning an old house on Franklin Avenue into a bar and restaurant we found out that the property we set our sights on was in an R-5 zone—basically residential but per-fectly fine to operate a hotel or a private club. I talked to Brother Bill about it and we agreed that the Academy of Magic Arts might be the answer. Bill loved the idea of bringing our dad's concept back to life. He offered to take on the enormous task of organizing a new not-for-profit club. Although Bill was a very successful executive at CBS Television his great love was magic. The rest is history!

The plan was I would lease the building, physically turn it into a club called the Magic Castle and sub-lease it to the AMA. Bill would put together a board of directors and work out the business details. Bill became "President for Life" of the Academy of Magical Arts. That was a half a century ago. The Larsen Brothers had no real idea of where we were heading but, it was a crazy idea and it just might—wait a minute—

It just did really work.

L-R: Dante, Erika, Heidi, Wendy, Charlie;
Bottom: Bill, Geri , Irene, Milt

The Castle is a very grand building and a tribute to all the people that have been working on it for the past 50 years but the heart and soul of the club is the solid foundation of The Academy of Magical Arts. It is a loyal membership of magicians and lovers of magic. That is totally a credit to my Brother Bill, and all the members of the boards over the years. Bill and Irene promoted the Academy at magic conventions throughout the world and the magic fraternity heard news of our club every month through the pages of Genii magazine. Bill was President for Life but sadly his life ended on February 12, 1993. Again, he left us much too soon at the age of 64 but his memory will be with us forever.

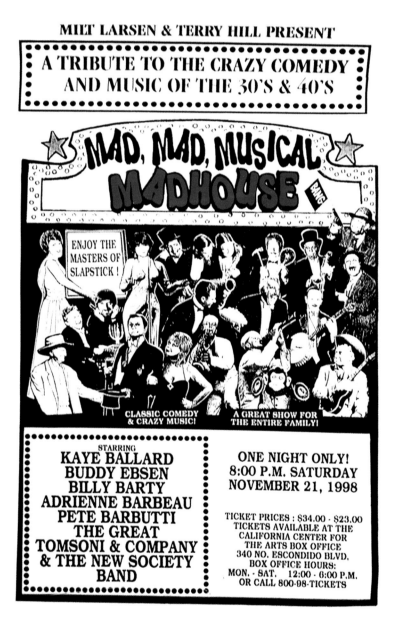

Terry Hill and I produced another stage show "Mad, Mad, Musical Madhouse" in 1998. This was a loving tribute to the great comedy bands and entertainers of the '30's and '40's. When it comes to comedy music most people think of Spike Jones and his City Slickers. Naturally we tipped our hat to Spike but we reminded the world of the great comedy acts like Professor Lamberti, who played the xylophone while strippers paraded behind him. He thought the applause was for him!

SIDETRACK—
CAESARS MAGICAL EMPIRE
A FIFTY MILLION DOLLAR + BET
AT CAESARS PALACE

In writing this book my researcher/editor Carol Marie (The Barracuda) and I tried to avoid any duplication of stories in our other Castle books, (not an easy task). In my Magic Castle: Hollywood Illusion book of anecdotes about the club and its personalities, I related the story about how Caesars Magical Empire came to be. I'll recap just a bit of that story and bring you up to date.

In Hollywood, it's not what you know it's whom you know that counts and I knew Henry Gluck. Who is Henry Gluck you ask? Well, he was a long-time friend, member of the Magic Castle, brother of Dick Sherman's wife Elizabeth and the Chairman of Caesars World Inc. It wasn't difficult to get a luncheon with Henry to pitch a casino game show idea I had, but he wasn't buying what I was pitching. He wanted a Magic Castle in Las Vegas. Caesars always had a soft spot for magic. Army Grant, Alan Bregman and I had talked about a dinner-and-magic theatre over twenty years ago but it never seemed to jell. Jimmie Grippo was the house magician for Caesars Palace Court for twenty years. I said there was no place in Las Vegas where people could enjoy intimate magic. Henry asked me if I could put 2,500 people a day through an *intimate* Las Vegas Magic Castle. If I could work this out, it was worth another lunch.

At the second luncheon I told Henry I had done extensive research and came up with an interesting fact: Julius Caesar had created an underground city for the magicians of his realm to keep them under his control. Caesar would be able to entertain senators and valued politicians and yet keep the devious magicians at bay underground. When the ruins of the lost catacombs of the conjurors were unearthed magic historians discovered it was the brainchild of the Roman General Lucullus, a famed epicure who was credited with importing the first cherry trees from Asia Minor in 79 B.C. Lucullus convinced Julius Caesar that magicians of the time should practice their art away from the public eye. He reasoned that these magicians, through their skills in magic, could convince the citizens that they were miracle workers. By controlling them, Caesar could use their powers for his own goals.

While other performers were entertaining the Roman masses by dodging lions in the coliseum, these magicians were treated royally and given their own world in which to practice their magical arts. What if we could re-create this hidden city? It would be a series of catacombs under the catacombs of Rome. Guests would gather in a large room filled with worldly delights to enjoy Caesar's hospitality. Then, at a given signal, the entire room became a huge elevator that would sink to a level below the known catacombs. Visitors would find themselves, escorted by beautiful slaves, to a magical dining area where they would experience a grand feast designed by General Lucullus. The General loved magic and the magicians loved to eat.

Henry asked me if this was true. I replied, "Julius Caesar isn't around to deny it. Why not?!" A man of action the Chairman of the Board of Caesars World simply said: "Let's build it!"

The Séance Room was a unique and intimate chamber of magic designed to host VIP guests.

After guests were escorted through the Catacomb Maze they were ushered into one of the ten door-ways leading to the dining chambers of the gods for a three-course meal, hosted by a sorcerer.

Mysterious Amphora Fountain

*The Chamber of Destiny was an opulent holding room that magically
transported the guests to the Magical Empire below.*

Gary Goddard's renowned theme park design company Landmark Entertainment was given the job. I was hired as Creative Consultant and paid handsomely to oversee the magic and provide Magic Castle type gimmicks and effects for the project. After four years of brainstorming, model building, researching, scripting, composing, computer programming, testing, casting, and rehearsing Caesars Magical Empire opened on June 18, 1996.

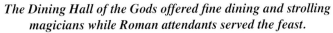

*The Dining Hall of the Gods offered fine dining and strolling
magicians while Roman attendants served the feast.*

The dragons of Wu-Han guarded the entrance to the Secret Pagoda, an ornate theater of Chinese origin where some of the best close-up magicians in the world performed nightly.

The designers did it justice: Celestial Courts, Chambers of Destiny, a Catacomb maze, Grotto Bar, Spirit Bar, Sanctum Secorum, Secret Pagoda, Infinity Hallway and dining chambers for sumptuous three-course feasts. Everything was designed down to minuscule detail. It was spectacular! This was a Las Vegas, Disney-like, Magic Castle creation with a 70-foot rotunda, a magical elevator that transported visitors to the sub-terranean catacombs below and over a dozen magicians that performed daily. Caesars

Magical Empire closed in 2002 after only six years in operation as Caesars underground magical realm to provide Celine Dion her own concert hall.

Our own Peter Pit, the unstoppable force of magic, was the very first act to perform on the stage of the Sultan's Palace at Caesars Magical Empire. After thirty solid years of Castle devotion and love, Peter moved to Las Vegas to work at Caesars Magical Empire and with his other Las Vegas clients. Peter and I worked closely booking acts for Caesar's. When I sold Henry Gluck on the concept of the Magical Empire, Alan Bregman was the talent booker for all of Caesars World. He had a personal list of the greatest names in Vegas history. He could call Frank, or Sammy or Dean at any time — they were all pals. Between the time we got the green light to build the 50 million+ Empire, Alan suffered a stroke and was incapacitated. His assistant took over his job. Linda Blair was a former entertainer and relied on Peter Pit and myself to suggest the acts for the new venture. Caesars employed fourteen magicians. Linda, like many of the Caesars Palace staff, couldn't quite figure out where or what the Empire was all about. One morning I received a call from Linda. She was concerned about a flash flood that had flooded much of the Las Vegas strip and the Caesars parking lots. She was worried that we might be out of business... after all, the catacombs were a hundred feet underground. I carefully explained that the elevator was an illusion and the entire building was safely above ground. She was amazed.

Part of the testing procedure involved building one of the twelve dining rooms in a warehouse in the Las Vegas industrial area. After watching a demonstration Arlene and I didn't want to wait for a cab so we started walking back to the hotel. It was a hot day and a hard walk. No cabs and no cars. Then a car came up behind us and honked — it was old magician friend Bill Smith and his wife. Bill is the owner of Advance Magic and well-known as the builder of illusions. They gave us a welcome lift to Caesars. Bill asked what we were doing and we told him about the new venture and introduced him to the project head at Landmark. He got the lucrative job of building all the special magic props for the Empire. Moral: Be kind to hitchhikers.

Santum Secorum

Max Maven was reduced in size to a small hologram doing magic on the spirit back bar.

Close-up Room

Hello Dolly Bar

Joe Hoffman

I met Joe Hoffman when I was writing the Jim Nabors Show in 1977. Joe was the Art Director. He had heard of John Shrum but had never met him. When John passed away, Joseph Hoffman took the art direction of the Magic Castle under his wing and started the renovation of the lobby to make the first impression upon entering the club a real experience, complete with a hand sculpted ceiling frieze. Joe spent hours of his time making the fountain area look like something out of a castle in Europe. Like John before him, Joe devoted hundreds of hours to the Castle, striving to make it the most magical place on earth. Joe did all this work for the love of the club. Joe had created a wonderful new look for the Close-up Gallery that involved a hanging framework. My hobby is woodworking so turning Joe's plan into reality was fun and an artistic challenge. Then he gave the Parlour of Prestidigitation a face-lift. The W.C. Fields bar was redesigned, as was the classroom entrance. Faux finishes, wood graining and stained glass added depth to his designs.

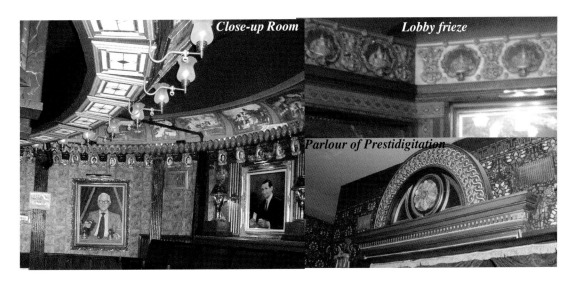

Close-up Room

Lobby frieze

Parlour of Prestidigitation

Magicians never have bad luck on Friday the 13th. Or so I had thought. Friday, the 13th of November 1998, I drove out to the valley to pick up a six-pack of seltzer for our "Big Band Ballyhoo" show in Arizona. I parked my convertible Chrysler LeBaron on Cahuenga across the street from my favorite liquor store for my weekly yogurt and lottery ticket purchase. A couple of minutes later I looked across the street and the car was gone! I have never had a car stolen before. It was a really weird feeling. A 911 call got quick action from two very understanding officers who couldn't resist a few

lines about the magician's vanishing car. They gave me a free ride back to the Castle that got a few more laughs from our smoking members outside as we drove up in the black and white. The reality of the missing car didn't really hit me until later. Arlene drove her car to the airport and we flew to Phoenix. We flew back on Sunday and Arlene drove to Santa Barbara so I really wouldn't have used my car anyway. Still the idea of the whole thing ruined my weekend. All of my Castle, house and apartment/office keys were in the car. What if the thief was smart enough to know where the keys fit? What about the compressor and nail gun in the trunk? Would a car thief hold up a bank with my air gun? And what about the six bottles of seltzer in the back seat? Would the guy go out and do his own version of "Truth or Consequences?"

I got a call from Officer Mesa and the nice folks at North Hollywood Police Station that my car had been found and was waiting for me at the impound lot. Remarkably, the car was unharmed in any way; the keys, the air gun, the seltzer bottles and all the trash were still in place. Apparently the thief merely saw an opportunity to get a free ride to wherever he was going. So I'm a very lucky guy who learned a really valuable lesson: Never, never, never leave your top down and your keys in the car—unless you want to be a magician with the disappearing automobile.

My lovely wife Arlene hand made centerpieces for many of the Academy of Magical Arts Awards Banquets. The Award Banquet in 1998 was particularly challenging and she worked for weeks on the design. Each centerpiece involved 8 wooden sticks drilled with 38 dowels and 76 holes. That's not too bad until you multiply the centerpiece by 70 tables: 560 sticks, 2,660 dowels and 5,320 holes. I helped by drilling those #*%##@ holes! They were wonderful centerpieces created by a rather remarkable person to honor a great magician, Harry Blackstone Jr.

Milt and Arlene

Geri watched her two sons grow up to carve their own notches in the world of magic. Mother's entire life was magic and music and she spread the warm glow of magic to everyone she ever knew. She was a beautiful and remarkable woman. My dear mother passed away at the age of 92 in 1998. She had three full and separate lives with three husbands, my dad—William Larsen Sr., Art Baker, and finally Rubin Jaffe. Bill and I had three wonderful fathers, and one incredible mother!

My mother was an excellent writer. Somewhere in our family tree the Conrads were linked with Henry Wadsworth Longfellow. Geri wrote a book of poetry and later a couple of novels, "Diary of a Magician's Wife" and "Nothing Up My Sleeve." Both would make great TV series ideas today. She also wrote a delightful children's book,

"Peterkin, the Magic Rabbit." In addition to her magical poetry she also painted the artwork for the book. "Peterkin, the Magic Rabbit" is a wonderful salute to my multi-talented mother and it is a credit to a lady I call *the barracuda*. Her name is Carol Marie Rettenwander who has always gone by the name of Carol Marie. She wrote the Magic Castle tour book (Milt Larsen's Magical Mystery Tour of Hollywood's Most Amazing Landmark, The Magic Castle) and edited my "Magic Castle:Hollywood Illusion"—an anecdotal recollection of the beginnings of the Magic Castle.

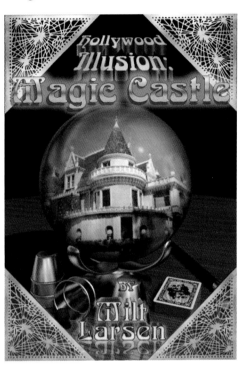

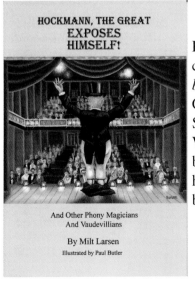

She also edited my crazy book about Professor Hockmann, illustrated by Paul Butler—my tongue-in-cheek response to the Masked Magician. Calling her *the barracuda* is a very complimentary and loving term. Carol, in the real world, is a film production accountant. She is the most efficient person I have ever known. When she tackles a project, like the beastly fish—the barracuda, she will not let go. None of my books would have ever been printed, including this one, if it hadn't been for *the barracuda*.

My writing mentor Snag Werris nailed it when he said, "Most writers can't write unless they have a deadline. The page is blank until you know that you won't get that paycheck if the script wasn't in on time." Carol Marie created those deadlines.

During one of her hiatuses, Carol Marie resurrected, edited and put together the unpublished children's poem and illustration book that my mother had penned, "Peterkin, the Magic Rabbit." On Mother's 100th birthday we honored her memory by finally publishing the book after about 60 years of it being on my office shelf. Thanks to the barracuda, Geri had a great 100th birthday (with Dad, Brother Bill, John Shrum, Dai Vernon, Jay Ose, Art Baker, Rubin Jaffe and Henry Wadsworth Longfellow) in a world we can only imagine.

NEW CENTURY 2000— FULL SPEED AHEAD

I worked as a consultant on a wonderful project, a three-hour television documentary special on the history of magic in 2000. The show, "Now You See It" was aired on the Learning Channel. Magical icons Carl Ballantine and Harry Anderson were taped at the Magic Castle. I had the honor of being interviewed for the show. Through the interviews and performances, it would be a real Who's Who of magic.

Harry Anderson

Carl Ballantine

Doug Henning said no thanks to an interview or providing archival footage for the show via his representation. That was a pity. Doug was a major influence in changing the art of magic. Before his hit Broadway show "The Magic Show" in the early '70's, magic was considered very much an ancient art. When Doug bounded on the scene as an energetic flower child he brought new youth and enthusiasm to our beloved art form.

Doug Henning

The Broadway show led to a series of hit TV specials which proved magic could be successful on television. Before his Broadway hit Doug studied magic with our own Professor Dai Vernon here at the Castle, made possible with a grant from the Canadian government. He was too young to be admitted to the Castle so we had to bring Doug in through the back door to study with Dai up in our third floor library.

By his own choice Doug had faded away from the active magic scene over the years. He was a modest and very private man as well as being very active in Canadian politics and plans for a future theme park. Doug Henning deserved a place in the history of magic and I was personally disappointed that he wouldn't be part of the "Now You See It" documentary. I tried to reach him personally to discuss the documentary to no avail. The following week Doug showed up at the Magic Castle with a group of super VIP's to enjoy the Young Adults Night. We had a nice chat and found that he knew almost nothing about the project. He not only agreed to allow the producers to use some footage from the Johnny Carson show but was also enthusiastic about being interviewed for the show. Doug had lost none of his love of the art of magic and he bubbled with energy as if he was still one of the junior magicians.

"A Night of a Thousand Laughs," a fund-raiser for the Alex Theater in Glendale, 2001, was a tribute to the late Steve Allen, produced by Terry Hill and myself and featured Bill Allen, Steve's son, conducting Steve Allen's seventeen piece band, Art Linkletter was emcee with George Bugatti, Sid Caesar, Norm Crosby, Stan Freberg, Don Knotts, Rich Little, Marilyn McCoo & Billy Davis, Louis Nye, Tom Poston, Mickey Rooney and Jonathan Winters. It was an incredible evening. Steve was a beloved professional who had the love and respect of everyone in show business.

L-R: Art Linkletter, Norm Crosby, Sid Caesar, Stan Freberg, Don Knotts, Rich Little
Bottom L-R:Marilyn McCoo and Billy Davis, Louis Nye, Tom Poston, Mickey Rooney, Jonathan Winters.

Milt, Johnathan, Billy McComb

One night at the Magic Castle I was chatting with The Amazing Johnathan whose outlandish comedy magic act was a sensation in Las Vegas. He asked me if I had ever thought of doing my comedy magic act in Las Vegas. He thought I might be a good act to open for Billy McComb who was the opening act for The Amazing Johnathan. I loved the idea. If nothing else I could say I played Las Vegas!

Arlene and I left early in the morning to drive from Santa Barbara to Las Vegas where I was thrilled that I was booked to do my carpenter act at the Golden Nugget Hotel. We habitually never listen to the radio on long trips, preferring to listen to CDs. Of course, I love to play my old radio shows, which, of course, Arlene changes to Strauss waltzes the minute I fall asleep. She drives, I sleep. I thought the date of September 11, 2001 would go down in history as the day Milt Larsen opened in Las Vegas. Instead, like Pearl Harbor, it was a day in infamy—a day we would like to forget but will always remember.

When we left home in Santa Barbara we knew nothing about the tragic events of September 11th, 2001. We stopped for gas and noticed the attitude of folks seemed strange but that was it. We went back to listening to the CDs. On the outskirts of Vegas we finally turned on the radio and all the shocking news poured forth. All of a sudden we were hearing news that was almost unbelievable.

Amazing Johnathan

That was an amazing night. Although every major show on the strip closed for fear of possible attacks on tourists' attractions, Johnathan decided to keep his show open. We played to a packed house and a somber audience replaced their helpless feeling, escaping to the world of wacky comedy. Johnathan was outrageous as always, hilarious and rightfully earns the title: Amazing. The Golden Nugget Hotel's Ballroom Theater is a beautiful room and well-suited to the intimacy of his show. At the end of the show Johnathan said a few moving words and the audience gave him a standing ovation. The next day every casino in Vegas stopped for three minutes of respectful silence. It was an incredible and very emotional experience—the familiar sound of bells and clanking slot machines was replaced by audible weeping of the inmates of Sin City.

I became a member of the Hollywood Chamber of Commerce in 2005. I got the opportunity to work with Johnny Grant, the seemingly tireless honorary mayor of Hollywood. He was a champion of Tinseltown who worked hard to maintain and even raise the image of the world's motion picture capital. Johnny was there when Bill and I received our star on the Hollywood Walk of Fame in 2006. I first met Johnny in the

Johnny Grant

'50's when Mr. Grant was a guest star on "Truth or Consequences." He was a member of the Magic Castle for many, many years. He was the true magician of Hollywood because he kept it alive. Johnny lived at the Hollywood Roosevelt just a block away from the Magic Castle. Sometimes I'd walk down the street and visit him. He'd be having breakfast and I'd join him. We would often discuss the old Warner Theater and the possibility of its restoration. Mr. Grant was instrumental in resuscitating Hollywood over the years by supporting such projects as the then Kodak Theater and the Hollywood & Highland retail and entertainment center. He was best known as the Hollywood host alongside more than five hundred celebrities he inducted into the Hollywood Walk of Fame. His mission in life was bringing the Tinseltown story to everyone. He hosted red carpet Oscar arrivals and Walk of Fame festivities, appeared in bit parts in movies and produced Hollywood's annual Christmas Parade.

The old phonograph records I collected are used today for a weekly radio show. Since our home is in Santa Barbara I was a frequent guest on a popular morning radio show on KZBN AM in Santa Barbara hosted by Ron "The Baron" Herron. The station was owned by Bob Newhart. They gave me a weekend spot for a show I called, "Hear Them Again for the First Time." I started playing the old 78 records that I claimed were so old they are brand new to today's generation. I recorded the show every week at my studio next to the Magic Castle in Hollywood. (Today's radio stations don't have the

About two dozen of them love Milt Larsen's fun-filled Weekend Radio Hour

HEAR THEM AGAIN *(for the first time!)*

equipment to play those old records. I have the original studio console turntables from NBC's Radio City at Sunset and Vine.)

The show featured crazy novelty songs from the roaring '20's and '30's, rare antique performances by many forgotten stars of yesteryear. Every week Oscar winning composer Richard M. Sherman honored Tin Pan Alley songwriters he met in his childhood through

Professor Harry Hockmann

his father, Al Sherman. And we were visited by an old vaudevillian Professor Hockmann who played one extremely rare acoustical record from the dusty vaults while recollecting unbelievable stories of the world's oldest magician. (Hockmann, of course, is my alter-ego.)

Not too long after I started the show on KZBN, Bob Newhart sold the station to the Santa Barbara News Press. The newspaper changed the format of the show to an all news and talk station, which meant it no longer had a license to Ventura's AM radio station KKZZ. After about a year on that station, they too changed their format and no longer played music but one of the stations liked "Hear Them Again For the First Time" and

Bob Newhart

put it on as a weekend feature. It has been running weekly ever since. The Sherman and Larsen segments about the songwriters spun off to another hour show on CRN called, "Hit Parade Cavalcade." All of this turned into another one hour radio show on the network's weekend schedule, "CRN's Classic Comedy Hour." I have always loved radio on my magical journey through life and obviously I do these shows for love rather than money. (Although you can always support the show with your sponsorship. For information: www.CRNTALK.com or www.CRN.net. We are now heard on cable radio on TV channels throughout the United States and throughout the world on the internet. Thanks for listening!

In 2006, we celebrated the 50th Anniversary of "It's Magic!" at the newly built Kodak theatre (now the Dolby Theatre) at Hollywood Blvd. and Highland just blocks from The Magic Castle. Designed by David Rockwell, the stage is one of the largest in the United States, specifically designed for the Annual Academy Awards (Oscars) with a seating capacity of up to 3,332 people. "It's Magic!" dedicated the performances to the memories of Bill Larsen, Jr., John Shrum, and Earl Witscher. We featured The Pendragons, Jeff McBride, Kevin James, Dimmare, Darren Romeo, Juliana Chen, Rich Bloch, Jason Latimer, Rick Thomas and the Passing Zone. Jason Alexander from "Seinfeld" was our host, directed by Dale Hindman.

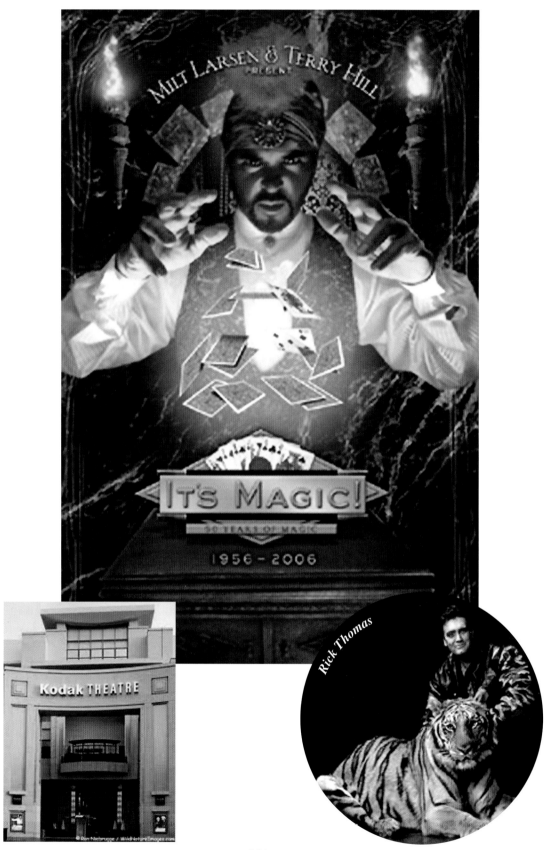

Kevin James

Jeff McBride

Darren Romeo

Passing Zone

Rich Bloch

Jason Latimer

The Pendragons

Juliana Chen

Dimmare

Jason Alexander

"It's Magic!" 50th Anniversary
Kodak Theater, Hollywood 2006

On September 15, 2006 the Honorary Mayor of Hollywood, Johnny Grant, and the Hollywood Chamber of Commerce President/CEO Leron Gubler were on hand to dedicate the 2,317th star on the Hollywood Walk of Fame to Bill and Milt Larsen. Guest speaker was "Price Is Right" host Bob Barker. Irene accepted the star plaque on behalf of her late husband. The star is located at the northeast corner of Hollywood Blvd. and Orange, directly across from the star of Harry Houdini. My old pal and longtime comedy song collaborator, Dick Sherman and his brother, Robert B. Sherman, were honored with a star just across the Boulevard. I kidded him about his star being out in front of "Hooters" and a lingerie shop. He responded by saying that the Larsen Brothers star was in the driveway to the famed Grauman's Chinese Theatre. I felt better when they built the fifty-million dollar Madame Tussauds Wax

Hollywood Walk of Fame Star dedication for the Larsen Brothers

Museum. Now Bill and I are in the sidewalk in front of the wax figure of Marilyn Monroe. The Larsen star is directly south of the Magic Castle and you are welcome to come and stand on our star anytime!

"Magic Castle After Dark" for the A&E Channel was a half-hour live-to-tape special featuring some incredible magicians from the World Famous Magic Castle in Hollywood with Executive Producers Jude Prest, Dale Hindman and Milt Larsen. It focused on the intimate magic of the Castle and its half hour vanished like magic. The executives at A&E dumped the show since they didn't want any competition to their

L-R: Nathan Gibson, Joel Ward, Shoot Ogawa
Christopher Hart, Andrew Goldenhersh,
Joycee Beck, Ivan Amodei

then very hot Criss Angel "Mindfreak" show. It premiered Saturday December 16th, 2006 after "Biography—Houdini" that aired at ten a.m. "Magic Castle *After Dark*," at 11 *in the morning*—like "Mindfreak" TV networks are weird!

My wife, Arlene, is the number one *themed fund-raisers* and party designer. It's amazing to watch her turn something very ordinary into something

extraordinary for the Magic Castle, the Awards Banquet or her fund-raisers. Some of her more memorable parties are the Royal Flush and the Surprise Parties.

Milt and Dale Hindman   *Arlene and Milt*

Terry Schoonhoven, artist, muralist, and friend of the Castle was Joe Hoffman's friend who was invited to create a piece of art to go with the new fountain renovation. What he created was a tiled mural that captured the essence of the Castle and the spirit of Bill, who the fountain honors. I remembered approaching Terry and asking him about the idea of doing something indelible that would commemorate Bill's life and contribution to the Castle.

The idea for making the fountain a tribute to Bill Larsen Jr. was Dale Hindman's and taking all these ideas and input, including the tour book and going through the Castle, Terry left that day smiling and assuring me that he would come up with something. Terry called me a week later and asked me if I wanted to see his concept for the mural. When I got to his studio, I saw laid out on a worktable his sketch of Milt and Bill. Terry had chosen the picture of the Lane Mansion, pre-Castle renovations, with Milt and Bill levitating the Castle to be, torn from its foundations of stability and upper class propriety. Terry's sense of humor put a rabbit climbing the steps to the missing front door. Above the rabbit head is an exclamation point. When I asked what that exclamation point was for he shrugged and smiled— "Magic" he whispered.

Bill's old *Lester Lake Guillotine* had been sitting at the Brookledge for many years. It is an original Thayer Lester Lake prop which was used by Bill Larsen Sr. Brother Bill can be seen using it in the film "Houdini." Johnny Gaughan rebuilt it for Bill and it is a beautiful piece of magical equipment. I asked Irene if I could use it for a week in the Palace. I didn't want to do the Carpenter Act this time around. Doing multiple shows for seven days creates an awful lot of broken glass and spilt milk. So I decided to go with a couple of standards from the Larsen family act. I performed it, using Dad's old patter, Monday and Tuesday but noticed it wasn't working right. On the last show Tuesday night my presentation of this classic effect would have made Valentino happy,

Standing L-R: William W. Larsen Sr, Geri, Milt;
Kneeling: Audience member

luckily the only thing that was hurt was my professional pride. Wednesday night I faked my way through a couple of dumb tricks having spent the better part of the day at Home Depot and in the shop with the guillotine. Thursday my wife, Arlene, came down from Santa Barbara to work with her decorating committee and brought along my wrist guillotine, same patter, smaller version.

Arlene and I were going to throw a huge party to celebrate our tenth year anniversary but we opted for a romantic dinner for two instead. I looked up the traditional wedding anniversary gift for year number ten and found it is tin or aluminum. So I got Arlene a can of beer.

Whitey Roberts was the last of the true vaudevillians. For years there was a small advertisement in the weekly Variety which simply stated: "Whitey Roberts—Always Working." That was a true statement. He worked actively up to the late '90's. He was a regular at our Mayfair Music Hall and the Variety Arts shows. Whitey's act was perfection. He was an elegant dancer and loved to dance with the ladies anywhere. Whitey was an encyclopedia of show business and added a great deal to the archives of the Society for the Preservation of Variety Arts. One of the most amazing collections of jokes, dozens of loose-leaf note books filled with thousands of jokes, each hand typed and carefully pasted in the books and indexed by categories was donated by Whitey. He used to say it was the finest joke collection in the world because he claimed he had used each and every joke in the books.

Carl Carlsson was a magician, juggler, plate spinner, bell ringer—you name it. I always considered him the ultimate vaudevillian. On "Truth or Consequences" I would come up with an idea for an act involving a switch on an old vaudevillian act. In pitching the idea at the writer's meeting our producer would say, "Great, but who does that act?" I would always reply. "The Carlssons." Then I'd call Carl and Ruth and ask if they did the act. Carl would always say they had the props and they did the act. "Yah —yah... ve do dat!" I'm sure they built the stuff overnight. They never let me down.

Jean Cantor was Bill's personal secretary and assistant. She started working at the Castle in the bookkeeping department. One day Bill came to me and said Jean was really a lousy bookkeeper and he was going to have to let her go. Before he could fire her, Jean told Bill that she was a lousy bookkeeper and her real talent was in administration. She wanted him to try her out as his personal assistant. The rest is history. She was an excellent assistant.

In the heyday of vaudeville there were many big time vaudeville circuits. The

Bob Hope

biggest was Keith-Albee who booked the Palace Theatres of the East Coast. The Orpheum Circuit started in San Francisco as a west coast operation. Later they merged and became Keith-Albee Orpheum later merging with Radio Pictures to form RKO. Gus Sun was considered the number one "small time" vaudeville circuit. He started a theatre in Springfield, Ohio shortly after the turn-of-the-century. In 1906 he was booking three houses and by the next year seventy houses in Ohio and Pennsylvania. By 1926 Gus Sun was booking over three hundred houses! The Gus Sun circuit was the proving ground for many future headliners. One of the youngsters proved to be Bob

Hope. My association with Bob was mainly in helping him research various vaudeville questions. He was always a gentleman and his daughter Linda and her staff were always a joy to work with.

Spike Jones was one of the more interesting people I have ever met. He was a fine musician and an absolute master of the sight gag. I always thought Spike got his original inspiration for the comedy band from The Milt and Frank Britton Band, popular in the '20's and '30's. He said he had heard of them but had never seen their act. The Britton Band made a Paramount short in the early '30's so I invited Spike over to the Brookledge and ran a print of it for him. He said the Britton Band was similar only in the fact that the slapstick was hilarious. Milt Britton's gimmick was that the band was absolutely elegant. As they played a classical selection one of the musicians accidentally hits another with his instrument. The mayhem builds and the orchestra ends up in total destruction. Spike loved it.

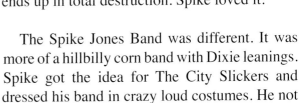

Spike Jones

The Spike Jones Band was different. It was more of a hillbilly corn band with Dixie leanings. Spike got the idea for The City Slickers and dressed his band in crazy loud costumes. He not only murdered the classics but he took on the greatest popular hits of the day. A song would start with an absolutely magnificent straight rendition and then all hell would break loose as Jones and some of the finest musicians in the business would murder the song. I produced an LP with the musicians who used to play with Spike. We called it the New Society Band and it featured such stars of the Jones band as George Rock on trumpet and Joe Siracusa on shotgun.

Sir Frederick Gas & The City Slickers

Sir Frederick Gas, in the tailcoat, who played a branch and twig like a violin brought a priceless donation to the Society—the Stradivarius of Twigs. He would play the branch as if it was a violin creating an eerie and peculiar sound with his voice. He gave me the original branch and the bow complete with phony leaves. It has its own violin case and it took its place alongside Billy Barty's bass fiddle and the Feedlebaum exploding cello.

Sandy Spillman presided over the Houdini Séance for most of the 1970's and into the '80s. He had planned a lecture on the upcoming schedule by all three of our primary séance mediums, E. Raymond Carlyle (Ed Fowler), Sandy Spillman and Leo Kostka. Sandy made a séance LP in 1973, which was released on our Electric Lemon label and is now a collector's item.

No one will ever fully appreciate the work member Tom Ruff has put into the creation of the new séance effects. He has introduced theme park technology into our show. I used to make séance gimmicks out of wood, paper clips and gaffers tape. Leo made the best out of stuff that would work some of the time. Tom has replaced miles of worn out wire and relays with state-of-the-art pneumatics. I call him the Phantom of the Attic since he spends hours creating his magic in the unseen spaces of the Castle. He does all this as a volunteer, moonlighting from his real job of running a major sound studio.

Medium Leo Kostka

Jeremy Beadle was a hugely popular television presenter. He fronted TV's hit candid camera show "Beadle's About." I worked with Jeremy as a consultant when he did a version of Ralph Edward's "Truth

Jeremy Beadle

or Consequences" in England. That show was called "Game For A Laugh." It was a pivotal show in the history of British television and was the first show that allowed ITV to win the Saturday night ratings battle with the BBC. His hugely popular "Beadle's About" TV show made him as familiar a face in the U.K. as Johnny Carson was in the States. When Jeremy entered a room people would run and hide fearing that they would be the next victims of his pranks. I didn't realize how really popular he was until we invited him to lunch with us in Santa Barbara on one of his visits to California. We lunched at the popular Harbor Restaurant on the wharf. As we were lunching a voice came from across the room, "Beadle's about!" and shortly his fans surrounded our table. Our visits to London were never complete without a pub-crawl with Jeremy. Once he gave Arlene and I a fabulous tour of Windsor Castle. Everyone seemed to know him and he had access to rooms normally off limits to tourists. When I complimented him on his knowledge of the Castle he explained that one of his first jobs was a Windsor Castle Tour Guide. He was a prolific writer and authored many books. He loved lists. Regular readers of my Magic Castle Friday Lunch News column know that I often start by recalling an event that happened in history. One of the books I use as a brain starter is Jeremy Beadle's "Today's the Day!"

Joe Weber and Lew Fields opened their Weber and Fields Music Hall in New York City in 1896. The biggest stars on Broadway loved playing the small music hall: Lillian Russell, Peter Dalley, Neville Collier, Trixie Friganza, David Warfield, Flo Templeton. They played it for fun and love, certainly not for the money. My early fascination with the comedy team of Joe Weber and Lew Fields goes back to the early '50's. I visited a favorite store that often had interesting books and memorabilia. The owner knew of my passion for the past and showed me a cardboard box. He said it was stuff he really couldn't sell because the box contained old scripts and other ephemera from an old comedy star. He would sell the entire box for twenty-five dollars. To me, it was like buying the interior of King Tut's Tomb. That little box contained material from Joe Weber's estate. In reading the scripts with handwritten notes by Weber, I found that their comedy routines were the basis of the classic comedy of the comedy team Abbott and Costello and their hilarious "Who's on First" baseball sketch.

This ignited a spark that grew into a glowing ember many years later when I brought up the idea of creating a musical show about Weber and Fields to Dick Sherman. Dick had collaborated with me for over a half a century on various projects. All through the years the idea of a musical about Weber and Fields kept surfacing.

Weber & Fields

In the early '80's Dick and I wrote some songs and I produced a show we called "Little Old Broadway" in the small theatre at the Variety Arts Theater in downtown Los Angeles. The show was fun and got good reviews but the writers knew it just didn't have what a really good musical must have—a story. In fact, we even called the show a "Revusical." At that time both Dick and I were busy with other activities and the project was put on the shelf. That glowing ember had become a forgotten ash.

Joe Hoffman was a good friend and art director for the Magic Castle and my other projects. He found the script in my office, read it and asked if he could research Weber and Fields to find that elusive story.

The story that Joe found is based on fact. In 1899 Weber and Fields were the unsung heroes of Broadway. As independent producers, they challenged the then all-powerful theater syndicate in New York. The *King of Broadway,* George M. Cohan, had worked with Weber and Fields before he became famous. With that as an inspiration, Joe, Dick and I started developing a new book for the musical. We enlisted the talents of a brilliant man who was a member of the Magic Castle. Bruce Gordon was a top *Imagineer* designer for Disney. He was well known to Dick and Joe and we asked him to come on board as Executive Editor. Bruce had a rare ability to see the flaws in our otherwise perfect work. He was very outspoken and was not afraid of making very construction criticism.

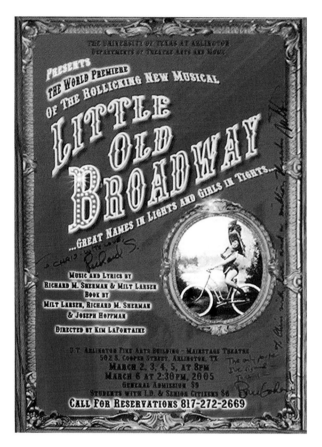

At that time Joe Hoffman had a longtime friend at the University of Texas in Arlington, Texas. Kim LaFountaine was head of the drama department. Every year the University was allowed to produce one original musical. Kim jumped at the chance to direct an original musical by one of the Sherman Brothers. Under Kim's direction, they produced a fully-staged version of "Little Old Broadway" in 2007. It was an amazing, professional production and it gave us confidence that today's world might be ready for a good old-fashioned, sing-able musical.

We were able to see the weak spots, delete them, write new material and create a new version with a change in the name—"Pazzazz!" (By the way, that was a word Weber and Fields coined back in 1896 to describe their extravaganzas at the Weber & Fields Broadway Music Hall. Your friendly computer spell checker will tell you it is spelled Pizzazz. That was a word used in Vogue Magazine back in the '30's. So, please note we are correct and the rest of the world is wrong! There is a wonderful World War I song about a mother singing of her son in the parade: "They Were All Out of Step But Jim."

Arlene and I decided to produce "Pazzazz!" ourselves. Normally, in the wonderful world of show business, a producer will option a play and then raise the money to produce it. We had a backer's party at our home in Santa Barbara and invited many of our millionaire friends to attend. Our friends were impressed and we said we'd get back to them with the investment details. We never did. Arlene and I decided we didn't really want any partners other than our own creative staff. The first rule of the theater is: "Never use your own money."

Well, what the hell, life had been good to us, so after all, how much could a musical cost? We found out! The Bank of Montecito had plenty of money and they were happy to loan us a bunch of it.

Arlene Larsen was Co-Executive Producer. As Arlene Zamiara she started in the costume business at the early age of sixteen, working with the Carousel Theatre in West Covina. She was lucky to have worked with some of the greats like Jack Benny, Reginald Gardner, Marilyn Maxwell and more. After the Carousel Theater closed, she moved over to television at the NBC studios to work on shows like Dean Martin, Phyllis Diller, Sonny and Cher, "Murder She Wrote," Air Wolf, Street Hawk and "Laugh-In." Shortly thereafter she started her own business "Zam" and worked in every media from television, theater, film nightclubs and rock music venues.

Arlene was involved in every aspect of the production of the musical. She created over one hundred-fifty elaborate costumes for "Pazzazz!" Joe Hoffman designed over a dozen scenic drops but they had to be made in a union scenery shop. Our musical director, Richard Allen, orchestrated the score for sixteen musicians. We hired a cast, casting director, director, choreographer, procured rehearsal halls, dealt with publicity,

Joey D'Auria as Lew Weber, Dale Kristien as Lillian Russell, Granada Theatre "Pazzazz!"

and on and on. Compared to the average cost of mounting a Broadway musical, we brought the show in at an amazingly low cost but it was still quite an investment. We broke in the musical at Citrus College and then opened for our world premiere at the Granada Theater in Santa Barbara.

The Granada Theatre, equipped with lovely Spanish fixtures and Moorish architecture, had fourteen dressing rooms on five levels and a huge Wurlitzer organ. It was Santa Barbara's first and only eight-story building that survived the 1925 earthquake with

Poster design by Al Rosson

almost no damage. The 1926 former vaudeville house was completely renovated in 2008 at the cost of over fifty million dollars to adapt the theater for live performances. The 1,400 seat vintage theatre was the perfect venue for "Pazzazz!" We were the first original musical to play the new performing arts center. The Granada production received excellent reviews but it still needed a lot of work. Our good industry friends who saw the show at Citrus College and Santa Barbara made very valuable suggestions and it was rewrite time again. Someone once said, "The final rewrite is the day the show closes."

Why did we decide to create a full scale, ready-to-roll Broadway touring company of a show that might not ever get to Broadway? In playing our "It's Magic!" in beautiful performing art centers up and down the West Coast and talking to the theater managers, we found there was a shortage of shows that would appeal to audiences of all ages. This would be a perfect show for them but in our estimation we still weren't ready. We did showcase versions at the Norris Theater in Rolling Hills, Walt Disney's El Capitan Theater in Hollywood and in 2011 we presented another full production at

"Pazzazz!" opening number, Danny Michaels as Times Square statue George M. Cohan

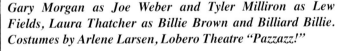

Gary Morgan as Joe Weber and Tyler Milliron as Lew Fields, Laura Thatcher as Billie Brown and Billiard Billie. Costumes by Arlene Larsen, Lobero Theatre "Pazzazz!"

Final cast finale, Lobero Theatre "Pazzazz!"

Santa Barbara's Lobero Theater. Now the show is ready and we're ready. Stay tuned!

We were dealt a crushing blow when Bruce Gordon passed away of a heart attack unexpectedly in 2007. Bruce would have undoubtedly foreseen many of the changes that became apparent in the "Pazzazz!" showcase versions. He was one of the most interesting people I have ever met and here's a spooky story about Bruce:

A few years back I decided it might be fun to enjoy a new car. I remembered that our old friend and first manager of the Castle, Don Culp, worked for Executive Car Leasing. I had leased a car from them in the past. Now I wanted to buy one but I recalled that Executive Car Leasing used to have really good deals on cars that were turned in when the leases ended. The Manager, Bob, said to check out their listings on their website and, if I saw one I liked, to give him a call.

I wanted a hardtop convertible and there was a Lexus SC430 listed with rather low mileage at a reasonable price. Both Dick Sherman and Bruce Gordon were Lexus owners so I decided to take a look. Bob said I could see it but it wasn't on the lot at the time. It seems his wife loved the car and took it home from time to time. Dale Hindman and I made an appointment to see the car the next day. I took one look at it and loved it.

It was a custom *Pebble Beach* sporty model with bright red leather upholstery. It was a car to make an older guy feel young. I bought it on the spot.

A few days later Joe Hoffman came into the office for a meeting and remarked that the new car looked like the Lexus Bruce Gordon used to drive. I remembered Bruce had a gold car, this one was black. No more was said until Dick Sherman came in and also remarked about the Lexus. We all agreed Bruce had had good taste and let it go at that.

The Lexus had a GPS gizmo. I seldom used one since Arlene and I always used Arlene's car for long trips. I hit the home button and when the home address came up, I recognized it as Bruce's home address. Yes, it was his car. Now when I drive it I feel the presence of our old friend and advisor telling me what's wrong with "Pazzazz!" As usual, Bruce is still always right.

Artist extraordinaire Joe hand painted the missing pieces of stenciling on the walls of the Parlour. Joe insisted The Magic Castle is a jewel and he was only polishing it to its proper shine. The Parlour is breathtaking with the new chairs. Every bit of the new color accents were hand-painted. The walls, and dome trim have never been more beautiful. Joe made some new atmospherical lighting and Tina Lee made the drapery.

Joe Hoffman put together the displays in the William W. Larsen Memorial Library, including one for Johnny Carson. On display are some of Johnny's personal magic props, his cards, linking rings, close-up pad, donated by his wife Alexis and nephew Jeff Sotzing. Carson began his show business career as a teenage magician and ventriloquist before serving in the Navy during World War II. Other displays include Geri Larsen, The Magic Lady, Billy McComb, Dante, and Johnny Platt.

**JOHNNY
CARSON
"THE GREAT
CARSONI"
1906-1998**

**GERI LARSEN
"THE MAGIC
LADY"
1903-1990**

**BILLY McCOMB
"WORLD'S
LARGEST
LEPRECHAUN"
1922-2006**

**HARRY JANSEN
DANTE
"SIM SALA BIM"
1888-1955**

**JOHNNY PLATT
"HADJI BABA"
1903-1990**

Sometime after John Shrum passed away in 1988 I met and found the late Joseph Hoffman to be willing to draft my ideas. I hired noted architect Edward Hunt to draw up many plans for future expansion. I have been blessed to have worked with artists who can explain graphically what I have in the back of my rather eccentric mind. After Joe Hoffman suddenly passed away member Kendall Bennet picked up the gauntlet and is working on many of my projects. Kendall is an art director at ABC TV.

I made the mistake of showing Joe a photo of Frank Bresee's family home in Hancock Park. In the backyard was one of the most beautiful lattice creations I have ever seen this side of Europe. Joe designed a magnificent latticework trellis for the Castle

fountain with all those curves, sweeps and contours, trickier than they look and quite challenging to make.

Puppet Magic: Jimmy Durante marionette

Joe personally created and painted the scenery for the puppet showcases. Alan McFarland did the animation aided and abetted by Tom Ruff. When you push a button at the bottom of the showcase, Jimmy Durante, the marionette created by the late Jack Shafton and donated by Verne Langdon, sings a snappy chorus of the Sherman and Larsen ditty: "The Magic Castle Shuffle." The Durante voice is by

Jack Shafton's Cowgirl and Horse

Magic Castle member Clark James. The second Puppet Magic Showcase displays Jack Shafton's "Cowgirl" and the "Horse."

For years my table at Friday lunch had the usual suspects— those crazy ticky-tacky-technical people are various talents that have helped design, invent, install, edit, and help create the various effects and gimmicks members enjoy at the Magic Castle and the creative team for our new stage musical "Pazzazz!" Chris Zamiara, my sister-in-law and assistant for many years, Dale Hindman, Alan McFarland, Tom Ruff, Richard Allen, and occasionally Carol Marie are the usual suspects. Over the years it has become a bare necessity that I mention Richard M. Sherman in every lunch menu whether or not he joined us for lunch.

If you want the true story of the Magic Castle stop reading this book right now and go to geniimagazine.com/genii_index/index.html. Thanks to Richard Kaufman, every issue of Genii for the past seventy-five years has been made available to Genii subscribers. My late brother, Bill Larsen Jr., started writing about the formation of the Academy of Magical Arts from the year before we opened The Magic Castle until his passing in 1993. From time to time Bill would tell his readers of my adventures in investigating the possibilities of another Magic Castle. For one reason or another, those plans didn't materialize. In 1969 Bill announced that I was in New York on business but while I was there, I was actively talking to our East Coast magician friends about the idea of creating another Magic Castle. I think the main spark plug for the idea was Mickey O'Malley. Mickey was a magician and also the staff artist for Genii magazine. He loved the Castle and he loved New York. We spent many happy hours in Mama Leoni's bar discussing the possibilities.

Obviously I wasn't looking for an old mansion on a hilltop in Manhattan but I was looking for a location with some kind of curious atmosphere. One of my favorites was a building that had been the Baldwin Piano showroom. The main thing I liked about it was an elevator that was like a beautiful polished mahogany paneled room big enough to lift a concert grand piano from floor to floor. I thought it would be a talking point to have an oriental carpet, chairs and tables on the ceiling and an upside-down chandelier on the floor. Upside-down magic posters would complete the illusion. Unfortunately someone else leased the building before I could make an offer.

Then I thought I found the perfect building. It was on 48th Street across from Rockefeller Center. Originally it had been President Taft's townhouse but it had lived its later years as a French restaurant. It had a room that would have been ideal for the Close-up magic the Magic Castle has become noted for and it was for lease on very reasonable terms.

We came close to serious negotiations when I received a call from a very good friend and a respected member of the magic fraternity. He was also a well-known banker in New York. He wanted to warn me that the people we were dealing with had business dealings, let's say, *left over from the days of prohibition*. He further explained that a lease with them was one-sided. They were assembling a block of properties and when they wanted to terminate the lease, you were out on the street. If you didn't agree to their terms you would simply be one more California kid with cement shoes at the bottom of the East River. He made his point and we looked elsewhere.

About that time we were also intrigued with the idea of a Magic Castle in San Francisco. Both Bill and I agreed the Barbary Coast was more our style than the East Coast. I found some wonderful grand mansions for sale but again, we decided to wait for another day. Bill and I always felt if there were ever to be another Magic Castle, it would not be a cookie-cutter imitation of the original but rather a similar but very different magical experience. Stay tuned.

Magicians have always loved celebrating Halloween. 13 is a lucky number. Black cats make nice pets. Broken mirrors can be good luck to magicians unless, of course, the mirror is part of an illusionary secret. Celebrating Halloween at the Magic Castle on October 31st every year is second only to celebrating New Years Eve. Over the years the parties got bigger and better. Members and their guests filled the club dressed in outlandish costumes—often undressed as the case may be. The celebration grew from a one night party on "All Hallows Eve" to several days in later years.

Jim Bentley as Houdini

One of the most elaborate Halloween events was held Halloween week of 2011. The events department came up with a catchy idea—the decor would be based on Dante's Inferno. The entire Castle would be decorated literally like Hell. The party was held every night leading up to the big climax on Halloween, October 31st. On the morning of Halloween the ladies in the third floor offices smelled smoke. The staff acted quickly and efficiently called the fire department and evacuated the building. Due to the quick action of our staff and the amazing magic of the Los Angeles Fire Department the fire was stopped before it spread through the attic and roof. That could have been disastrous especially if it had happened later when our Halloween party was underway.

As it was, the fire was contained before it became a major conflagration so there were no injuries. In Santa Barbara, Arlene and I received the first calls from Dale Hindman and Erika Larsen to turn on the TV news. It was an eerie feeling watching smoke pouring out of my pet project of the last 50 years. We felt very helpless but all we could do was watch and pray. When Erika called with the good news that the fire was out we knew the Castle was in the best possible hands. I elected to return on the train as usual Tuesday morning. I heard reports of the heroic efforts of the firemen rescuing the priceless antiques and art work in the building and when I got to the Castle Tuesday morning I realized the magnitude of the damage and the challenges that we would now face.

Most of the actual fire was limited to the office and attic, however the water damage was very extensive. By the time I arrived, our landlord, West McDonough, Dale Hindman, Jim Bentley and Erika were meeting with insurance representatives, restoration specialists, contractors and various inspectors. (They had spent the evening trying to dry out and save my collection of Prohibition temperance glass slides in the Irma Room bar.) Work was already well underway removing the truckloads of soggy carpeting and obviously unsalvageable materials. Jim Bentley was hired as project director for the mammoth restoration project ahead.

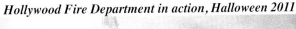
Hollywood Fire Department in action, Halloween 2011

If you have ever experienced a fire or earthquake or anything that puts a dent in your life as you know it, you can identify with the myriad of necessary steps that must be taken to comply with updating to the building codes of today. The Lane Mansion was built in 1910 and at that time it was considered a modern residence with everything built up to code. Here's what young whippersnappers have to understand about the complexities of today's world: After the fire the main problem was water damage. If water was detected within the old

lath and plaster walls and ceilings they had to be demolished. This literally uncovered the fact that most of the wiring in the affected areas was *knob and tube*; rubber and cloth insulated wires running between the wood joists and through porcelain tubes in the joists—all very legal from 1890 to the early '30's. When the Lane home was built the house was wired for both gas and electricity. I had fun showing the electricians the gas pipes when the walls were uncovered. To comply with the building and safety code all the old wiring had to be removed and replaced with approved conduit, etc. to bring the wiring up to current code. It was an unexpected development that added many days to the restoration time line. The fire insurance experts and contractors agreed that the restoration of the mansion would mean closing the main portion of the house for about six months. Using our special gift of magic the club re-opened partially in just ten weeks, January 15, 2012.

During the rebuilding of the Castle the club remained in business serving dinners and having shows by utilizing the showroom annex which was not affected by the fire. When Randy Sinnott became Treasurer of the Academy of Magical Arts, he had found the club was very under insured. Randy is a well-known Los Angeles attorney who specializes in insurance cases. Under his suggestion the AMA policies were brought up to date and increased. Thanks to him the Castle was properly insured and there was no problem covering the losses and the reconstruction.

In the 50 years history of the Academy of Magical Arts there have only been 8 Presidents: Bill Larsen Jr (1961- Feb 1993); Ron Wilson (Feb 1993-Feb 1994); Irene Larsen (Feb 1994-Feb 1996); Mark Wilson (Feb 1996-Feb 1998); Dale Hindman (Feb 1998-Feb 2006); Gay Blackstone (Feb 2006-Feb 2008); Robert Lamoureux (Feb 2008-April 2011) and Neil Patrick Harris (Apr 2011-present). They have all devoted thousands of hours working tirelessly to make our dream come true—that goes for all the members of the boards, the committees, the members of the AMA and all our faithful employees over the years.

In the early days of the Castle, we had to make physical changes and improvements happened with no money and a lot of ingenuity. Dealing with leftover building materials and surplus stores left something to be desired as far as being 100% *up to code*. Thanks to the Halloween fire it is incredible that the Academy of Magical Arts can look to the future with a century old mansion that is now up to 2012 Los Angeles building codes.

At this writing we are looking forward to the Castle's Fiftieth "Golden" Anniversary. The official date of the Magic Castle opening is January 2, 1963 and it is more successful now than it has ever been. Fifty years ago my brother and I gave life to our father's dream of a club for magicians. Little did we realize that a half century later the Magic Castle would become what it is today. I think we proved that nothing is impossible.

In this book I have tried to chronicle the fun times I have had on my magical journey over the past eighty years. There have been very good times and very bad times. The good times have greatly outnumbered the bad. Win or lose, I did it my way.

My train ride on the magic track has been rewarding in every aspect, that light at the end of the tunnel stays bright and magnetic. There are many mysteries to explore. I hope to open many doors that will lead to new projects in my life. In addition to working with the Board of Directors, the Board of Trustees, the management and the staff of the Academy of Magical Arts and constantly working on new ideas for the Magic Castle, my dreams for the future include many other entertainment projects.

Plans beyond the scope of the Hollywood Magic Castle fall under the aegis of our corporate entity Magic Castles Inc. and Brookledge Corporation. I am President and Arlene Larsen is Vice President. Dale Hindman, who was President of the Academy of Magical Arts for eight years, is our Executive Director. One of Hollywood's legendary entertainment attorneys, Edward Blau, handles our legal affairs. Our CPA is Harvey Dunn.

The Larsen Enterprises (Magic Castles Inc & Brookledge Corporation) offices are hidden away next door to the Magic Castle. They are actually part of a 1930's nine-unit apartment building that is now part of the Glover family's *Magic Castle Hotel.* Our part of the complex includes my personal apartment, Dale Hindman's executive office, my radio studio, my vintage recording archives, and other technical rooms.

I spend about half the week at home in Santa Barbara with my lovely wife, Arlene, and our two character dogs, Whizzer and Angel. Arlene and I were married late in life. We have no children unless you count the five thousand members of the AMA… they are all kids because magicians never get old. We are proud of our *children*. When we hear of our young members enjoying success in the world of magic it is the reward of a lifetime.

Over the years I have driven my friends and associates crazy with visions of ideas that never quiet happened. I have wonderful plans by John Shrum, Hubbell Braden, Edward Hunt, Joe Hoffman and others on good ideas that just never quite jelled. At

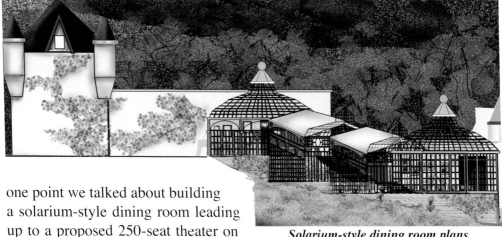

one point we talked about building a solarium-style dining room leading up to a proposed 250-seat theater on the parking lot above the Palace an-

Solarium-style dining room plans

nex. How about a five story parking garage with a park on the top level and another Magic Castle Hotel? Plans for the expansion of the Castle? You name 'em -- I've got

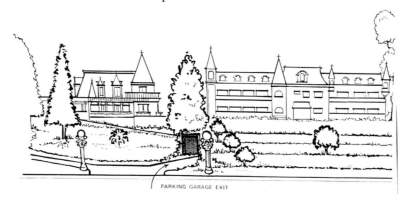

PARKING GARAGE EXIT

'em. They now dwell in the plan files in my studio/office next door to the Castle. Joe Hoffmann called it my dream file. ABC-TV Art Director Kendall Bennett is now working with me on future plans.

Far from retiring we have many projects in the works. Magician Rich Bloch has our license to provide an intimate *Magic Castle at Sea* series of shows for the very exclusive Celebrity Cruise ships. We are providing Magic Castle magicians for a theme park in Nagasaki Japan; a 20th Century Fox feature film will shortly go into production based on the concept of The Magic Castle; my longtime partner Terry Hill and I have a number of "It's Magic!" shows booked well into 2014.

We hope to announce plans soon for the future of the Sherman and Larsen stage musical "Pazzazz!" That may include a reality TV show and the theatre restoration project in downtown Los Angeles.

In my spare time I now host three one-hour radio shows on the air every week. They are all on CRN—The Cable Radio Network. Hear Them Again (for the first time); Hit Parade Cavalcade with Dick Sherman and Classic Comedy Hour. (See www.CRNi.Net for information.) Like they say: "Life begins at eighty!"

Downtown L.A. theatre restoration plans by Joe Hoffman

I'm reading the final proofs of my book. Carol Marie has done fabulous job of putting together the rambling stories about my life in magic in the past. Where she found some of the pictures I'll never know. In my long and magical life there are still so many stories that remain untold. It is amazing how many magicians I have met. If I have omitted your favorite anecdote just let me know. Carol and I like writing books. Life is good and I'm in excellent health, which is to say I'm still climbing the ladder of excitement and expectation.

Now it's time to get back on the train and enjoy the future.

Gone, but not forgotten!

I could devote pages to writing about the dearly departed major stepping-stones in my magical journey. Within the stories you have just read—or will be reading later if you skip to the end of books like I do—there have been incredible talents who have been there to help me along the way. I have always been a dreamer, but I always seemed to have someone at my side to make my dreams come true. If you are reading this and are not on this list, REJOICE! You are still among the living. So, while my train rests at the side of the track waiting for another train to pass, here is my honor roll of fallen heroes:

Bill Larsen, Art Baker and **Rubin Jaffe**—My three wonderful fathers.

"Snag" Werris—My mentor in the fine art of comedy writing. Snag was the epitome of a *gag* writer. He was a former burlesque banana who taught me to pay attention to comedy structure and clean material.

Harrison "Red" Baker—My first writing partner and **Robert "Bobby" Lauher**, my writing partner from 1957 until his untimely passing in 1973.

Ralph Edwards—Ralph gave me my first real job as a writer for "Truth or Consequences." He was like a second father to me and allowed me to *moonlight* away from my job in order to build the Magic Castle.

Floyd Thayer and my grandfather, **Sam Conrad**—My teachers in wood turning and box building.

Ed Wynn, Steve Allen, Walt Disney and **Ernie Kovacs**—My role models who helped me prove that nothing is impossible. In my book they were all magicians.

Don Damaskin—Don was a "Jack of All Trades," in the early days of building a Magic Castle, Mayfair Music Hall and Variety Arts theatre. He lived too short a life.

Shirley Carroll—Shirley and her late husband Norman were publicists for Ringling Brothers. Without them the idea of "It's Magic!" might have been abandoned after the first two years. They helped create a new interest in the art of magic and that led to my train ride and my Magical Journey.

Barbara Logan and **Eleanor St. Germain**—A tragic plane crash took the life of my fiancé in 1965 and Eleanor helped me through a very difficult time as my right-hand-lady at the Castle, Mayfair and Variety Arts.

John Shrum, Joe Hoffman and **Bruce Gordon**—Three of the greatest losses in my life. All three died unexpectedly and they all left a great deal of unfinished work to be done. **John Shrum** was with me from the first day of the Castle and brought his skills as senior art director for NBC and the Art Director of Johnny Carson's "Tonight Show" to create and design magic to the Magic Castle, "It's Magic!," the Mayfair Music Hall and the Variety Arts. They were all his *standing sets*. John passed away at the age of 53 in 1988.

Joe Hoffman was the art director for the Jim Nabors Show when I met him. He stepped into Shrum's very large shoes to become my official Castle designer until his passing in 2011 at the age of 61. Joe also co-authored the book for the Sherman & Larsen musical "Pazzazz!" and created the scenery for the show.

I got to know **Bruce Gordon** when we started working on our musical, "Pazzazz!" He was a true genius working on major attractions for Walt Disney. His advice on our show was invaluable. He passed away suddenly at the age of 54 in 2007.

Bob Busch—Bob was the only reason I regretted giving up cigars at an early age. He was with the Edison Company and once told me that the reason we had so many power outages in Montecito was because someone kept tripping over the extension cord.

Ernie Evans—who taught me the fine art of saving yesterday's demolition trash that is considered today's *Architectural Antiques*.

Thomas O. Glover—Without his faith in a young comedy writer with crazy ideas there would be no Magic Castle. He shared my vision for the future.

ALOHA GOOD FRIENDS – 'TIL WE MEET AGAIN.

Afterword

By all rights, I should have known Milt far before I actually met him. In my late teens I remember hearing the Back Porch Majority at Ledbetters sing Sherman-Larsen's "Smash Flops." I worked on "The Waltons" which was edited by a friend of Milt's, Gene Fowler, who donated the hat collection in the Inner Circle. I was an independent script typist (before computers) and worked for Anthony Hopkins, Richard Maibaum, Rachel Welch, Anthony Newley's Broadway musical "Chaplin" and William Reed Woodfield (of Magicana fame) who first introduced me to the Magic Castle. I was the Administrative Director for Gazebo Theatre One in Santa Barbara where I worked with Gary Goddard and Anthony Jenkins years before the Landmark Caesars Magical Empire project. I

The Barracuda, Carol Marie

was a theater junkie and worked with many of the experimental theaters in Los Angeles—including the LA Actors Theater when they moved downtown—the same time Milt had acquired the Friday Morning Club and started the SPVA. I worked with Anson Williams (from Victory Canteen) who was a director on a television series where I was employed.

But I didn't meet Milt until I became a member of the Magic Castle and started taking his monthly tours. His curiosity was piqued by the number of times I repeated the tour and we struck a friendship that has lasted for years. He became my antique restoration mentor, my book writing/editing/desk-top publishing co-author/publisher and has been a valued and good friend.

Throughout the years, he has presented many challenges—the first task he gave me was to alphabetize over 3,000 78 records in his office, by vocalists last name. That took a little while…

Then there was the Tour Book. Not coming from a magical background I had a lot of research to do in the library, Genii magazine, archival photos, etc. and I had to learn Pagemaker and Photoshop. That took a little while…

Next was cataloging the SPVA collections. I catalogued boxes of photos, frames, books, theater playbills, and made scrapbooks for the unprotected ephemera of Earl Carroll, Mayfair Music Hall, SPVA, "It's Magic!" and the Magic Castle and other smaller collections. That took a little while…

(And unfortunately, Milt's got another three garages and one container full of more ephemera that I haven't been able to get to.)

William W. Larsen Sr. Memorial Library

Then there was re-cataloguing the entire AMA library and the ephemera and donated props from the back room, instigating a security system, upgrading viewing equipment—and with Milt's amazing physical library make-over the library now looks like a rich, beautiful working library. I had help with this project with my shelf elves: Joanne and Larry Lazar, Dave Knackstedt, Allan Hayden and Tom Meseroll, Rich and Phyllis Cowley. Even with them that took a little while…

1908 Farmhouse in Ashland, Oregon

Then there were the other books… Thank goodness for Joe Hoffman and now Kendall Bennett.

And, when I wasn't busy, every time I could, every Wednesday night, I gleaned from Milt how to cheaply restore a 1908 farmhouse in Ashland, Oregon—still not complete, but adorned with architectural treasures from his mother's house in Montecito and left-overs from the Magic Castle.

My mantra, whenever Milt asked me if I could do something… was:

Interesting that my "bumble bee can't fly" graphic was a dog trying to keep up with a train! I wouldn't trade a moment of any of my projects with the Amazing Milt and appreciate his continued support and challenges! The Magic Castle now has four of my original stained glass art windows in the turret above the valet station… the first magical-themed windows ever to grace The Magic Castle.

Thanks Milt! For everything! And I'm waiting for the next challenge… cm